C++ For Dummies®, 3rd Edition

Declarations

```
// declaration of a simple type
[const] type objName [ = expression]; // declaration of a class object
[const] type objName[(argument list)]; // if no arguments, then the
                                        // default constructor is invoked
// declaration of a function
type fnName([argument list]); // if empty, the argument list is
                              // assumed to be void
```

Declarations have one of the following forms. The intrinsic types are

```
[<signed | unsigned >]char
[<signed | unsigned>] [<short | long>] int
float
double
long double
```

Users may also define their own types using the `class` or `struct` keywords:

```
<struct | class> ClassName [ : [public] BaseClass]
{
  public:
    // public data members
    type dataMemberName;
    // public member functions
    type memberFunctionName([arg list]) [{...}]
    // const member function
    type memberFunctionName([arg list]) const [{...}]
    // virtual member functions
    virtual type memberFunctionName([arg list]) [{...}];
    // pure virtual member functions
    virtual type memberFunctionName([arg list]) = 0;
  protected:
    // repeat for any protected members};
};
```

C++ For Dummies®, 3rd Edition

Cheat Sheet

Here, in a nutshell, are a few rules to live by. I've used the following contractions in these rules:

`[feature]`	feature is optional
`<feature1 | feature2>`	either feature1 or else feature2
`...`	unspecified number of statements or expressions

Expressions

Expressions have both a value and a type. Expressions take one of the following forms:

```
objName                          // for a simple object
operator expression              // for unary operators
expr1 operator expr2             // for binary operators
expr1 ? expr2 : expr3            // for the ternary operator
funcName([argument list]);       // for function calls
```

Operators

	Operator	*Cardinality*	*Associativity*
Highest precedence	() [] -> .		left to right
	! ~ + - ++ — & * (cast) sizeof	unary	left to right
	* / %	binary	left to right
	+ -	binary	left to right
	<< >>	binary	left to right
	< <= > >=	binary	left to right
	== !=	binary	left to right
	&	binary	left to right
	^	binary	left to right
	|	binary	left to right
	&&	binary	left to right
	||	binary	left to right
	?:	ternary	right to left
	= *= /= %= += -= &= ^= |= <<= >>=	binary	right to left
Lowest precedence	,	binary	left to right

IDG BOOKS WORLDWIDE

Cheat Sheet $2.95 value. Item 0389-8.
For more information about IDG Books, call 1-800-762-2974.

...For Dummies®: Bestselling Book Series for Beginners

C++ FOR DUMMIES®

3RD EDITION

C++ For Dummies®

3rd Edition

by Stephen R. Davis

IDG Books Worldwide

IDG Books Worldwide, Inc.
An International Data Group Company

Foster City, CA ♦ Chicago, IL ♦ Indianapolis, IN ♦ New York, NY

C++ For Dummies®, 3rd Edition

Published by
IDG Books Worldwide, Inc.
An International Data Group Company
919 E. Hillsdale Blvd.
Suite 400
Foster City, CA 94404
www.idgbooks.com (IDG Books Worldwide Web site)
www.dummies.com (Dummies Press Web site)

Library of Congress Catalog Card No.: 98-85435

ISBN: 0-7645-0389-8

Printed in the United States of America

10 9 8 7 6 5 4 3

3B/SS/QT/ZZ/IN

Distributed in the United States by IDG Books Worldwide, Inc.

Distributed by CDG Books Canada Inc. for Canada; by Transworld Publishers Limited in the United Kingdom; by IDG Norge Books for Norway; by IDG Sweden Books for Sweden; by Woodslane Pty. Ltd. for Australia; by Woodslane (NZ) Ltd. for New Zealand; by TransQuest Publishers Pte Ltd. for Singapore, Malaysia, Thailand, Indonesia, and Hong Kong; by ICG Muse, Inc. for Japan; by Norma Comunicaciones S.A. for Colombia; by Intersoft for South Africa; by Le Monde en Tique for France; by International Thomson Publishing for Germany, Austria and Switzerland; by Distribuidora Cuspide for Argentina; by Livraria Cultura for Brazil; by Ediciones ZETA S.C.R. Ltda. for Peru; by WS Computer Publishing Corporation, Inc., for the Philippines; by Contemporanea de Ediciones for Venezuela; by Express Computer Distributors for the Caribbean and West Indies; by Micronesia Media Distributor, Inc. for Micronesia; by Grupo Editorial Norma S.A. for Guatemala; by Chips Computadoras S.A. de C.V. for Mexico; by Editorial Norma de Panama S.A. for Panama; by American Bookshops for Finland. Authorized Sales Agent: Anthony Rudkin Associates for the Middle East and North Africa.

For general information on IDG Books Worldwide's books in the U.S., please call our Consumer Customer Service department at 800-762-2974. For reseller information, including discounts and premium sales, please call our Reseller Customer Service department at 800-434-3422.

For information on where to purchase IDG Books Worldwide's books outside the U.S., please contact our International Sales department at 317-596-5530 or fax 317-596-5692.

For consumer information on foreign language translations, please contact our Customer Service department at 1-800-434-3422, fax 317-596-5692, or e-mail rights@idgbooks.com.

For information on licensing foreign or domestic rights, please phone +1-650-655-3109.

For sales inquiries and special prices for bulk quantities, please contact our Sales department at 650-655-3200 or write to the address above.

For information on using IDG Books Worldwide's books in the classroom or for ordering examination copies, please contact our Educational Sales department at 800-434-2086 or fax 317-596-5499.

For press review copies, author interviews, or other publicity information, please contact our Public Relations department at 650-655-3000 or fax 650-655-3299.

For authorization to photocopy items for corporate, personal, or educational use, please contact Copyright Clearance Center, 222 Rosewood Drive, Danvers, MA 01923, or fax 978-750-4470.

About the Author

Stephen R. Davis, who goes by the name of Randy, has been a programmer and author at E-Systems in Greenville, Texas, for 15 years. He currently specializes in Java and C++ programming and software engineering issues. Randy fights for computer time with his wife Jenny and son Kinsey.

Randy can be reached for compliments at `srdavis@ACM.org`. Send all complaints to `device NUL:`.

ABOUT IDG BOOKS WORLDWIDE

Welcome to the world of IDG Books Worldwide.

IDG Books Worldwide, Inc., is a subsidiary of International Data Group, the world's largest publisher of computer-related information and the leading global provider of information services on information technology. IDG was founded more than 30 years ago by Patrick J. McGovern and now employs more than 9,000 people worldwide. IDG publishes more than 290 computer publications in over 75 countries. More than 90 million people read one or more IDG publications each month.

Launched in 1990, IDG Books Worldwide is today the #1 publisher of best-selling computer books in the United States. We are proud to have received eight awards from the Computer Press Association in recognition of editorial excellence and three from Computer Currents' First Annual Readers' Choice Awards. Our best-selling *...For Dummies®* series has more than 50 million copies in print with translations in 31 languages. IDG Books Worldwide, through a joint venture with IDG's Hi-Tech Beijing, became the first U.S. publisher to publish a computer book in the People's Republic of China. In record time, IDG Books Worldwide has become the first choice for millions of readers around the world who want to learn how to better manage their businesses.

Our mission is simple: Every one of our books is designed to bring extra value and skill-building instructions to the reader. Our books are written by experts who understand and care about our readers. The knowledge base of our editorial staff comes from years of experience in publishing, education, and journalism — experience we use to produce books to carry us into the new millennium. In short, we care about books, so we attract the best people. We devote special attention to details such as audience, interior design, use of icons, and illustrations. And because we use an efficient process of authoring, editing, and desktop publishing our books electronically, we can spend more time ensuring superior content and less time on the technicalities of making books.

You can count on our commitment to deliver high-quality books at competitive prices on topics you want to read about. At IDG Books Worldwide, we continue in the IDG tradition of delivering quality for more than 30 years. You'll find no better book on a subject than one from IDG Books Worldwide.

John Kilcullen
Chairman and CEO
IDG Books Worldwide, Inc.

Steven Berkowitz
President and Publisher
IDG Books Worldwide, Inc.

Eighth Annual Computer Press Awards 1992

Ninth Annual Computer Press Awards 1993

Tenth Annual Computer Press Awards 1994

Eleventh Annual Computer Press Awards 1995

IDG is the world's leading IT media, research and exposition company. Founded in 1964, IDG had 1997 revenues of $2.05 billion and has more than 9,000 employees worldwide. IDG offers the widest range of media options that reach IT buyers in 75 countries representing 95% of worldwide IT spending. IDG's diverse product and services portfolio spans six key areas including print publishing, online publishing, expositions and conferences, market research, education and training, and global marketing services. More than 90 million people read one or more of IDG's 290 magazines and newspapers, including IDG's leading global brands — Computerworld, PC World, Network World, Macworld and the Channel World family of publications. IDG Books Worldwide is one of the fastest-growing computer book publishers in the world, with more than 700 titles in 36 languages. The "...For Dummies®" series alone has more than 50 million copies in print. IDG offers online users the largest network of technology-specific Web sites around the world through IDG.net (http://www.idg.net), which comprises more than 225 targeted Web sites in 55 countries worldwide. International Data Corporation (IDC) is the world's largest provider of information technology data, analysis and consulting, with research centers in over 41 countries and more than 400 research analysts worldwide. IDG World Expo is a leading producer of more than 168 globally branded conferences and expositions in 35 countries including E3 (Electronic Entertainment Expo), Macworld Expo, ComNet, Windows World Expo, ICE (Internet Commerce Expo), Agenda, DEMO, and Spotlight. IDG's training subsidiary, ExecuTrain, is the world's largest computer training company, with more than 230 locations worldwide and 785 training courses. IDG Marketing Services helps industry-leading IT companies build international brand recognition by developing global integrated marketing programs via IDG's print, online and exposition products worldwide. Further information about the company can be found at www.idg.com.

1/24/99

Dedication

To my friends and family who help me to be the best Dummy I can be.

Author's Acknowledgments

I find it very strange that only a single name appears on the cover of any book, but especially a book like this. In reality, many people contribute to the creation of a *...For Dummies* book. From the beginning, editorial manager Mary Corder and editorial agent Claudette Moore were involved in guiding and molding the book's content. During development, I found myself hip-deep in edits, corrections, and suggestions from project editors Kelly Ewing and Colleen Williams (third edition), and Susan Pink (first and second editions); and technical reviewers Jeff Bankston (third edition), Garrett Pease (second edition), and Greg Guntle (first edition) — this book would have been a poorer work but for their involvement. And nothing would have made it into print without the aid of the person who coordinated the first and second editions of the project, Suzanne Thomas. Nevertheless, one name does appear on the cover and that name must take responsibility for any inaccuracies in the text.

I also have to thank my wife, Jenny, and son, Kinsey, for their patience and devotion. I hope we manage to strike a reasonable balance.

Finally, a summary of the animal activity around my house. For those of you who have not read any of my other books, I should warn you that this has become a regular feature of my *...For Dummies* books.

My two dogs, Scooter and Trude, continue to do well although Trude is all but blind now. Our two mini-Rex rabbits, Beavis and Butt-head, passed on to the big meadow in the sky after living in our front yard for almost a year and a half. We acquired two cats, Bob and Marly (both female, by the way), during the writing of *MORE C++ For Dummies*. Marly died of kitty leukemia, but Bob and the family have carried on.

A friend of my sister-in-law was secretly harboring a pot-bellied pig named Penny in her (the friend's, not Penny's) apartment last winter. Due to some sort of piggy indiscretions, the cover was blown and the apartment manager threatened Penny with bodily harm (apparently he didn't keep kosher). We were forced to spirit Penny away in the back of my Explorer under the cover of darkness. Penny arrived safely at her new quarters (outside this time), where she continues to thrive.

If you would like to contact me concerning C++ programming, pot-bellied pigs, semi-blind dogs, or free-roaming rabbits, feel free to drop me a line at `srdavis@ACM.org`.

Publisher's Acknowledgments

We're proud of this book; please register your comments through our IDG Books Worldwide Online Registration Form located at `http://my2cents.dummies.com`.

Some of the people who helped bring this book to market include the following:

Acquisitions, Development, and Editorial

Project Editors: Colleen Williams, Kelly Ewing

Senior Acquisitions Editor: Jill Pisoni

Media Development Manager: Heather Heath Dismore

Associate Permissions Editor: Carmen Krikorian

Copy Editor: Gwenette Gaddis

Technical Editor: Jeff Bankston

Editorial Manager: Colleen Rainsberger

Editorial Assistant: Darren Meiss

Production

Project Coordinator: Regina Snyder

Layout and Graphics: Cameron Booker, Lou Boudreau, Angela F. Hunckler, Jane E. Martin, Drew R. Moore, Anna Rohrer, Brent Savage, M. Anne Sipahimalani, Rashell Smith

Proofreaders: Christine Berman, Kelli Botta, Nancy Price, Christine Sabooni, Rebecca Senninger, Janet M. Withers

Indexer: Steve Rath

Special Help

Joell Smith, Software Developer

General and Administrative

IDG Books Worldwide, Inc.: John Kilcullen, CEO; Steven Berkowitz, President and Publisher

IDG Books Technology Publishing: Brenda McLaughlin, Senior Vice President and Group Publisher

Dummies Technology Press and Dummies Editorial: Diane Graves Steele, Vice President and Associate Publisher; Mary Bednarek, Director of Acquisitions and Product Development; Kristin A. Cocks, Editorial Director

Dummies Trade Press: Kathleen A. Welton, Vice President and Publisher; Kevin Thornton, Acquisitions Manager

IDG Books Production for Dummies Press: Michael R. Britton, Vice President of Production and Creative Services; Cindy L. Phipps, Manager of Project Coordination, Production Proofreading, and Indexing; Kathie S. Schutte, Supervisor of Page Layout; Shelley Lea, Supervisor of Graphics and Design; Debbie J. Gates, Production Systems Specialist; Robert Springer, Supervisor of Proofreading; Debbie Stailey, Special Projects Coordinator; Tony Augsburger, Supervisor of Reprints and Bluelines

Dummies Packaging and Book Design: Patty Page, Manager, Promotions Marketing

♦

The publisher would like to give special thanks to Patrick J. McGovern, without whom this book would not have been possible.

♦

Contents at a Glance

Cartoons at a Glance

By Rich Tennant

page 213

page 49

page 97

page 361

page 7

page 263

page 149

Fax: 978-546-7747 • E-mail: the5wave@tiac.net

Table of Contents

Introduction

Welcome to *C++ For Dummies,* 3rd Edition. Think of this book as C++: *Reader's Digest Edition,* bringing you everything you need to know without the boring stuff.

About This Book

C++ For Dummies, 3rd Edition, like all *...For Dummies* books, concentrates on you and your needs.

Like its C counterpart, this book is a tutorial unlike most *...For Dummies* books. It is meant to be read from front to back (not in one sitting, of course — the family starts to get anxious waiting that long).

This book will not turn you into a C++ "language lawyer." (That's a person who is really into the details of a computer language — a real language nerd — like me.) Although I do touch on just about every aspect of the language, I spend more time on features that are at the heart of the power of C++ and less time on the "power user" features that you don't need yet. The follow-up book to this one, *MORE C++ For Dummies* (written by me and published by IDG Books Worldwide, Inc.), goes into detail on some of the more technical features of the language.

In addition, this book does not cover Windows programming. Learning to program Windows in C++ is really a two-step process. First, you need to master C++. That accomplished, you can move on to Windows. And for that, you could do worse than (watch out for shameless plugs) *Windows 95 Programming For Dummies,* by yours truly (published by IDG Books Worldwide, Inc.).

Unlike other C++ programming books, *C++ For Dummies,* 3rd Edition, considers the "why" just as important as the "how." The features of C++ are like pieces of a jigsaw puzzle. Rather than just present the features, I think it's important that you understand how they fit together.

If you don't understand why a particular feature is in the language, you won't truly understand how it works. After you finish this book, you'll be able to write a reasonable C++ program, and, just as important, you'll understand why and how it works.

This book cannot teach you how to install your compiler — there are too many different compilers, and they change all the time. In addition, I can't go into the details of entering the program, getting it compiled, and so on. As long as you can edit a file, and compile, link, and execute the resulting program, you know enough for this book. (I do, however, devote a chapter to compiler options.)

About the CD

In this edition, unlike in the first edition, I'm including a CD-ROM to spare you the trouble of typing the many examples in the book. Unfortunately (or fortunately, depending on your preferences), *C++ For Dummies,* 3rd Edition, includes numerous extremely small examples (often no more than three or four lines). I decided that it wouldn't be worth the trouble of finding such small examples on the enclosed CD. Therefore, the accompanying CD includes all programs in the book but does not include snippets.

You can find the programs in the corresponding chapter file on the CD. The CD also includes a 25-Minute Workout (questions and answers to correspond with the first five parts of the book) in the Workout folder. The questions for each part are in the Question file. The answers for each part are in the corresponding part file. See the Installation Instructions in the back of the book for more about the CD.

What Is C++?

C++, as the name implies, is the next generation of the C programming language: the result of adding new-age academic computer linguistic thinking to that old workhorse C.

C++ is, at its core, C. It's almost completely upwardly compatible. Anything C can do, C++ can do, too. C++ can even do it the same way. But C++ is more than just C with a new coat of paint slapped on. The extensions to C++ are significant and require some thought and some getting used to, but the results are worth it. This book will help you get from C to C++ as painlessly as possible.

This book teaches you Standard C++, which is endorsed by the ANSI C++ Standards Committee and 9 out of 10 dentists. This is the version of C++ implemented in Borland C++, Turbo C++, Visual C++, Symantec C++, and C++ from most other companies.

Vendors stick as close as possible to this standard, so everything in this book should apply to any other version of C++ as well. When I do come across something unique to the Borland or Microsoft variants, I flag it with the Nonstandard icon (more on that in a minute).

Who Are You?

This book assumes that you already know at least some C. If you don't know C at all, stop now, casually slip this book back on the shelf (without attracting undue attention), and look right next to it for *C For Dummies, Volume I* (by Dan Gookin and published by IDG Books Worldwide, Inc.). (Remember where you put this book, though, because you'll want to come back.)

If your knowledge of C is a bit rusty, but you basically know it or at least knew it at one time, keep fumbling for your credit card. Part I reviews the most important aspects of C and lets you polish your skills quickly.

How This Book Is Organized

Each new feature is introduced by answering the following three questions:

- *What* is this new feature?
- *Why* was it introduced into the language?
- *How* does it work?

Small pieces of code are sprinkled liberally throughout the chapters. Each demonstrates some newly introduced feature or highlights some brilliant point I'm making. These snippets may not be complete and certainly don't do anything meaningful.

Note: Due to the margins of the book, very long lines of code continue to a second line. This arrow (⮐) appears at the end of those lines of code to remind you to keep on typing — don't press the Enter key yet!

At the end of each part . . .

To help you retain the material I present, I include two aids: an example program at the end of the first five parts and an exercise section on the CD.

I think it's important to see the features of C++ working together in a complete program. I get distracted, however, when I'm forced to wade through many different example programs. I spend more time figuring out what each program does than understanding the language features it contains. In addition, I have difficulty comparing them because they don't do the same thing.

To avoid this, I use one simple example program, BUDGET. This program starts life at the end of Part I as a functionally oriented C program. Then I rewrite BUDGET to incorporate the features presented in each new part.

By the time you reach the end of Part VI, BUDGET has blossomed into a completely object-oriented C++ debutante ready for the object-oriented cotillion. Some may find this a ghastly waste of time. (If so, just skip it and keep it to yourself — I convinced my editor that it was a really neat idea.) However, I hope that as you see BUDGET evolve, you will see how the features of C++ work together.

The second aid is the 25-Minute Workout (exercise) section in the Workout folder on the CD. Give the questions a try. (I present hints and warnings to steer you in the right direction.) After you finish your solutions, compare them to mine, which are provided along with an explanation in the corresponding part file.

Part I: Charting a Course: A Review of C

In Part I, I make sure everybody is on the same sheet of music. If you already feel comfortable with your knowledge of C, you can breeze through this part. If you're really feeling confident, you might skip it altogether, but be sure to scan the BUDGET program and test your knowledge by answering the questions on the CD.

Part II: Getting Your Feet Wet: The Non–Object-Oriented Features of C++

In Part II, you are introduced to the non–object-oriented features of C++, including a new comment style, inline functions, and stream I/O. These features make C++ a better C without making it a new language in any significant way. These features can be mastered fairly quickly because they don't require you to change your functional ways.

Part III: Wading In: Introduction to Classes

In Part III, you venture far enough into C++ that you start to see the differences between it and C. I introduce the concept of object-oriented programming and discuss classes. Both of these make C++ a truly different language from C.

Part IV: Warming to the Water: Getting Comfortable with Classes

The introduction to object-oriented programming with classes is a big step. This requires you to reexamine your functional programming ways and rethink problems that you thought you had solved a long time ago. Part IV gives you more time to let object-oriented programming sink in.

Part V: Plunging In: Inheritance

Inheritance is what separates the object-oriented wheat from the procedural chaff. Understanding this most important concept is the key to effective C++ programming and the goal of Part V. There's no going back now — after you've completed this part, you can call yourself an Object-Oriented Programmer, First Class.

Part VI: Advanced Strokes: Optional Features

By the time you get to Part VI, you know all you need to program effectively in C++. I touch on remaining, optional issues. You can read the chapters in this part in any order you like, using them as you would a reference.

Part VII: The Part of Tens

What *...For Dummies* book would be complete without the lists of ten? In the first chapter in Part VII, you find out the best ways to avoid introducing bugs into your programs.

Have you noticed how many different compiler options there are these days? How do I know whether I want my v_table pointer to follow my member pointer? And what's the alternative to fast floating point? Slow floating point? In the second chapter in Part VII, I guide you through these options, pointing out those that are important and those that are better left alone.

What You Don't Need to Read

C++ is a big pill to swallow. There are easy parts and not-so-easy parts. To keep from swamping you with information that you may not be interested in at the moment, technical stuff is flagged with a special icon. (See the section "Icons Used in This Book.")

In addition, certain background information is stuck into sidebars. If you feel the onset of information overload, feel free to skip these sections during the first reading. (Remember to read them sometime, though. In C++, what you don't know will hurt you — eventually.)

Icons Used in This Book

This is technical stuff that you can skip on the first reading.

Tips highlight a point that can save you a lot of time and effort.

Remember this. It's important.

Remember this, too. This one can sneak up on you when you least expect it and generate one of those really hard-to-find bugs.

This reminds you about some C feature you may have forgotten.

This indicates a nonstandard feature specific to compilers from Borland or Microsoft.

Now What?

Learning a programming language is not a spectator sport. I'll try to make it as painless as possible, but you have to power up the ol' PC and get down to some serious programming. Limber up the fingers, break the spine on the book so that it lays flat next to the keyboard (and so that you can't take it back to the bookstore), and dive in.

Part I

Charting a Course: A Review of C

ONE DAY IT REALLY HIT BERTHA JUST HOW OBSESSED HER HUSBAND HAD BECOME WITH HIS COMPUTER.

In this part . . .

Part I is a quick review of the C language. It is not intended as an introduction for those who are unfamiliar with C (except as something to keep *B* and *D* from bumping into each other). It is not even a complete review of C. Instead, Part I reviews the concepts that are critical for understanding C++ and can cause problems.

C is an apparently simple but often subtle language. Because C++ builds and expands on features in C, grasping these subtleties is important to the understanding of C++.

Chapter 1

C, C Dick, C Jane

In This Chapter

- Short history of C
- Declarations 101 — the simple stuff
- Storage class, or "Where did I put that variable?"
- Function declarations
- Actually doing something: C expressions

If you know nothing about C, this chapter is designed to bootstrap you into the C language enough so that you will be able to pick up the thread of the remainder of the book. As such, it covers some of the real beginning stuff like a little about the history of the language, some of the basic storage types, and very basic expressions. This will set you up for some of the slightly more advanced C features covered in the remainder of this part.

How Did We Come to C?

The C language was born at AT&T Bell Labs in 1972. C was the proud progeny of Dennis Ritchie, who then used C to port the UNIX operating system to an early DEC PDP-11 to which he had access.

AT&T bundled a C compiler called K&R C with the UNIX operating system when it began shipping UNIX to universities. (K&R C was named after Brian Kernighan and Dennis Ritchie, who wrote the first book describing the C language. Today K&R C is also known as Classic C.) Everyone who bought a copy of UNIX received a C compiler for free. Most liked C. Besides, UNIX was written in C, so if you wanted to understand UNIX, you had to learn C. The fact that C was free didn't hurt, either. The result was an instant standard.

As C became more popular, companies began introducing their own C compilers, including compilers that ran under operating systems other than UNIX. Each of these compilers introduced enhancements designed to address some perceived limitation of the original language. But enhancements that everyone doesn't agree with mean incompatibilities, so demand increased for a national standard. The American National Standards Institute (ANSI) version of C appeared in 1987. This version, variously known as ANSI C or Standard C, incorporated many significant improvements over Classic C, not the least of which was the fact that you could compile your program on almost any Standard C compiler.

Over the years, Classic C has fallen into almost total disuse outside the UNIX community. Even there, Standard C is the preferred lingua franca. When I refer to C in this book, I refer exclusively to the ANSI standard C. C++ is based on and is almost completely upward compatible with ANSI C.

Declaring Simple Variables

One of the first topics that causes confusion to beginning C programmers is the declaration of different types of objects.

Declaring variables starts out simply. All variables must be declared before they're used in order to establish their type. A type may be user defined or one of the built-in intrinsic types. Table 1-1 lists the intrinsic variable types.

Table 1-1 Built-In Variable Types

Type	*Meaning*
`char`	Character
`int`	Integer
`float`	Single-precision floating point
`double`	Double-precision floating point

The `char` and `int` types can be adorned with the descriptors `unsigned` or `signed` and `long` or `short`. The default for `int` is `signed`. The default for `char` is actually neither `signed` nor `unsigned`; however, many compilers allow you to treat otherwise unspecified `char`s as either `signed` or `unsigned`. Both `float` and `double` types are always `signed`.

A few extra floating points

In addition to the variable types in Table 1-1, most PC-based compilers allow the declaration of a *long double*, which is 80 bits wide. Eighty bits corresponds to the width of the internal registers in the Intel floating-point units (FPUs). On the 80386 and earlier processors, the FPU was a separate chip bearing the designation 80x87. On the 80486 and later, the FPU is built in. Motorola has a similar FPU called the 68881, which uses the same 80-bit format internally.

The following are all legal declarations:

```
int i;              /*default is signed                  */
char c;
unsigned char uc;
long int li;
unsigned short int si;
signed long sl;     /*int is assumed                     */
```

The size of each built-in variable type is not specified in the ANSI standard and therefore can vary according to the CPU and compiler. All the standard says is that a `short int` is the same size or smaller than an `int` which is, in turn, the same size or smaller than a `long int`. Most compilers running on a standard PC have the data allocation sizes shown in Table 1-2. (Compilers typically support the smaller `short int` and `int` sizes for DOS and Windows 3.1 and the larger sizes for Windows 95 and NT.) The include file `limits.h` gives the ranges for each built-in variable type for the current compiler and can be used to write machine-independent programs.

Table 1-2 Typical Size of Simple Types on the PC

Type	*Size*
`char`	8 bits
`short int`	8 or 16 bits
`int`	16 or 32 bits
`long int`	32 bits
`float`	32 bits
`double`	64 bits
`long double`	80 bits

Declaring Storage Class

In addition to declaring a variable's type, you also declare each variable as local to a function or global. A variable that is local to the function may only be accessed by that function. Global variables may be accessed by all functions. Local variables may also be declared `auto`, `static`, or `register`.

Global variables

Variables declared outside any function are called *global variables*. Global variables are created when the program starts and stay around until the program ends.

Global variables are accessible to any function declared in the same C file. Global variables declared in one C file can be made accessible to a second C file by including an `extern` declaration in the second C file.

You can specifically limit the scope of a global variable to the .C file in which it was created by declaring it static. Static variables are not accessible by other modules, even those with an `extern` declaration.

The following demonstrates the accessibility of global variables:

```
FILEA.C:
       int x;        /*potentially visible everywhere  */
static int y;        /*visible only inside FILEA.C     */

FILEB.C:
extern int x;        /*gives FILEB access to FILEA's x */
extern int y;        /*this doesn't work               */
```

Global variables reside in an area called the *data segment*. Because the number and size of all global variables is known before the program starts, the global segment is preallocated as part of the executable program.

Local variables

A variable declared in a function is called a *local variable*. A local variable is visible only to the function in which it's declared. That is, one function cannot access another function's local variables by name. There is no `extern` for local variables.

Local variables may be declared `auto`, `static`, or `register`. Because the default is auto, you'll almost never actually see the keyword `auto` (`auto` is short for *automatic,* I guess).

An *auto variable* is created when the program enters the function containing the auto declaration and is destroyed when the program exits the function.

A *static local variable* is created the first time the function is called but continues to exist and retains its value through subsequent returns and calls. For example:

```
void fn(void)
{
   int autoVar;                /*autoVar starts life here*/
   static int staticVar = 0; /*value first time fn() is called*/
   autoVar = 10;
   staticVar = 20;
}                              /*autoVar ends life here*/
int main()
{
   fn();
   fn();
   return 0;
}
```

The first time `fn()` is called, the variable `staticVar` is initialized to 0. Unless specifically initialized, local variables contain an unknown and unpredictable value when they're created. The second time `fn()` is called, `staticVar` starts out life with the value it had when the program last exited `fn()`.

Static local variables are kept in the data segment along with global variables. Auto variables are stored on the function's stack.

A *register variable* is like an auto variable in that it's created at the beginning and destroyed at the end of the function. However, a register variable is not stored in memory but cached in a register of the processor. Because register variables are not in memory, they have no address.

An interesting note: When I declare a variable `register`, it's only a request. The compiler (like my wife) is free to ignore me.

TIP

In the old days, when compiler optimizers weren't very good, a programmer could significantly improve the performance of a program by declaring the proper variables `register`. As optimizers improved, compilers were able to cache variables into registers in such a way as to optimize performance. Experience showed that a good optimizing compiler could do a better job than a person. Programmers usually just screwed things up by using up registers with the wrong variables. So don't use the `register` keyword. (Most modern compilers ignore the `register` keyword anyway because they know they can do better.)

Declaring Functions

A *function declaration* establishes the number and type of arguments to the function as well as the type of the returned value, if any. A function declaration with no code is called a *function prototype*.

Always declaring a function before using it is good programming style. This allows the compiler to compare the way the function is called with the way it's declared. If the function is called improperly, the compiler can flag the call with a compiler error, saving you the trouble of finding the error yourself.

Function prototype declarations are often made in a `.h` include file to allow their easy inclusion in multiple `.c` files. Here's a function prototype in `multiply.h`:

```
/*the following is a prototype declaration*/
int multiply(int firstArg, int secondArg);
```

And here's `multiply.c`, which defines `multiply()`:

```
#include "multiply.h"
/*this is the actual definition of the function*/
int multiply(int firstArg, int secondArg)
{
   int result;

   result = firstArg * secondArg;
   return result;
}
```

Other .c files that include functions that call multiply() appear as follows:

```
#include "multiply.h"
/*some other functions...*/
int someOtherFn(int a, int b)
{
   /*...other code...*/
   return multiply(a, b);  /*compiler compares this call...*/
}                          /*...to the prototype*/
```

Here the multiply() function takes two integer arguments, multiplies them, and returns the integer result. Because function someOtherFn() uses multiply(), the module that contains it includes the .h file multiply.h. The prototype for multiply() contained in multiply.h ensures that the function is used properly.

If a function doesn't return a value, its return type is void. If it takes no arguments, its argument type is void. For example:

```
void noReturn(int x, int y);
int  noArguments(void);
void neither(void);
```

If no return type is specified, C assumes type int. If you leave the argument list empty, C doesn't check the number and type of arguments when the function is called. This can be specified explicitly using ellipses, as follows:

```
returnsAnInt(void);
void unspecifiedArguments();
void alsoUnspecifiedArguments(...);
```

If a function is not prototyped, C attempts to infer a prototype from the way the function is first used. This is what I call the Miranda prototype. ("If you cannot afford a prototype, one will be provided for you.")

WARNING!

The prototyping rules for C and C++ are different. The C rules are described here, in Part I. The C++ rules are presented and contrasted with the C rules in Part II.

TIP

Always provide prototypes for all your functions. In addition, inform your compiler that you want it to generate a warning if it encounters a function that is used without a prototype. This step may seem like a hassle, but it will save you time debugging problems that the compiler could have found for you.

Mastering the Ins and Outs of C Expressions

An *expression* is a C statement that has a value. Most executable C statements are expressions of one type or another. Expressions consist of smaller expressions, which I call *subexpressions,* linked by operators. Consider the following example:

```
void fn(void)
{
    int x;
    int y = 2;
    x = 5 + 2 * y;        /*expression in question*/
}
```

You can quickly recognize `2 * y` in this code snippet as a subexpression whose value is 4. You may not recognize, however, that within this subexpression is another subexpression, `y`, which evaluates to 2. The constant 5 is yet another subexpression whose value is 5.

Besides a value, every expression also has a type. The type of the subexpression `y` is `int`. Likewise, the type of the subexpression `2 * y` is `int`.

In the example snippet, the complete expression, including the assignment operator, is

```
x = 5 + 2 * y
```

In C, unlike most other languages, assignment is just another operator. The assignment operator says "take the value on the right and stuff it into the variable on the left and *return the resulting value and type of the thing on the left.*" I stress the end of the sentence because it highlights the fact that assignment is an operator.

Smooth operators

Given that expressions consist of subexpressions linked together by operators, it's important to know what the operators are.

Table 1-3 is a complete list of the operators in C. Every operator has a syntax, a precedence, and an associativity. The syntax specifies the way in which the operator is used. The precedence specifies the order in which operators are executed. Higher precedence operators are evaluated before lower precedence operators. Finally, associativity specifies whether operation is from left to right or right to left. In the example expression

```
x = 5 + 2 * y
```

the multiplication was performed before the addition because the multiplication operator has a higher precedence than the addition operator.

Table 1-3 Operator Precedence

	Operator	*Associativity*
Highest precedence	() [] -> .	left to right
	! ~ + - ++— & * (cast) sizeof	right to left
	* / %	left to right
	+ -	left to right
	<< >>	left to right
	< <= > >=	left to right
	== !=	left to right
	&	left to right
	^	left to right
	|	left to right
	&&	left to right
	||	left to right
	?:	right to left
	= *= /= %= += -= &= ^= |= <<= >>=	right to left
Lowest precedence	,	left to right

Some operators, such as the – operator, seem to appear twice in Table 1-3. These operators have two forms: a one-argument, or *unary,* form and a two-argument, or *binary,* form. The unary form always has higher precedence than the binary form.

Operators fall into several broad categories: mathematical, bitwise, logical, assignment, and miscellaneous. The following sections present tables that identify these various operators along with notes on operators that may be confusing or may cause trouble.

Mathematical operators

Table 1-4 shows the mathematical operators. These operators are designed to work on numbers, such as `int`s, `float`s, and `double`s.

Table 1-4 Mathematical Operators

Operator	*Meaning*
+ (unary)	Effectively does nothing
- (unary)	Reverse the sign of the argument
+ (binary)	Addition
- (binary)	Subtraction
* (binary)	Multiplication
/	Division
%	Modulo (returns the remainder after division)
++	Increment
--	Decrement

The increment and decrement operators come in both a prefix and postfix version. The value of the variable is the same with either version, but the value of the expression itself is different. Consider the following:

```
void fn()
{
    int z;
    int x = 5;
    int y = 5;
    z = ++x;          /*value of z is 6*/
    z = y++;          /*value of z is 5*/
}
```

Both `x` and `y` end up with the value 6. But `++x` is the value of `x` after the increment, whereas `y++` is the value of `y` before the increment.

Bitwise operators

Table 1-5 introduces the bitwise operators. These operators allow the programmer to set, test, and clear individual bits in integer variables.

Table 1-5 Bitwise Operators

<table>
<tr><th>Operator</th><th>Meaning</th></tr>
<tr><td>~</td><td>Bitwise inverse</td></tr>
<tr><td>& (binary)</td><td>Bitwise AND</td></tr>
<tr><td>|</td><td>Bitwise OR</td></tr>
<tr><td>^</td><td>Bitwise eXclusive OR</td></tr>
<tr><td><<</td><td>Left shift</td></tr>
<tr><td>>></td><td>Right shift</td></tr>
</table>

When left shifting, a zero is always shifted into the least significant bit. When right shifting an unsigned integer, a zero is shifted into the most significant bit. When right shifting a signed integer, however, the compiler is free to copy the sign bit. There is no rotate operator in C.

Logical operators

Logical operators take the place of Boolean operators used in other languages. Logical operators work with integers. (Their counterparts in other languages work on Boolean values.) See Table 1-6.

Table 1-6 Logical Operators

<table>
<tr><th>Operator</th><th>Meaning</th></tr>
<tr><td>!</td><td>Logical inverse</td></tr>
<tr><td>&&</td><td>Logical AND</td></tr>
<tr><td>||</td><td>Logical OR</td></tr>
<tr><td>==</td><td>Equality (1 if left and right arguments are equal; 0 otherwise)</td></tr>
<tr><td>!=</td><td>Inequality (logical inverse of ==)</td></tr>
</table>

All logical operators use the rule that 0 is false and all other numbers are true. These operators generate either a 0 (false) or a 1 (true). The result of any of these operators can be stored in a variable or used in a larger expression.

The && and `||` operators practice short-circuit evaluation. Consider the following example:

```
if ((x == y) && (y == z))
```

If `x` is not equal to `y`, the overall condition is false whether or not `y` is equal to `z`. There is no need to evaluate the second subexpression if the first subexpression fails. This is called *short-circuit evaluation*.

A similar short circuit is performed on `||`. If the first subexpression in a logical OR is true, the overall condition is true and the program skips the evaluation of the second subexpression. Normally this is good because it results in a slightly faster program. Sometimes, however, short-circuit evaluation can cause unexpected results.

Consider the following:

```
if (g() && f())
```

The `g()` function is called first. If it returns a zero, the `f()` function is not called. Now if `f()` should do more than just perform some test, you may not see the results that you expect.

Assignment operators

Table 1-7 introduces the assignment operators, the operators that perform some type of assignment. Most assignment operators also perform some other operation.

Table 1-7 Assignment Operators

Operator	*Meaning*
=	Assignment
*=	Multiply by
/=	Divide by
%=	Modulo by
+=	Add to
-=	Subtract from
&=	AND with
^=	eXclusive OR with
|=	OR with
<<=	Left shift by
>>=	Right shift by

The assignment operator (=) takes the value on the right and stores it in the variable on the left. The value and type of the expression correspond to the resulting value and type of the left-hand variable.

The other assignment operators are merely shorthand. In every case, the following equivalence is true

`z #= x` is the same as `z = z # x`

where # is a valid binary mathematical or bitwise operator.

Miscellaneous operators

Table 1-8 shows the remaining, miscellaneous operators.

Table 1-8 Miscellaneous Operators

Operator	*Meaning*
( )	Function call
[ ]	Array index
.	Member of the structure
->	Member of the structure pointed to
?:	Ternary operator
,	Comma operator

The ternary operator is often confused with a control structure. It works as follows:

```
a ? b : c;
```

If `a` is true, the result of the operator is the value of `b`; otherwise, the result is the value of `c`. The ternary operator uses short-circuit evaluation, too. If `a` is true, `c` is not evaluated; if `a` is not true, `b` is not evaluated.

The comma operator is really useful. It means evaluate the subexpression on the left of the operator and then evaluate the subexpression on the right. The value and type of the expression correspond to the subexpression on the right. Now how about that for an operator? It's a "get out of the way" operator; that is, it basically doesn't do anything.

Actually, the comma has a few obscure uses. One of the uses of the comma operator is to cram extra stuff into the clauses of a `for` loop. For example:

```
for(x=0,  y = 100; x < y; x+=10, y-=10)
```

This initializes two loop counters and causes one to count up while the other counts down.

Special operator considerations

You can override the precedence of the operators by using parentheses. Consider the following example:

```
void fn(void)
{
    int a = 2;
    int b = 3;
    int c;

    c = 2 + a * b;      /*multiplication first; c = 8*/
    c = (2 + a) * b;    /*addition first; c = 12*/
}
```

Without parentheses in the first expression, a is multiplied by b and the result is added to 2 because multiplication has a higher precedence than addition. In the second expression, 2 is added to a and the result is multiplied by b because of the parentheses.

Except for the three short-circuit cases noted in the section "Logical operators," the order of evaluation of subexpressions at the same precedence level is not known. Consider the following example:

```
z = f() * g();       /*don't know order functions are called*/
```

Because ( ) has a higher precedence than *, both functions are called before the multiplication is performed. Fine. The problem is that the programmer doesn't know which function is called first. The compiler is well within its rights to call f( ) first and then g( ) or to change its mind and call g( ) first.

Parentheses have no effect on this particular property. The only way to affect the order is to break the expression into two statements, as follows:

```
z = f();             /*now f() is called first... */
z *= g();            /*...followed by g()         */
```

Chapter 2

C Pointers

In This Chapter

- Declaring pointers to simple variables
- Using pointers
- Operations on pointers
- Passing pointers to functions
- Allocating and using memory off the heap

This chapter covers that most dreaded of topics — pointers. The mere mention of the word sends otherwise battle-hardened programmers shrieking to the vending machine for more caffeine-laden cola to calm their nerves. But it needn't be that way. Pointers are a powerful arrow in every C programmer's quiver, and it behooves us all to master them.

Declaring and Using Simple Pointers

A *pointer variable* is a variable that contains an address, usually the address of another variable. Consider the following example:

```
void fn()
{
   int i;
   int *pI;

   pI = &i;          /*pI now points to i*/
   *pI = 10;         /*stores 10 in i  */
}
```

Pointer variables are declared like normal variables except for the addition of the unary * character. In an expression, the unary & means "the address of," and the unary * means "pointed at by." Thus, you would read the first assignment as "store the address of i in pI." The second assignment is "store 10 in the location pointed at by pI."

To make this more concrete, assume that this function's memory starts at location 0x100. In addition, `i` is at address 0x102 and `pI` is at 0x106. The first assignment is shown in Figure 2-1. Here you can see that the value of `&i` (0x102) is stored in `pI`.

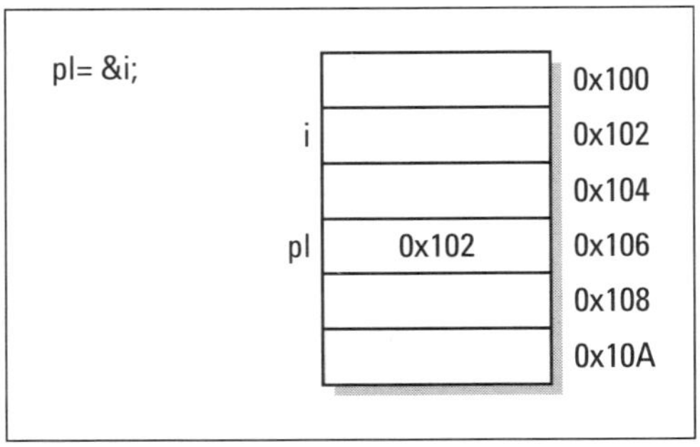

Figure 2-1: Storing the address of i in `pI`.

Figure 2-2 demonstrates the next assignment. The value 10 is stored in the address contained in `pI`, which is 0x102 (the address of `i`) — that is, `*pI` is the location pointed at by `pI`.

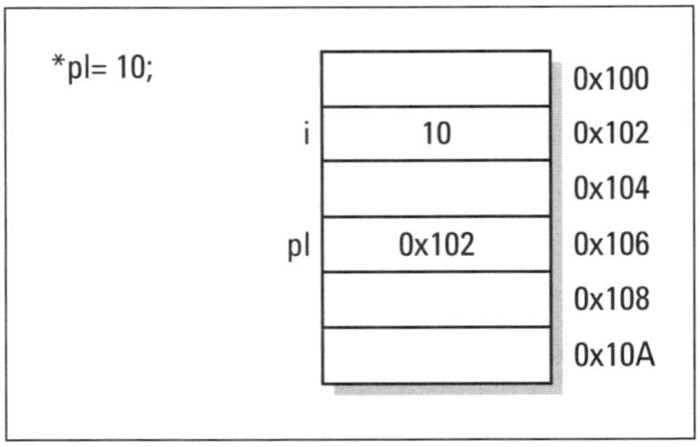

Figure 2-2: Storing 10 in the address pointed at by `pI`.

Remember that every expression has a type as well as a value. The type of the `&i` expression is pointer to integer, written as `int*` in C-ese. Comparing this to the declaration of `pI`, you see that the types match exactly.

Similarly, because `pI` is of type `int*`, the type of `*pI` is `int`. Expressed in plain English, the type of the thing pointed to by `pI` is `int`.

The pointer type `char*` serves the role of a separate string type. Any string of characters in quotation marks is assumed to be of type `char*`. In addition to the characters you code, C adds a trailing 0, which is used as a string terminator. This string terminator is convenient because it's easy to test for a 0 in loops. (Remember that 0 is the only value that is considered false.)

For example, consider the following function, which makes all the characters in a string passed to the function uppercase:

```
#include <ctype.h>
void upperCase(char *pS)
{
   while (*pS)
   {
      if (islower(*pS))
      {
         *pS = toupper(*pS);
      }
      pS++;
   }
}

void fn()
{
   char *pString;
   pString = "Davis";
   upperCase(pString);
}
```

In function `fn()`, the assignment to `pString` is allowed because both `pString` and `"Davis"` are of type `char*`. The value of the subexpression `"Davis"` is the address of a string consisting of `'D','a','v','i','s'`, and a terminating `'\0'` added by C.

The call to `upperCase()` passes the address of this string. In the `while` condition in `fn()`, `*pS` is true for every character in the string except the terminating '\0', which C tacked on the end of the string for us. When this character is encountered, the loop is terminated, which causes the program to exit the function. The function `toupper()`, whose prototype is included in `ctype.h`, returns the uppercase version of whatever you pass it.

Operating on Pointers

In the code snippet in the preceding section, notice the `pS++` in the function `fn()`. From this, you can infer that some of the operators are defined on pointer types as well. By "defined on pointer types," I do not mean defined on the object pointed at by a pointer, as in the following example:

```
void fn(void)
{
    int i = 5;
    int *pI = &i;
    int b;
    b = 2 * *pI;
}
```

*pI is an integer. (It is the integer pointed at by pI.) Like any other integer, *pI is subject to all the operations defined for other integers. Well, then, what operations other than * are defined for pI itself? (See the following sections to find out the answers.)

Incrementing pointers

The ++ operator is defined for pointers. To see the results of incrementing a pointer variable, look at the graphical computer, shown in Figure 2-3. Assume that the string "Davis" is stored beginning at location 0x100, one character per byte, and that pS points to the beginning of that string.

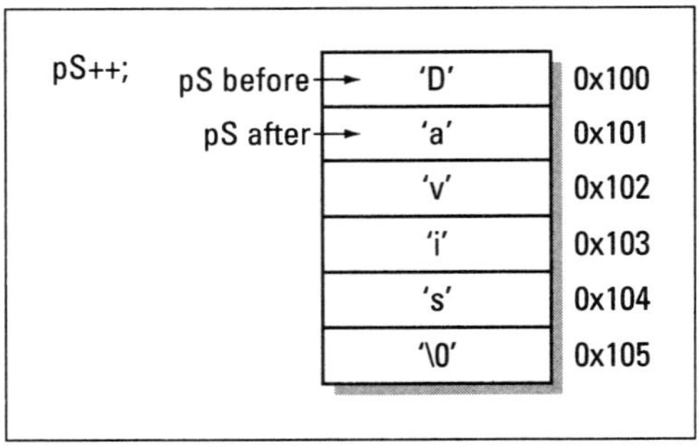

Figure 2-3: Incrementing a character pointer.

If pS started out pointing at the 'D' with a value of 0x100, it makes sense that adding 1 to pS results in a value of 0x101, which happens to be the address of 'a', the next character in the string. Repeating the process moves the pointer to 'v', then to 'i', then to 's'. Finally, pS points to the trailing '\0'.

The designers of C thought this was really neat, and so do most C programmers. But what if a character requires more than one byte? Or what if pS pointed not to a string of characters but to an array of integers, each of which takes multiple bytes on the PC? Then the addition wouldn't work as well because 0x101 would not correspond to an even address.

The inventors of C made up a rule to retain the neat addition trick for all storage types, even those that take more than a byte: Pointer variable addition is always defined in terms of the size of the thing pointed at. For example, if `pS` points to 2-byte integers, `pS++` adds 2 instead of 1 to `pS`. If `pS` points to some complex structure such as a structure containing 50 characters, `pS++` might add 50 to the value of `pS`. Stated another way, if `pS` is the address of a house, `pS++` moves `pS` to the next house down the block, irrespective of the size of the house.

Defining other operations on pointers

What other operators besides ++ are defined for pointers? Well, ++ moves the pointer one house up the block, and -- moves it one house down the block, to use the analogy defined in the earlier section. In fact, any variation of integer addition or subtraction is defined. The result is always a pointer. For example:

```
void fn(void)
{
    int i;
    X *pX;

    pX + i;
}
```

Thus, if `i` is an integer and `pX` is a pointer to type `X`, `pX + i` is a pointer to `X`, `i` elements away from `pX`. That is, `pX + i` points to the `i`th house down the block.

The only other operation defined for pointers is the subtraction of two pointers of the same type. This results in an integer that is the number of elements between the two pointers. In other words, subtracting the address of one house from that of another results in a count of the number of houses between the two addresses.

Arrays and Pointers: Can You Ever Get Them Together?

A direct relationship exists between adding to a pointer and indexing an array. Consider what it means to index into an array of integers.

```
void fn(int i)
{
    int array[10];
    int *pI;
    array[i] = 0;         /*store 0 into the i'th element*/

    pI = &array[0];
    *(pI + i) = 0;        /*has the same effect as previous*/
}
```

array[i] refers to the ith element in array. This is similar to the effect of adding to a pointer. If pI points to the 0th element of the array, pI + i points to the ith element. Thus, storing a value at pI + i has the same effect as storing a value at array[i].

In fact, C interprets the index operator, [], in the following way:

> array[x] is interpreted as *(array + x)

To highlight this relationship, C has a rule that if you give the name of an array without an index, you mean the address of the first element. Thus, array and pI are both of type int*. In fact, all the following statements are legal:

```
void fn(int i)
{
    int array[10];
    int *pI;

    pI = array;          /*both are of type int* so types match*/
    pI[i] = 0;           /*this is now same as array[i] = 0  */
    *(array + i) = 0; /*this is also same as array[i] = 0 */
}
```

Compare the declaration of a pointer to that of an array:

```
int *pPointer;
int array[10];
```

The pointer declaration allocates space for an address but doesn't allocate space for the integer(s) to which the pointer points. The array declaration allocates space for the integers but doesn't allocate space for a pointer; instead, it treats the address of the array like a constant.

Keeping this relationship between arrays and pointers in mind can often help make sense out of the pointer ravings you find in many C programs.

Passing Pointers to Functions

Arguments to C functions are always passed by value. That is, when the call is made, only the value of the variable is passed. A function cannot change that value in the calling function. Consider the following example:

```
void fn(int i)
{
    i = 10;           /*this is legal and the...*/
                      /*...value is now 10 in fn()*/
}


int main()
{
    int i = 0;

    fn(i);            /*only the value 0 is passed to fn()*/
    return 0;         /*i is still 0 upon returning*/
}
```

If you want to change the value of a variable in the calling function, you must explicitly pass the address of the variable, as the following example demonstrates:

```
void fn(int *pI)
{
    *pI = 10;
}


int main()
{
    int i = 0;
    fn(&i);       /*this passes the address of i*/
    return 0;     /*now the value of i is 10    */
}
```

In this case, the address of `i` is passed to the function `fn()`. When `fn()` stores 10 in the integer pointed to by `pI`, it overwrites the old value of `i`.

Because the name of an array without a subscript is equal to the address of the array, calling a function with a simple array name passes the address of the array. The following snippet demonstrates this:

```
void zero(int i, int *pArray)
{
   pArray[i] = 0;
}


int main()
{
   int array[100];

   zero(10, array);
   return 0;
}
```

Declaring Pointers to Functions

Storing and manipulating the address of a function is also possible, in addition to the manipulations on data pointers you've seen so far in this chapter. However, the following doesn't declare a pointer to a function:

```
int *pFn();
```

Instead, this declares a function that returns a pointer to an integer. The `()` takes effect first because it has a higher precedence than `*`. To get the desired effect, parentheses are required:

```
int (*pFn)(float);
```

Now the `*` takes effect first. This is read as "pFn is a pointer to a function that takes a float argument and returns an int." In use, its semantics are similar to those of an array:

```
int anotherFn(float f);  /*some function, somewhere*/
void myFunc(float x)
{
   int (*pFn)(float);     /*declare a pointer to a function*/

   pFn = anotherFn; /*function name alone refers to itsÆ address*/
   (*pFn)(x);       /*call the function pointed at by pFn*/
}
```

The extra parentheses are necessary when calling `*pFn` (again) because the precedence of `()` is higher than that of `*`.

Allocating Heap Memory

The *heap* is an amorphous blob of memory from which your program can allocate chunks through a group of Standard C library calls, the most common of which is `void* malloc(size_t size)`. `malloc()` accepts as its argument either an `int` or a `long` (depending on your compiler), which represents the number of bytes of memory to allocate. `malloc()` returns a pointer to the memory allocated or a zero if it couldn't fulfill the request, usually because there isn't as much contiguous heap memory on hand as you asked for.

You can do whatever you want with the memory block returned from `malloc()`. When you're finished, however, you must remember to replace the memory block by calling `free()`, passing it the same pointer returned to you by `malloc()`. If you don't, your program will slowly starve itself by running out of heap memory (unless it ends before that). When your program terminates, any memory you have checked out of the heap is automatically returned for you.

TECHNICAL STUFF

So what good are pointers to functions?

I have a lot of mottoes to get me through life. One of them is "Not everything in the world that can be done is worth doing." Take bungee jumping, for example. Pointers to functions can be very useful in some unusual cases. One of these is the callback function.

The *callback function* works like a return address on a registration form. When a program executes under a graphical operating system, such as Windows or UNIX X-Windows, it can register itself to be alerted when certain events occur (for example, when the operator clicks the mouse in a window).

As part of the registration, the program provides the address of the function to be called. When the event occurs, the operating system calls that address, passing a structure containing a description of what happened. The following pseudocode gives you a feel for how a callback function works:

```
/*callbackFunction - is called when
   EVENT_NAME occurs;
   pPacketOfData points to a structure that
   describes
   what just happened*/
void callbackFunction(struct Packet
     *pPacketOfData);
int main()
{
   /*other stuff and then...*/
   /*here, register callbackFunction as a
   function to be called
       when event EVENT_NAME occurs*/
  register(EVENT_NAME, callbackFunction);
   /*...life goes on*/
}
```

Somewhere deep in the bowels of the operating system, `call- backFunction` address is stored in a pointer to a function, like `pFn` declared earlier, and called indirectly when the event is detected.

Heap memory is nice because it's dynamically allocated — that is, heap memory is allocated at run time. This is great if you don't know how much memory you'll actually need until run time. In addition, heap memory allows you to use all available memory in the machine without the need to know how much that is at compile time.

Chapter 3

User-Defined Types: The C Structure

In This Chapter

- Declaring and initializing structures
- Declaring and using pointers to structures
- Working with structures and functions
- Retrieving structures off the heap

In addition to the intrinsic types, programmers may define their own types using the C keyword `struct`. To master C++, you need to have a complete understanding of the C structure. In this chapter, I tell you all you need to know about the C structure.

C Structures 101

A structure is defined and accessed as follows:

```
struct MyStruct
{
   int   firstElement;
   float secondElement;
};

void fn()
{
   struct MyStruct ms;
   ms.firstElement = 0;   /*refers to the integer member*/
   ms.secondElement = 1.0;/*refers to the float member*/
}
```

Structures differ from arrays in that elements in an array must each be of the same type, but elements in a structure can be of different types. Because a structure's elements can be of different types, however, they must be declared and referenced by name rather than by subscript. Thus we see the names `firstElement` and `secondElement` assigned to the two members of `MyStruct`.

You must differentiate between a structure and an instance of a structure. (An instance of a structure is also known as an *object*.) In the preceding snippet, the structure is `MyStruct`; the object is `ms`. To use an example closer to home: *Reader* is a class of people who read books, and you are an instance of class *Reader*. You may also be an instance of class *Snoozer* by now.

Arrays and structures can be mixed and matched. You can have an array of structures, as demonstrated by `ms` in the following, or a structure containing an array, as does `MyStruct`.

```
struct MyStruct
{
   float anElement;
   int   anArray[10];
};

void fn()
{
   struct MyStruct ms[20];

   ms[10].anElement = 10.0;
   ms[10].anArray[5] = 5;
}
```

Structures can be initialized when declared, as the following example demonstrates:

```
struct MyStruct
{
   int   firstElement;
   float secondElement;
};

void fn()
{
   struct MyStruct simple = {1, 2.0};
   struct MyStruct array[2] = {{1, 2.0}, /*array[0]*/
                               {1, 2.0}};/*array[1]*/
}
```

The only mathematical operator that is defined for structures is the assignment operator. Assignments such as the following are allowed if the source and destination types match:

```
void fn(MyStruct source)
{
   struct MyStruct target;

   target = source;      /*copy the source into the target*/
}
```

Such an assignment performs a binary copy of the source to the target.

Pointers to C Structures

This chapter offers a quick overview of pointers to simple objects. The following example shows how to declare and use a pointer to a structure object:

```
struct MyStruct
{
   int firstElement;
   float secondElement;
};

void fn()
{
   struct MyStruct mc;
   struct MyStruct *pMC;

   pMC = &mc;             /*point pMC to the object mc     */
   pMC->firstElement = 1;/*reference the first element...*/
                          /*...of the object pointed...   */
                          /*...to by pMC                  */
   pMC->secondElement= 2.0; /*you get the idea           */
}
```

The type of `pMC` is `struct MyStruct*` , which you read as "pMC, is a pointer to a MyStruct object." The -> operator is used to access members of structures pointed to by a pointer type. This is very similar to the way that `int*` was a "pointer to an int" as demonstrated in Chapter 2.

Just as `array[i]` was really a shorthand for `*(array + i)`, so `pMC->firstElement` is also a shorthand. Consider the following: If `pMC` is a pointer to an object of structure `MyClass`, `(*pMC)` must be the object pointed to by `pMC`. Thus, I could have written `(*pMC).firstElement`.

(The parentheses are necessary because . has higher precedence than *. Refer to Chapter 1 if you're not sure which operators have precedence.) Thus, the following equivalence holds true:

`pMC->firstElement` is equivalent to `(*pMC).firstElement`

Operations on pointers to structures

The same operations that are defined for pointers to intrinsic types (see Chapter 2) are defined for pointers to user-defined types and with the same effect. For example, the following function initializes the `pName` field in an array of structures:

```
struct MyStruct
{
   char *pName;
   /*...other stuff...*/
};

void fn(int number, struct MyStruct *pMS)
{
   while (number > 0) /*loop until count exhausted*/
   {
      pMS->pName = (char*)0;
      number--;      /*decrement the count*/
      pMS++;         /*go to next element in array*/
   }
}
```

Because addition is defined on pointers to structures, the index operator `[]` is also defined. Thus, this example function could have been written as follows:

```
void fn(int number, struct MyStruct *pArray)
{
   int i;

   for (i = 0; i < number; i++)
   {
      pArray[i].pName = (char*)0;
   }
}
```

Notice that the pArray[i] is not a pointer to an object but an object. Hence, it requires the . operator, not the -> operator.

Using pointers to structures

Pointers to structures are used in many of the same ways as pointers to intrinsics. However, pointers to structures are used also in one way that is unique to structures: with linked lists.

Intrinsic objects such as ints and floats have no way of "pointing to" each other. The only practical way that multiple intrinsic objects can be grouped is the array. The array, however, is inconvenient for many applications. In particular, inserting or removing an element from the middle of an array is difficult.

Structure objects can include pointers to other objects. This allows the objects to be connected in many ways that are more convenient to handle. For example, the following structure allows for the implementation of a linked list:

```
struct LList
{
   /*include whatever data you like*/
   int whatEverData;

   struct LList *pNext;      /*ptr to next object in list*/
};
struct LList *pFirst;        /*ptr to first object in list*/
```

The pointer pFirst is intended to point to the first element in the list. In each element of the list, pNext points to the next element. In the last element, pNext contains 0.

A singly linked list is traversed easily. For example, the following function traverses a linked list of LList structures looking for an element with whatEverData set to 0:

```
void fn(struct Llist* pFirst)
{
   struct Llist *pLL;

   /*start with the first; continue until pLL is 0;
     link from one element to the next each time*/
```

(continued)

(continued)

```
    for (pLL = pFirst; pLL; pLL = pLL->pNext)
    {
        if (pLL->whatEverData == 0)
        {
            /*...whatever processing you want here...*/
        }
    }
}
```

You can see linked lists in use in a working program in BUDGET4 at the end of Part IV.

Structures and Functions

When a structure object is passed to a function, a copy of the object must be made and given to the function. (C always passes by value — see Chapter 2.) Changes made to the structure object by the function don't affect the object's value in the calling function. For small objects, this may be what is desired. Copying large objects, however, can result in considerable overhead in both time and memory.

Passing the address of a structure object, as demonstrated in the following snippet, is generally more efficient.

```
struct MyStruct
{
    int lotsOfData[10000];
};

void fn1(MyStruct ms);
void fn2(MyStruct *pMS);

void fn()
{
    struct MyStruct ms;
    fn1(ms);    /*this passes some 10,000 integers to fn1()*/
    fn2(&ms);   /*this passes a single pointer*/
}
```

Here the call to fn1() results in an entire ms, some 10,000 integers being copied onto the stack and passed to fn1(). The call to fn2(), however, copies only the address of the existing ms object onto the stack.

Allocating Structures from the Heap

Structure objects can be allocated from the heap, as the following code snippet shows.

```
#include <malloc.h>
struct MyStruct
{
   int data;
   /*...whatever other data you want...*/
};

struct MyStruct *getNewMS(int someData)
{
   struct MyStruct *pMS;
   pMS = (struct MyStruct*)malloc(sizeof struct MyStruct);
   if (pMS)
   {
      pMS->data = someData;
   }
   return pMS;
}
```

The sizeof MyStruct returns the number of bytes in a MyStruct object. This number is passed to malloc(), which attempts to allocate that much memory off the heap. If the request is successful, malloc() returns a nonzero pointer. This pointer must be recast into the proper type before being assigned to pMS. The function getNewMS() stores whatever data it wants into this new object. Finally, getNewMS() returns this pointer to the calling function.

getNewMS() continues to allocate MyStruct objects until heap memory is exhausted.

The C Version of the Budget Program: BUDGET1.C

As I mention in the Introduction of this book, Parts I through V end with an example program. In Part I, the program starts life as a straight C program. In Parts II through V, I add C++ features covered in that particular part. This lets you see how C++ programs differ from C programs. By comparing the new features with the old, you can come to appreciate their beauty. (Okay, maybe that word's a little strong, but a good program does get me choked up sometimes.)

Before you look at the first version of the example program, you should know something about my coding style. I use the following conventions:

- Types, such as structures, start with an uppercase letter.
- Variables start with a lowercase letter.
- Pointers start with the letter *p*.
- Each word (except the first) in a multiword variable name starts with an uppercase letter.
- Macros and #defined constants appear in all uppercase.

In addition, I try to be consistent about where I place open and close braces and how far I indent.

The BUDGET program is a simple checkbook and savings register program. Here's what it does:

1. Allocates a savings account entry, allocates a checking account entry, or exits.
2. Assigns an account number.
3. Begins accepting transactions, consisting of deposits and withdrawals. A transaction of zero signals the end of this entry.
4. After the user chooses to exit, the program displays the ending balance of all accounts, the subtotals of all checking and savings accounts, and the total of all accounts.

Avoiding needless coding errors

We humans have a limited amount of CPU power between our ears. We need to direct our CPU power toward getting our programs working, not toward figuring out simple stuff (such as indentation).

Be consistent with how you name variables, where you place open and close braces, and so on. This is called your coding style. When you have developed a style, it's just as important that you stick to that style to minimize wasted human CPU time. After a while, your coding style will become second nature. You'll find that you can code your programs with less time and read your programs with less effort.

When working on a project with several programmers, it's important that you all use the same style to avoid a Tower of Babel effect with conflicting and confusing styles. In addition, I strongly suggest that you enable every error and warning message that your compiler can produce. Even if you decide that a particular warning is not a problem, why would you want it suppressed? You can always ignore it. More often than not, even a warning represents a problem that needs to be corrected.

Some people don't like the compiler finding their slip-ups because they think it's embarrassing and they think that correcting things to get rid of the warnings wastes time. Just think how embarrassing and time-consuming it is to painstakingly search for a bug only to find that it's a problem your compiler could have told you about hours ago.

You can find further bug-avoiding techniques in Chapter 28.

This program must mimic a few bank rules concerning transactions:

- Never let the balance become negative. (Your bank may be friendly, but I bet it's not that friendly.)
- Never charge for making a deposit.
- Charge 20 cents per check if the balance is less than $500; otherwise, checks are free.
- Charge $5 for each withdrawal from a savings account after the first withdrawal, which is free.

The following program should be straight ANSI C; no tricks. Feel free to compile this with your C++ compiler. If you want to make sure that I'm not slipping in any C++, be sure that the name of the program ends in .C and that the "C++always" compiler option isn't set.

```
/*BUDGET1.C - calculates your bank account balances.
             There are two types of accounts:
                   Checking - $.20 per check if
                                  balance < 500
```

(continued)

(continued)

```
                    Savings  - $5.00 per withdrawal
                               (first is free)
*/
#include <stdio.h>

/*the maximum number of accounts you can have*/
#define MAXACCOUNTS 10

/*Checking - this describes checking accounts*/
struct Checking
{
   unsigned accountNumber;
   float    balance;
} chkAcnts[MAXACCOUNTS];

/*Savings - you can probably figure this one out*/
struct Savings
{
   unsigned accountNumber;
   float    balance;
   int      noWithdrawals;
} svgAcnts[MAXACCOUNTS];

/*prototype declarations, just to keep us honest*/
void initChecking(struct Checking *pCO);
void processChecking(struct Checking*pCO);

void initSavings (struct Savings  *pSO);
void processSavings (struct Savings*pSO);
int main();

/*main - accumulate the initial input and output totals*/
int main()
{
   char     accountType;     /*S or C*/
   unsigned keepLooping;     /*0 -> get out of loop*/
   float    chkTotal;        /*total in checking accounts*/
   float    svgTotal;        /*total in savings accounts*/
   float    total;           /*total of all accounts*/
   int      i;
   int      noChkAccounts;   /*no. of checking accounts*/
   int      noSvgAccounts;   /*no. of savings accounts*/

   /*loop until someone enters X or x*/
   noChkAccounts = 0;
```

```
  noSvgAccounts = 0;
  keepLooping = 1;
  while (keepLooping)       /*Note 1*/
  {
     printf("Enter S for Savings,"
            " C for Checking,"
            " X for exit\n");
     scanf("\n%c", &accountType);

     switch (accountType)
     {

case 'c':
case 'C':            /*Note 2*/
   if (noChkAccounts < MAXACCOUNTS)
   {
      initChecking(&chkAcnts[noChkAccounts]);
      processChecking(&chkAcnts[noChkAccounts]);
      noChkAccounts++;
   }
   else
   {
      printf("No more room for checking accounts\n");
   }
    break;

    case 's':
    case 'S':
           if (noSvgAccounts < MAXACCOUNTS)
           {
              initSavings(&svgAcnts[noSvgAccounts]);
              processSavings(&svgAcnts[noSvgAccounts]);
              noSvgAccounts++;
           }
           else
           {
              printf("No more room for savings accounts\n");
           }
           break;

        case 'x':
        case 'X':
           keepLooping = 0;
           break;
```

(continued)

(continued)

```
        default:
            printf("I didn't get that.\n");
      }
   }

   /*now present totals*/
   chkTotal = 0.0F;              /*Note 3*/
   printf("Checking accounts:\n");
   for (i = 0; i < noChkAccounts; i++)
   {
      printf("Account %6d = %8.2f\n",
             chkAcnts[i].accountNumber,
             chkAcnts[i].balance);
      chkTotal += chkAcnts[i].balance;
   }
   svgTotal = 0.0F;
   printf("Savings accounts:\n");
   for (i = 0; i < noSvgAccounts; i++)
   {
      printf("Account %6d = %8.2f (no. withdrawals = %d)\n",
             svgAcnts[i].accountNumber,
             svgAcnts[i].balance,
             svgAcnts[i].noWithdrawals);
      svgTotal += svgAcnts[i].balance;
   }
   total = chkTotal + svgTotal;
   printf("Total for checking account = %8.2f\n", chkTotal);
   printf("Total for savings account  = %8.2f\n", svgTotal);
   printf("Total worth                = %8.2f\n", total);
   return 0;
}

/*initChecking - initialize a checking account*/
void initChecking(struct Checking *pChecking)
{
   printf("Enter account number:");
   scanf("%d", &pChecking->accountNumber);
   pChecking->balance = 0.0F;
}

/*processChecking - input the data for a checking account*/
void processChecking(struct Checking *pChecking)
{
   float transaction;
```

```
   printf("Enter positive number for deposit,\n"
          "negative for check, 0 to terminate");
  do
  {
    printf(":");
    scanf("%f", &transaction);

    /*is this a deposit?*/
    if (transaction > 0.0F)
    {
       pChecking->balance += transaction;
    }

    /*how about a withdrawal?*/
    if (transaction < 0.0F)
    {
       transaction = -transaction;
       if (pChecking->balance < transaction)
       {
          printf("Insufficient funds: "
                 "balance %f, check %f\n",
                 pChecking->balance, transaction);
       }
       else
       {
          pChecking->balance -= transaction;

          /*if balance falls too low, charge service fee*/
          if (pChecking->balance < 500.00F)
          {
             pChecking->balance -= 0.20F;
          }
       }
    }
  } while (transaction != 0.0F);
}

/*initSavings - initialize a savings account*/
void initSavings (struct Savings  *pSavings)
{
  printf("Enter account number:");
  scanf("%d", &pSavings->accountNumber);
  pSavings->balance = 0.0F;
  pSavings->noWithdrawals = 0;
```

(continued)

(continued)

```
}

/*processSavings - input the data for a savings
account*/
void processSavings(struct Savings *pSavings)
{
   float transaction;

   printf("Enter positive number for deposit,\n"
          "negative for withdrawal, 0 to terminate");
   do
   {
      printf(":");
      scanf("%f", &transaction);

      /*is this a deposit?*/
      if (transaction > 0.0F)
      {
         pSavings->balance += transaction;
      }

      /*how about a withdrawal?*/
if (transaction < 0.0F)
      {
         transaction = -transaction;
         if (pSavings->balance < transaction)
         {
            printf("Insufficient funds: "
                   "balance %f, check %f\n",
                   pSavings->balance, -transaction);
         }
         else
         {
            if (++pSavings->noWithdrawals > 1)
            {
               pSavings->balance -= 5.00F;
            }
            pSavings->balance -= transaction;
         }
      }
   } while (transaction != 0.0F);
}
```

A sample run of this program follows (just enough to give you an idea of how it works):

```
Enter S for Savings, C for Checking, X for exit
S
Enter account number:123
Enter positive number for deposit,
negative for withdrawal, 0 to terminate:200
:-50
:-50
:0
Enter S for Savings, C for Checking, X for exit
C
Enter account number:234
Enter positive number for deposit,
negative for check, 0 to terminate:200
:-25
:-20
:0
Enter S for Savings, C for Checking, X for exit
X
Checking accounts:
Account    234 =   154.60
Savings accounts:
Account    123 =    95.00 (no. withdrawals = 2)
Total for checking account =   154.60
Total for savings account  =    95.00
Total worth                =   249.60
```

Here's how the BUDGET1.C program works. Two `struct`s, `Checking` and `Savings`, contain the information needed for checking and savings accounts. To keep the program as simple as possible, I allocate storage for these accounts from two arrays, `chkAcnts` and `svgAcnts`.

The downside of the array approach as opposed to dynamic memory allocation is that only a maximum number of accounts can be accommodated (`MAXACCOUNTS`).

The main program is divided in two sections: the accumulation section, where the deposits and withdrawals are accumulated into accounts, and the display section. The accumulation section prompts the user for S, C, or X and then inputs a character (see the `Note 1` comment in the listing).

If the user enters `C`, control passes to the checking account case (`Note 2`). If the maximum number of checking accounts hasn't been reached, a new one is allocated, initialized [`initChecking()`], and processed [processChecking ()]. When the maximum number of accounts is reached, further attempts to add accounts are rejected with an error message.

The initChecking() function merely asks for the account number and initializes the balance to 0. The program assumes that a deposit must precede any withdrawal.

The processChecking() function accepts transactions. Positive transactions are assumed to be deposits, negative transactions are withdrawals, and zero exits the function. (I know this is crude, but trees are a valuable national resource.) Deposits are accepted without comment, but withdrawals must go through a few hoops (such as ensuring that enough money is in the account).

Savings accounts are processed in a similar fashion to checking accounts by functions that are laid out the same but with slightly different names. The charging algorithm for savings account withdrawals, however, is different than the one for checking account withdrawals.

When the user enters X, the main() function passes control to the display section of the program (Note 3). At that point, the program loops through all the accounts, spitting out the balances and adding them in the chkTotal and svgTotal variables.

You can note a few general points about the program. First, information about checking and savings accounts is strewn throughout the program. Although I was careful to write processChecking() and processSaving() functions (which not all C programmers do), members of these structures are referenced in many other places. This can lead to side effect errors, in which changing a value in one place accidentally changes it somewhere else.

Also notice that despite the obvious similarities between savings and checking accounts, I was forced to write separate functions because relating two structures is impossible unless they are identical.

TECHNICAL STUFF

I could have written an Account structure that is either a savings account or a checking account depending on the value of some internal variable. This type of structure is called a *variant record.* C even encourages variant records by supplying the union keyword. Using variant records, however, makes the resulting code more complicated. Whenever the accounts should be treated differently, the code must check the type of account and act accordingly. This has the effect of distributing even more information about the internals of an Account throughout the code.

Although other (maybe even better) ways exist to implement this program, it serves nicely as the basis for our investigations. As you progress in your knowledge of C++, you will see this pure C program morph into a full-blown, object-oriented C++ program.

Part II

Getting Your Feet Wet: The Non-Object-Oriented Features of C++

The 5th Wave By Rich Tennant

"SO I SAID, 'WAITER! WAITER! THERE'S A BUG IN MY SOUP!' AND HE SAYS, 'SORRY, SIR, THE CHEF USED TO PROGRAM COMPUTERS.' AHH HAHA HAHA THANK YOU! THANK YOU!"

In this part . . .

Now it's time to look at the features that make C++ a better C. Eventually, I discuss the features that make C++ an OO language (as in "object-oriented," not as in "oh-oh, I made a mistake trying to learn C++"). But I start with the basics.

Chapter 4

Some Simple Stuff

In This Chapter

- Getting a new comment style
- Declaring variables anywhere
- Introduction to the reference type and two new type specifiers, `const` and `volatile`

In this chapter, you start your journey through C++ by covering a few simple additions to the language. First, C++ adds a new comment style. Second, C++ lets you define your variables anywhere in a function instead of only at the beginning. Third, C++ defines some new type specifiers.

A New Comment Style

Besides the old C standby /* */ comments, C++ defines a new kind of comment. Anything following // on the same line is considered a comment.

Why do I need it?

The C++ alternate form of comment closes itself automatically with the end of the line. With the old comments, if you forget to close the comment properly with a */, anything up to the next */ is treated as if it were a comment. This new style is self-closing, so the problem doesn't arise. This argument is pretty weak, but then such a simple addition doesn't need much justification. Maybe Stroustrup just got tired of typing */.

How does it work?

The following code uses the old style of comments:

```
area = PI * r * r; /*did you remember how to
                  calculate the area of a circle?*/
```

Notice how tempting inserting code into the blank space is? If you did insert code into the blank space, however, whatever you added would be commented out. For example:

```
area = PI * r * r; /*did you remember how to
vol = height * area; calculate the area of a circle?*/
```

The assignment to `vol` is in the comment.

In the new style of comments, anything to the right of // up to the new-line character is considered a comment. However, because the new-line character terminates the comment, a new // is required if the comment is spread over more than one line. For example:

```
area = PI * r * r; //did you remember how to
                   //calculate the area of a circle?
```

Not only does this look slightly more balanced, it avoids the problem of unintentionally commenting out code. The following works as expected:

```
area = PI * r * r;  //did you remember how to
vol = height * area;//calculate the area of a circle?
```

Here, the assignment to `vol` is not part of the comment.

NONSTANDARD

Several compilers, including Borland C++, allow the // form of comment to be used even when compiling in C mode. Be careful, though; if you try to move C code with C++ comments to a different C compiler, you may have to do a lot of editing.

TECHNICAL STUFF

The // comment feature is unusual in the world of C++ in that it treats a new line differently than any other form of white space. (White space consists of characters such as spaces, tabs, and new-line characters.)

Variable Declarations Anywhere You Want

In C, variables must be declared at the beginning of the function, before any executable statements. C++ drops this restriction. Well, okay, it relaxes this restriction a whole bunch.

Why do I need them?

To a certain extent, "Why do I need them?" is another case of "Why not?" Whenever I wanted an index for a `for` loop, for example, I always found it inconvenient to have to search for the beginning of the function I was in so that I could declare the index. Because I always forgot to set an editor bookmark, I then had to search for my old location in the program after I declared the variable before restarting — what a waste of time.

In C++, all this nuisance is unnecessary. I can declare the variable right where I need it. It makes the code slightly easier to read as well because the reader can see the type of the variable immediately.

Besides the convenience, being able to declare variables in the middle of a function allows you to initialize variables with values calculated previously in the function.

How do they work?

In C, global variables can be declared anywhere you like at the module level; local variables, however, must be declared at the beginning of the function. In C++, you can declare a variable almost anywhere. This means that I don't have to jump all over the place with the editor. I can simply write things like the following:

```
void makeCopy(char *pT, char *pS)
{
   //first check for zero pointer
   if (pS == 0)
   {
      *pT = '\0';
      return;
   }

   //copy the block
   int i;           //C wouldn't let us get away with this
   for (i = 0; pT[i] = pS[i]; i++)
   {
   }
}
```

A variable exists from the point it is declared to the end of the function. Thus, in the preceding example, it would be illegal to try to reference `i` before the declaration at the end of the function. Just as always, it's illegal to declare two variables with the same name.

You can't access a variable before it is declared. In addition, you have to be careful not to jump around a declaration. If you attempt to use a variable whose declaration has been avoided, the results are unpredictable. Even if you don't attempt to access the variable, the compiler may not like it. For example, the Borland C++ compiler complains about the following code snippet:

```
//absValue - this is a silly way to take
//           absolute value
int absValue(int i)
{
   if (i > 0)      //if i <= 0 ...
   {
      int j = -i;  //...then the declaration of j is skipped
   }
   return max(i, j);
}
```

You can't declare a variable in a few places, such as:

- **In a conditional.** For example, the following is not allowed.

  ```
  if (int i = f())
  ```

- **In the second or third expressions of a `for` loop.** Neither of the following examples is allowed.

  ```
  //example 1
  int i;
  for (i = 0; int j = array[i]; i++)

  //example 2
  MyClass *ptr;
  for (ptr = first; ptr; MyClass *p = ptr++)
  ```

  The following, however, is allowed.

  ```
  //example 3
  for (MyClass *ptr = first; ptr; ptr++)
  ```

  Note that the scope of a variable declared in this way is limited to the `for` loop.

- **In the call to a function.** For example, the following is not allowed.

  ```
  result = fn(int temp = a);
  ```

In general, declare a variable immediately before the separately identifiable block of code in which the variable is used. There's no point in declaring variables in the middle of complex constructs, except to show how clever you can be. Often, this kind of cleverness can backfire by generating bugs.

I mention the following only to keep some book reviewer off my case and to impress you with my knowledge of C. The rule for C requires only that variables be declared at the beginning of a block. (A *block* is a section of code surrounded by braces.) Defining blocks anywhere in a function is possible, but I don't think I've ever seen it, and I'm certainly not going to suggest that you do it.

Constant Variables

Declaring a variable constant using the `const` keyword is possible. After you've declared a constant variable, its value cannot be changed.

Why do I need them?

One reason for using a constant variable instead of a numeric constant is because it enables you to assign a meaningful name to the constant. Consider the following example:

```
double speedOfLight = 2.9979E08;      //[meters/s]
double avogadrosConstant = 6.023E23; //[molecules/mole]
int    radiusOfEarth = 3959;          //[miles]
```

I know that most of you instantly recognize 3959 as the mean radius of the earth in miles, but others don't. By declaring a variable `radiusOfEarth` and using it instead of this strange number, the meaning is clear to all.

Unfortunately, declaring a variable to hold a constant introduces a potential error: What if someone changes it? Assume for a minute that the radius of the earth shouldn't change. (If the radius of the earth actually does change, whether or not your program works is of absolutely no concern.) You would like to be able to declare a variable so that you get to use its name, but flag it unchangeable so that the compiler won't let anyone muck with it. Ta da! That's what `const` does.

Some may note that the capability to give constants recognizable names already exists in C through the use of `#define`. This is partially true. However, `const` variables are more flexible, as you will see. (For example, a `const` can be a structure object; a `#define` can be only a simple number.) Besides, the general trend in C++ is away from using the preprocessor for everything except `#include`.

How do they work?

To declare a constant variable, just tack the keyword `const` on the front of the declaration. For example:

```
const int radiusOfEarth = 3959; //[miles]

void someFn()
{
   radiusOfEarth = 0;           //illegal
   int r = ++radiusOfEarth;     //also illegal
}
```

The first assignment is illegal. The declaration of `r` is also illegal because it has the side effect of changing the constant.

Because the value of a `const` variable can't be changed, if it is to have any value except zero it must be initialized when defined, as in the previous examples. For example, the following is not allowed:

```
const int radiusOfEarth;
radiusOfEarth = 3959;    //this is not allowed, remember?
```

`const` variables must be initialized when declared. (You'll never get another chance.)

`const` variables don't have to be initialized with a constant. They can be initialized also with the results of an expression. For example:

```
const int radiusOfEarthInMiles = 3959;
void fn()
{
   //example 1
   const int radiusOfEarthInKM = 1.609 *
                radiusOfEarthInMiles;

  //example 2
  const double distanceFromSun = calcDistanceFromSun();
}
```

There is one difference between the two cases shown, however. The compiler knows everything it requires to calculate the value of `radiusOfEarthInKM` at compile time (that is, while generating the code). It cannot calculate the value of `distanceFromSun`, however, without executing the function `calcDistanceFromSun()`, which won't happen until the program executes.

So? Well, `const` variables whose values are known at compile time can be used to allocate arrays and things like that, but `const` variables whose values are not known at compile time can't. It's easier to show you than to explain it:

```
const int maxNameLength = 20;
const int numberOfNames = 100;

void fn()
{
   //this is allowed because both values are known
   //at compile time
   char blockForNames[maxNameLength * numberOfNames];

   //the following is not allowed because longestName
   //is not known until the program executes
   const int longestName = calcLongestName();
   char anotherBlock[longestName * numberOfNames];
}
```

Like all variables, a `const` variable can be declared external, as in the following example:

```
extern const int radiusOfEarth; //defined somewhere else
```

In this case, the value of the variable is not known at compile time, and so it cannot be used to declare the size of arrays. In addition, this declaration does not attempt to initialize the value of the variable — the module that allocates the space gets to do that. Aside from these facts, an `extern const` is no different than other `const` variables.

The `const` keyword is part of ANSI C as well (borrowed from C++). In C, however, `const` variables are more like regular variables and less like constants. For example, `const` variables in C cannot be used to initialize arrays whether or not their value is known at compile time.

Applying `const` to pointers

The `const` keyword can be applied to pointers. However, this introduces an interesting ambiguity. Where does the `const` go? Before the type? After the type but before the variable name? The answer is *either*, but the results are different. Consider the following examples:

```
int main()
{
    const char * pCC = "this is a constant string";
    char * const cpC = "this is also a string";

    *pCC = 'a'; // assignment #1 - illegal
    *cpC = 'b'; // assignment #2 - legal

    pCC = "another string"; // assignment #3 - legal
    cpC = "another string"; // assignment #4 - illegal
    return 0;
}
```

What is and isn't constant in the declaration of `pCC` and `cpC`? The rule is that the "const-ness" applies to the thing immediately to the right of the `const` keyword.

The four assignments help sort it out. Compiling the preceding example generates an error message on assignments 1 and 4. Thus, `pCC` is a normal pointer to a constant character string. That is, although `pCC` can be changed (assignment 3), the character string to which it points cannot (assignment 1).

By comparison, `cpC` is a constant pointer to a normal character string. Thus, the string pointed to by `cpC` can be changed (assignment 2), but the pointer itself cannot (assignment 4).

Volatile Variables

There is yet another storage class called `volatile`. This storage class has the same syntax as `const`, but almost the opposite meaning. Tagging a variable `volatile` tells the compiler that the value of the variable may change at any time.

Why do I need them?

Compilers try to cache into registers the value of frequently used variables. This results in fewer memory accesses, making the program faster. If a memory location may change at any time, however, the compiler must reload the variable every time it's referred to. Declaring a variable `volatile` precludes the compiler from caching it.

What could possibly change the value of a variable without the program knowing about it? On some processors, data input is via special memory locations whose value magically changes as data comes pouring in. In addition, memory locations that are shared between processes on multiprocessing operating systems such as Windows NT and UNIX should be flagged as `volatile`.

The Referential Type Specifier

C++ retains the pointer types introduced by C. In addition, C++ introduces something called reference variables. *Reference variables* allow you to declare a variable that acts as an alias to some other base variable. After you declare the reference variable, accessing it has the same effect as accessing the base variable.

For example, in the following code snippet, `i` is an `int`. Adding the ampersand squiggle to the declaration of `refI` makes it a reference, in this case to `I`:

```
int i;
int &refI = i;
```

Any subsequent reference to `refI` is the same as referring to `i` directly. Thus, the following statements have the same effect:

```
int i;
int &refI = i;        //declared refI as an alias for i
int *pI;

i = 2;                //sets i to 2 (what else?)
refI = 3;             //sets i to 3

pI = &i;              //&i return address of i
pI = &refI;           //&refi also returns address of i
```

Notice that even `&refI` returns the address of `i`.

Why do I need it?

At first blush, this looks just about worthless. If accessing refI has the same effect as accessing i, why not just access i itself and be finished with it?

Reference variables solve in a very convenient way a nuisance that has been confusing programmers almost from the day they first went to C. Consider the following simplistic code segment:

```
void changeArgument(int I)
{
    I = 10;
}
int main()
{
    int i = 5;
    changeArgument(i);
    //the value of i here is still 5

    return 0;
}
```

It's pretty obvious that the programmer wants the function changeArgument() to change the value of I not only in changeArgument() but also in main(). Because C always passes function arguments by value, however, that's not what happens. When changeArgument() is called, the value 5 is passed (because that's what i contains when the call is made). By the time the value gets to changeArgument(), no connection exists between I and i.

Declaring I to be reference to i solves the problem. Now, I becomes an alias to i. Anything you do to I also affects i — even setting its value to 10.

How does it work?

The following shows how the preceding function would look with I declared as a reference:

```
void changeArgument(int &refI)    //just add the squiggle
{
    refI = 10;             //looks like a normal assignment
}
int main()
{
    int i = 5;
```

```
    changeArgument(i);     //no change to the call
    //the value of i is now 10

    return 0;
}
```

Adding the & character to the declaration of refI makes it a reference variable. Now when main() calls changeArgument(), refI becomes a reference to i. Any change to refI affects i directly.

C STUFF

C programmers handle this problem by passing the address of the variable to the function. The function can then dereference the pointer back to the original variable. It looks like this:

```
void changeArgument(int *pI)
{
    *pI = 10;
}
int main()
{
    int i = 5;
    changeArgument(&i);
    //the value of i here is now 10

    return 0;
}
```

You can see that what gets passed to changeArguments() this way is not 5 but the address of i. This lets the function "reach back" into i and change its value.

Reaching back into i and changing its value works okay, but it confuses people who aren't used to C pointers. (Sometimes it even confuses those who are.)

C++ is doing the same thing. The variable refI is like a pointer that C++ initializes with the address of i. Every time refI is used, C++ applies the * automatically. Thus, at the machine language level, the C++ reference solution is doing the same thing as the C solution, but references let C++ worry about the grungy details of taking addresses and dereferencing pointers. (This is fine with me because computers are a lot better at handling grungy details than I am.)

After a reference variable has been declared, you can do nothing to access the reference variable itself. That's why a reference variable must be initialized when it is declared — there is no other time when you have the opportunity to grab the reference variable without slipping through to the base variable. Reference variables declared as arguments to functions are initialized when the function is called.

A reference variable must be initialized when it is declared.

TIP

Passing variables to functions by reference can also save a considerable amount of memory and time. Normally when an object is passed to a function by value, the entire object is copied to the stack for the function to use. This is not a problem for small objects like integers and floats, but it can add up to a large amount of memory and time for large structures. Passing the object by reference causes the address of the object to be passed to the function. This address is the same size, irrespective of the size of the object.

Consider the following example:

```
struct ReallyBigArrayType
{
   int reallyBigArray[10000];
} reallyBigObject;
void fn1(ReallyBigArrayType rbo);
void fn2(ReallyBigArrayType &refRBO);
```

To call `fn1()`, a 10,000-word object must be copied to the stack. To call `fn2()`, however, only a single address must be copied.

Chapter 5

Functions, I Declare!

In This Chapter

- Formulating function prototypes
- The joys of strong typing
- Defining and using inline functions
- Overloading function names
- Providing default arguments to functions

In this chapter, I discuss function prototypes. You may remember from your C days that function prototypes are not exactly a new feature to C. Even old K&R C allowed programmers to declare the return type of a function (although they couldn't declare the function argument types). Nobody did, of course, because it wasn't required unless the function returned something other than `int` or `void`. ANSI C expanded the concept of function prototypes by allowing function arguments to be prototyped as well. C++ expands on the concept even further. In addition, C++ makes such prototypes a requirement.

Function Prototypes

C++ wants to know the type of each function called. The function type includes the type of the value returned by the function and the number and type of each argument. The programmer provides this information by including a prototype declaration of the function before calling the function.

The prototype declaration looks just like a function definition except that it has no code. (In computerese, we say the function has no body, like my hair.)

Here I am using the politically correct terms *declaration* and *definition* currently in style among language lawyers. A declaration introduces a name into the program. ("Good day Mr. Program. This is function f(). Function f(), this is Mr. Program.") A definition is a declaration that also tells the program all there is to know about the function. Thus, these are declarations:

```
struct MyStruct;
int max(int x, int y);
```

Whereas these are definitions:

```
struct MyStruct
{
   int a;
   int b;
};

int max(int x, int y)

{   return (x > y) ? (x) : (y);
}
```

Notice that a definition is automatically also a declaration.

Why do I need them?

I have a central rule (actually, I have a lot of central rules, but this one is way up near the top of the list): If a machine can do the work instead of me, let it. In K&R C, calling functions with the wrong arguments is probably the most common programming error. Strict function prototyping makes this error a thing of the past.

If you provide a function prototype declaration, the compiler can carefully compare each use of the function with the prototype to determine whether you have used the function properly. Calling the function with the wrong arguments sets off more alarms than leaning on a parked Porsche. And correcting the problem is easy when you've got bird dog C++ pointing straight to it.

Why do I want my compiler complaining at me?

Now why is it that I want my compiler harrassing me about my code? Doesn't my boss hassle me enough? Besides, it's embarrassing to have a mere machine complaining, especially if it's right. (I don't have to worry about that with my boss.)

Humans and computers don't communicate well. They don't think alike or talk alike. You need to tell the compiler all you can about what you want it to do. You also want to turn the compiler into a skeptical curmudgeon — and avoid miscommunication — by enabling all the warning messages possible.

People didn't always have this idea. The first computer languages (such as FORTRAN) took the opposite approach. The motto was: Less work for the programmer. Someone says, "Hey, no sense forcing the programmer to declare variables. We'll just use the first letter to determine the type and go from there." Great idea. Not!

Now if you misspell a variable name in FORTRAN, does the compiler tell you about it? Heck no. It just makes up a new variable with a slightly different name and a random value, and then pushes on. When you finish coding and the program doesn't work, you can debug the program and eventually find the misspelling.

But there's the rub: You, the human, must find a problem that the computer can find automatically. What fun.

This concept of "make sense out of whatever the programmer throws at us" was taken to its illogical extreme by IBM in the language PL/1. This compiler had a special Check Out version that was undauntable — it would make some kind of sense out of absolutely anything you provided it.

When I was just a wag in college, I was always looking for a way to have fun and show my superior intelligence. I just loved to torture PL/1 with existential statements like `IF`. That's it, just `IF`, not followed by anything. Believe it or not, PL/1 would construct what it thought I meant. (It derived `IF (.TRUE.) CONTINUE;` through some entertaining but amazingly complex logic that I really don't want to go into.)

Of course, what it thought I meant was wrong. I know it was wrong because I didn't mean anything at all. I was just having fun and wasting valuable CPU cycles. (People worried about wasted CPU cycles back then.)

Anytime you leave these types of decisions up to the computer, you are asking for trouble, because the computer might be wrong. Even if the computer is right most of the time, it will be wrong when you can least afford it, and you will spend time trying to find the misunderstanding.

How much better your programming life — and your personal relationships — will be if you just get these issues on the table up front and don't leave anything open to possible misinterpretation.

The moral is

- Be honest in your relationships.
- Enable all warnings.
- Leave nothing to the computer's deranged imagination.
- If you are ever on a computer language standards committee, remember PL/1.

How do they work?

A prototype declaration looks just like a function definition without any code — just the function name, return type, and arguments followed by a semicolon. Consider the following example:

```
int max(int a, int b);
```

The preceding example declares `max()` to be a function that takes an integer followed by another integer and returns an integer. The statement doesn't say anything about what `max()` does with the integers it receives or how `max()` generates the integer it returns. That's left to the definition. The prototype just allows the compiler to check subsequent attempts to call the function and flag any that are wrong.

TIP

Place your definitions in a `.CPP` file. Place the prototype declarations in an `.H` file of the same name. Include the `.H` file in the `.CPP` file. During compilation, the compiler will check the definitions against the prototype declarations and flag any differences. You can then include the `.H` file in any file that calls one of the functions. The compiler compares the use of the function to the prototype declaration for accuracy.

For example, if `max()`, `min()`, and other functions were defined in a `MATH.CPP` file, you might define `MATH.H` as follows:

```
//MATH.H
int max(int a, int b);
int min(int a, int b);
```

The application file then appears as follows:

```
#include "MATH.H"
void myFunc(int a)

{    a = max(a, -a);          //make sure a is positive
                              //...etc...
}
```

If a function returns nothing, it should be declared as returning `void`. As in C, `void` in C++ is the word for "nothing." If the function takes no arguments, it should be declared with `void` arguments or with an empty argument list, as in `example3()`:

```
void example1(int a, float b); //takes an int and a float
                               //and returns nothing
void example2(void);           //takes nothing and returns
                               //nothing
void example3();               //same as example3(void)
```

When C++ sees an empty argument list, it assumes that the argument is `void`.

In C, a prototype declaration with no arguments means any number of arguments of any type. In this way, ANSI C maintains maximum compatibility with legacy K&R C code, which didn't prototype the function arguments. (Over the years, a company can develop a large amount of code. This code is called *legacy code*. It represents a considerable investment and must be rewritten, at amazing cost, if the company changes to computer systems or languages that are not upwardly compatible. For this reason, ANSI C stays as upwardly compatible as possible with the older K&R C, and C++ stays upwardly compatible with ANSI C.)

If the function takes a variable number of arguments or if you don't want to say what arguments it takes, you may declare a function with ellipses, as in the following example:

```
void example4(...);           //any number of any type of args
```

The ellipses mean any number of any type of arguments. Ellipses can also be mixed with known arguments. For example, `printf()` is commonly declared as a function that takes a pointer to a character followed by an unknown number of unknown arguments:

```
int printf(char* pChar, ...);
```

In a prototype declaration, only the types of the arguments are necessary, not the names of the arguments. The argument names, if present, are ignored. What should the compiler do with them anyway? When the function is called, you can use any argument names you like.

Thus, a function that takes two character pointers, for example, can be declared as follows:

```
int copyString(char *, char *);
```

Strongly typed function pointers

Pointers to functions need to be strongly typed as well. Consider the following example:

```
void function1(int, char*, float);
void function2(int, int);
void fn()
{
   void (*pFn)(int, char*, float);
   pFn = function2;        //this is not // allowed; types don't match
   pFn = function1;        //types match here
   (*pFn)(10, 10);         //error here too - // wrong arguments
   (*pFn)(10, "ten", 10.0); //arguments // match again
}
```

The pointer `pFn` is a fully typed function pointer. This is read as "pFn is a pointer to a function that takes an int, a char*, and a float and returns a void" (or "returns nothing"). In techno shorthand, its type is `void (*)(int, char*, float)`.

The first assignment to `pFn` generates a compiler error because the arguments to `function2` are not the same as those specified by `pFn`. In addition, the first attempt to call the function is an error because the use doesn't match the declaration.

This is generally a bad idea, however, because the name of the variable can tell the reader a lot more about the role of the argument than simply its type.

Compare the preceding prototype declaration with the following:

```
int copyString(char *pTarget, char *pSource);
```

Now, what do the left- and right-hand arguments do?

Inline Functions

C++ allows functions to be defined with the new keyword *inline*. An *inline function* appears like a normal function in use, but it doesn't act the same. Calling an inline function from several different locations does not result in multiple calls to a single function; rather, the code for the inline function expands in place wherever the function is used.

Why do I need them?

When a normal function is compiled, the code is put in one location. Every place where the function is called, the compiler sticks in code to jump to that one function. (The program stores the return address so that the function knows where to return when it's finished.) Because only one copy of the code is produced, the resulting executable (.EXE) file is smaller than if the code was duplicated in all the places that it's needed. The program may be slightly slower, however, because it takes time to make the call.

The overhead of making the call discourages extremely performance-minded programmers from writing small functions even when it may be desirable to do so. Inline functions allow programmers to retain a highly modular style without incurring any overhead.

Can't I do that in C?

C programmers attempt to use `#define` macros, which are defined as follows, to do the same thing that inline functions do:

```
#define square(a)  a * a
```

Unfortunately, macros are tricky. They are processed by a separate preprocessor that has a slightly different syntax than "real" C. Further, because the C compiler sees the output of the preprocessor, which is different than the input you and I see, macros can generate errors that are difficult to track down.

The preceding macro can be easily confused. (Actually, the programmer who tries to use the macro will be confused.) Consider the following example:

```
int squareOfSum(int r1, int r2)
{
   return square(r1 + r2);
}
```

As simple as this function appears, it's not correct. (It's embarrassing when a function with one statement is wrong.) When the preprocessor expands `square()`, it does so directly, without frills. Thus, what the compiler sees is the following:

```
int squareOfSum(int r1, int r2)
{
   return r1 + r2 * r1 + r2;
}
```

Because multiplication is performed before addition, this is interpreted as follows. (Go and check the operator precedence rules in Part I if you don't believe me.)

```
int squareOfSum(int r1, int r2)
{
   return r1 + (r2 * r1) + r2;
}
```

Although this and most other problems with macros can be solved, macros are still undesirable because the problems are usually difficult to find.

Inline functions are part of the C++ language and are not processed by the preprocessor. Thus, inline functions do not share the problems of macros. So forget about macros and use inline functions instead.

How do they work?

To inline a function, the programmer adds the keyword `inline` in front of the definition. For example:

```
inline int max(int a, int b)
{
   return (a > b) ? a : b;
}
```

Notice the verb usage in the first sentence. To "inline a function" is to make a function an inline function. A normal (that is, non-inline) function is known in C++ jargon as an *outline function*. This also has a verb form: To outline a function is to force an inline function outline. Also notice that `inline` is now a keyword. If you like to name your C variables "inline," you'll have to find another name now. Have you noticed how I can ramble on about the silliest things?

An inline function is invoked just like any other function. Rather than generating a single function that each invocation jumps to, however, the code for an inline function is expanded in place. Thus, the following does not generate a conventional function call:

```
int betterSalary, mySalary, urSalary;
betterSalary = max(mySalary, urSalary);
```

Because the code body is necessary to expand an inline function, you must define an inline function before it can be used — a prototype declaration is not enough. It is common to define inline functions in the same `.H` files in which you prototype your outline functions.

Inline functions are the only type of function that you should define in an include file. Conventional outline functions should not be defined in include files.

Inline functions are useful only for small functions. The disadvantage of expanding a large function inline outweighs the small gains from inlining the function. The break-even point for an inline function is about three executable lines.

How much faster is faster?

To demonstrate the types of improvement you can expect using inline functions, I timed the following program:

```
//inline max function
inline int maxi(int x, int y)
{
    return (x > y) ? x : y;
}

//outline version of the same thing
int maxo(int x, int y)
{
    return (x > y) ? x : y;
}

int main()
{
   int i, j = 5000, k, loop;

   //first straight
   for (loop = 0; loop < 10000; loop++)
   {
      for (i = 0; i < 10000; i++)
      {
         k = (i > j) ? i : j;
      }
   }

   //now as an inline function
   for (loop = 0; loop < 10000; loop++)
   {
      for (i = 0; i < 10000; i++)
      {
```

(continued)

(continued)

```
            k = maxi(i, j);
        }
    }

    //now as an outline function
    for (loop = 0; loop < 10000; loop++)
    {
        for (i = 0; i < 10000; i++)
        {
            k = maxo(i, j);
        }
    }
    return 0;
}
```

The straight and inline versions of the loop showed identical execution times (about 7 seconds). The outline version of the loop took about two times longer to execute (14 seconds). Advantage: inline.

I then repeated the experiment with a more complicated version of the `max()` function. (Okay, the additions are nonsensical, but that doesn't make any difference.)

```
inline int maxi(int x, int y)
{
    x = (x * 4) >> 2;         //this has no effect
    y = (y * 4) >> 2;         //but what does the compiler
    //know?
    x = (x * 4) >> 2;
    y = (y * 4) >> 2;
    return (x > y) ? x : y;
}
int maxo(int x, int y)
{
    x = (x * 4) >> 2;
    y = (y * 4) >> 2;
    x = (x * 4) >> 2;
    y = (y * 4) >> 2;
    return (x > y) ? x : y;
}
```

The resulting `maxi()` function ran only 25 percent faster than the outline version (15 versus 20 seconds). Virtually deuce.

Because an inline function is expanded as part of each line that calls it, you cannot single step an inline function with the debugger. The entire inline function executes as a single line no matter how many lines it contains and no matter how much havoc those lines might cause.

This is a problem during debugging. To debug an inline function, you should first change it to an outline function. To do this, you can just remove the `inline` keyword and recompile. Because this is a hassle, most compilers provide a compile-time switch that automatically outlines all inline functions. For the Borland C++, Turbo C++, and Microsoft Visual C++ compilers, this switch is under the C++ compiler options. When you have finished debugging, recompile without the compiler option switch to re-inline the inline functions.

Even if you declare a function to be inline, several things may force the function outline. For example, including any type of looping statement (such as a `for` loop) in a function usually forces it outline. You shouldn't declare a function like that inline anyway, because the time that it takes to execute the loop overshadows any minor gain from declaring the function inline. Depending on the compiler, other things may force a function outline as well. (The draft standard for C++ allows for all sorts of things.) For example, under the default project settings for the Visual C++ compiler while debugging, functions declared inline are automatically outlined. To get the preceding numbers, I had to turn inlining back on while leaving other optimizations off.

Function Overloading

Unlike most other languages, C++ allows functions to have the same name if it can tell the functions apart by the number and type of the arguments to the function during use. For example, the following two functions are not considered the same:

```
int date(int   year);
int date(char *pPerson);
```

That is, applying the function `date()` to a `year` is different than applying `date()` to a `pPerson`. This use of the same name for two different functions with different arguments is known as overloading the function name.

Why do I need it?

Why not? I have two friends named David, and I have no trouble telling them apart; their hair color is different and one has a broken arm. I have no trouble telling `date(1993)` and `date(someGuy)` apart, so why should the computer?

Function overloading is useful in avoiding an annoyance. In C, I am forced to use different names for similar functions. For example, consider the following set of C `square()` functions. Each is designed to return the square of its argument:

```
int    squareInt(int);   //square for int
float  squareFlt(float); //square for float
double squareDbl(double);//square for double
```

If I had more functions, I would need a set of . . . `Int` functions, each with a corresponding . . . `Flt` and . . . `Dbl` function. With function overloading, this isn't necessary:

```
int    square(int    i);
float  square(float  f);
double square(double d);
```

You could argue, "Why have all those silly functions? Just define the double version and use it for floats and ints as well." This is not a convincing argument. (If it were, I wouldn't have mentioned it.) Squaring a double-precision floating point number takes a lot more computing than squaring an integer. Besides, I could think of other examples (just give me a moment) in which using a single function wouldn't work anyway.

How does it work?

Not too much goes into declaring overloaded functions: Declare them as you would any other function. Just make sure that the arguments are sufficiently different to allow the functions to be differentiated in use.

TECHNICAL STUFF

The technical term for differentiating two or more overloaded functions by the way they are used is *disambiguation,* believe it or not.

For example, I may implement the previously mentioned set of square functions as follows:

```
int square(int i)
{
   return i*i;
}
float square(float f)
{
   return f*f;
}
double square(double d)
{
   return d*d;
}

int main()
{
   int    i = 2;
   float  f = 3.0;
   double d = 4.0;
   i = square(i);   //calls square for ints
   f = square(f);   //calls square for floats
   d = square(d);   //calls square for doubles
   return 0;
}
```

Compile and execute this program to convince yourself that this works. Single step through each function call. It's amazing the first time you do it. When I was learning C++ (many moons ago), executing this program was the first time I got the feeling that C++ was not just a jazzed up C.

The argument types are said to be part of the function's extended name (also called the *function signature*). Thus, the name of the function may be `square()`, and the extended name is `square(int)` (pronounced "square int").

What constitutes sufficiently different?

Okay, so I've said that C++ can tell two or more functions with the same name apart as long as the arguments are sufficiently different. The problem is: What constitutes "sufficiently different"? Obviously the following functions are different:

```
int fn(int i);
int fn(char c);              //different argument type
int fn(int i, int j);        //different no. of arguments
int fn(int *pI);             //pointer to an int is not the
                             //same type as an int
```

Different pointer types are sufficiently different as well:

```
int fn(int  *pI);
int fn(char *pC);          //char* is not same as int*
```

Signed-ness (for example, `int` versus `unsigned int`) and `const`-ness are also sufficiently different to tell functions apart. But if you do something like the following, you're probably just trying to confuse yourself and anyone else who may come along and try to read your code:

```
int fn(int i);
int fn(unsigned i);          //this is a different function
```

So what's not different enough?

So what types of differences don't qualify as different enough? Functions cannot be differentiated by their return type. For example, the following functions are not sufficiently different:

```
int   fn(int i);
float fn(int i);        //must differ by more
                        //than return type
```

A simple type cannot be overloaded with a reference type:

```
int   fn(int  i);
int   fn(int &refI);    //not different enough
```

Functions with non-specific arguments cannot be overloaded for obvious reasons. Consider the following example:

```
int fn(int i, ...);      //int followed by anything
int fn(int i, float f);  //int followed by a float
int main()
{
   fn(1, 2.0);           //which one?
}
```

Finally, all C functions, including those that make up the Standard C Library, cannot be overloaded.

Print what you want about me, but don't mangle the name

How does C++ keep functions with the same name straight during the link step? For example, suppose MOD_A.CPP has two functions, f(int) and f(char). If a function in a separate module calls one of these functions, how does the linker keep them straight?

C++ uses a complex technique called *name mangling* to sort the versions of functions with the same name at link time. A complete discussion of name mangling is too complicated to go into here. The main point is that the types of the arguments become part of the function name that is passed to the linker. For example, the previous two functions might be called something like f_i() and f_c(). For the most part, you can ignore name mangling. However, you do need to be aware of two cases in which name mangling causes a problem.

Case 1

C doesn't allow function overloading and therefore has no use for name mangling. Therefore, when declaring a C function, you need to tell C++ not to mangle it. C++ extended the extern keyword to allow you to do this, as follows:

```
extern "C" int printf(char *, ...);
```

This declares printf() to be a C function. Because printf() isn't a C++ function, its name doesn't get mangled. If you have more than one C function to declare, you can combine them as follows:

```
extern "C"
{
   int firstCFunc();
   int secondCFunc();
   int thirdCFunc();
}
```

Such a block can also include an include file:

```
extern "C"
{
#include "myInclud.h"
}
```

In this construct, all the functions declared in the include file are declared as C functions.

Normally, you have to enclose an include file in an extern "C" block only if you have a library of C routines that you link with your programs and for which you don't have the source.

If you forget to declare a C function properly, you get an obscure link-time error rather than a compile-time error. Consider the following example:

```
int printf(char*,...);
int main()
{
   printf("Hello world\n");
   return 0;
}
```

C++ assumes from the prototype that `printf()` is a C++ function. It then mangles the name to add the `char*` and . . . signature to the extended name. When C++ then tries to link, the linker sees no connection between the C++ function `printf(char*, . . .)` and the C function `printf()`. The result is the following:

```
Error: undefined external function printf(char*, . . . )
```

You can solve the problem by including the proper standard C library `.H` file, which declares functions correctly by using extern "C" blocks where necessary:

```
#include <stdio.h>
int main()
{
   printf("Hello world\n");
   return 0;
}
```

This works as expected.

Case 2

In general, you cannot link object files from two different C++ compilers. Name mangling is not standardized, and functions won't link correctly. For example, if your friend compiles a file with the Microsoft compiler and gives you the `.OBJ` file to link with your Borland modules, it won't work. Just recompile your friend's source code, and things should work out fine.

Default Arguments to Functions

C++ allows functions to be declared with default arguments. If a default argument is not provided in the call, the default value is provided automatically. In the following function, the second argument defaults to zero. Thus the calls on line 2 and line 3 are equivalent:

```
//the second argument defaults to zero if not present
int sampleFunc(int x, int y = 0);
int main()
{
    sampleFunc(1, 2);      //Line 1 - this is okay;
                           //         don't use the default
    sampleFunc(1, 0);      //Line 2
    sampleFunc(1);         //Line 3 - same as line 2
    return 0;
}
```

Because the call on line 3 provides only one argument, C++ provides the default second argument of 0 from the prototype declaration.

Why do I need them?

Default arguments are another cutesy feature. I can't think of any overpowering reason for it, but it can be sort of nice. For example:

```
int calculateWeeklyPay(int payRate, int hoursWorked = 40);
```

This function is designed to calculate the pay an employee will receive for one week's employment. Because the normal work week is 40 hours, I put that in as the default; if an employee works something other than 40 hours, however, that's allowed as well.

How do they work?

Default values can be provided for more than one argument, but they must be specified from right to left. For example, if you have a function that takes two arguments, you can't provide a default value for only the first (left) one.

Defaults are filled in by the compiler in a strictly right-to-left fashion as well, even if the types would seem to indicate that the programmer had some grander scheme in mind. Consider the following:

```
void fillInGrade(char *pLName, char *pMI = "NMI", int age = 0);
int main()
{
   fillInGrade("Davis", 37); //not legal
   return 0;
}
```

You and I can see that what's missing in the call is the middle initial argument, but C++ makes no attempt at this type of interpretation. If two arguments are provided in the call, the third argument must be the one that's defaulted, resulting in the following (mis)interpretation:

```
int main()
{
   fillInGrade("Davis", 37, 0); //interpretation of preceding
   return 0;
}
```

Because the integer 37 cannot be converted to a pointer or to a character, an error is generated.

You can get the desired effect of a default middle argument using function overloading, as in the following example:

```
void fillInGrade(char *pName, char *pMI, int age = 0);
inline void fillInGrade(char *pName, int age = 0)
{
   fillInGrade(pName, "NMI", age);
}
```

Now a call such as `fillInGrade("Davis", 37)` invokes the inline function, which turns right around and calls the first function with the `pMI` argument filled in with the desired default. This is why default arguments are not really necessary — the clever use of function overloading can generate the same effect.

Being overloadingly argumentative

Default arguments can sometimes confuse function overloading. Consider the example in the preceding section. Suppose you had the following (clever) function declarations:

```
void fillInGrade(char *pName, char *pMI = "NMI", int age = 0);
void fillInGrade(char *pLast, char *pFirst);
```

A call like the following is ambiguous:

```
int main()
{
    fillInGrade("Davis", "Stephen"); //which one?
    return 0;
}
```

You and I can see that this call is trying to access the second function. But the compiler, being stupid, doesn't know that you're not trying to call the first function with a default age of 0. Because the compiler can't decide which of the two functions you mean to call, it generates an error.

When both overloading and providing default arguments, make sure that all the possible ways that the functions can be called are unambiguous. When in doubt, don't use default arguments for overloaded functions.

Importance of Function Declarations

The function declaration is optional in K&R C but is a requirement in C++. Rather than being forced to eat in K&R's kitchen, function declaration can take its rightful place at the head of the table in C++. Function declarations not only allow the compiler to do a better job of error detection, they also allow the same function name to be overlaid with different meanings.

Chapter 6

Stream Input and Output

In This Chapter

- Introducing stream I/O
- What's wrong with `printf()`?
- Using stream I/O
- Drawing parallels between C I/O and stream I/O

C++ defines a new input/output mechanism in addition to `printf()`. This mechanism, called `stream I/O`, is based on redefining the << operator to perform output and the >> operator to perform input.

When redefined, << is known as the *insertion operator* and >> is called the *extraction operator* to differentiate them from the left-shift and right-shift operators.

Why Do I Need Streams After the Rivers of printf()s I'm Used To?

The change to stream I/O is probably the most difficult adjustment for the beginning C++ programmer. "What? Take my `printf()`? You'll have to pry it from my cold, dead fingers." To me, `printf()` and `scanf()` are like my old, beat-up work car. They work, I'm familiar with them, but if the truth be known, they break down sometimes and they don't carry very much. To say the same thing in computerese, they're not type safe and they're not extensible.

The case for stream I/O: Part 1

Ladies and gentlemen of the jury, consider the first charge first (that's logical): strong typing. Prototype declarations save you from yourselves in lots of different cases, but they aren't much help with scanf() and printf(). The number and type of function arguments that printf() and scanf() expect depend on information encoded in the first argument. This information isn't available to the compiler, so the compiler cannot check the calls to printf() and scanf() to see whether they are proper.

If I call either function improperly, there's nothing that C or C++ can do to help me out. Usually, this is not a big problem with printf(); I get garbage for output and check what's wrong.

The situation with scanf() is much worse. Consider the following example:

```
int i = 10;
scanf("%d", i);
```

The call is in error because I should have passed the address of i instead of the value of i. However, without a descriptive prototype to tell it otherwise, the compiler does not complain. The compiler assumes that the value scanf() gets (10 in this example) is an address, and it stores the integer read into that address. In this case, the value that scanf() reads is stored in location 10.

I can only hope that this mistake is fatal so that I am alerted to the problem. (On modern operating systems it is.) If it isn't, I've just overwritten some random location that will eventually come back to haunt me. This (and premature hair loss) are the kinds of problems that keep systems programmers awake at night.

The case for stream I/O: Part 2

Now, jury members, consider the second charge before you today, that of extensibility. But before you do that, what is extensibility anyway? *Extensibility* means that you can add to the definition of your I/O mechanism to handle any new structures that you might create.

printf() knows how to output strings, integers, and floating points. That's basically it. Sure, you can change the number of significant digits, change the base to 10 or 16, control whether the left or the right is padded with spaces or zeros, and control a host of other things, but these features are window dressing. You can't teach printf() to output a new structure of your own invention.

Stream I/O is extensible. For example, having defined a structure `MyStruct`, I can teach the insertion operator how to output one of those and I can teach the extraction operator how to read one. The details of how to do this are left to Chapter 23.

How Does Stream I/O Work?

Before you can use I/O streams in your program, you must include `iostreams.h`. This include file is one of the standard include files provided by C++.

Depending on the environment, `iostreams.h` is a very big include file. Therefore, you might want to enable the precompiled headers switch if your compiler supports that. Both Borland and Microsoft do. (Look in the compiler options menu under the C++ options.)

Precompiled headers is a feature in which the compiler saves in a separate file the result of compiling the include files. The next time you compile your module, the compiler rereads that file instead of recompiling the sometimes enormous include files. It does this as long as you don't edit one of the include files or change the order in which they're included in the module. This feature greatly increases the speed of compilations, except for the first one.

Note that precompiled headers also work for different source files if they include the same include files in the same order. The basic rule is: Include files in the same way and your compilations will be faster all day. (Check your compiler documentation for details.)

The `iostream.h` include file defines some default devices. These are shown in Table 6-1. Standard input is normally the keyboard. Standard output and standard error output are normally the screen.

Table 6-1 The Standard Stream Devices

C++ Name	*Device*	*C Name*	*Default Meaning*
cin	Keyboard	stdin	Standard input
cout	Screen	stdout	Standard output
cerr	Screen	stderr	Standard error
cprn	Printer	stdprn	Printer

Table 6-1 also shows the corresponding default devices in C. Remember that `printf()` is just shorthand for `fprintf(stdout,...)` and `scanf()` is shorthand for `fscanf(stdin,...)`.

The object `cout` corresponds to the default output (usually the display), just like `stdout` does with `fprintf()`. Likewise, `cin` corresponds to the default input (usually the keyboard), just like `stdin` does with `fscanf()`.

The following function outputs to the display whatever name is passed to it:

```
#include <iostream.h>
void outName(char *pName)
{
   cout << "My name is";
   cout << pName;
   cout << "\n";
}
```

Both insertion and extraction operations can be strung on a single line. Thus, the preceding function and the following one have the same effect:

```
#include <iostream.h>
void outName(char *pName)
{
   cout << "My name is "
        << pName
        << "\n";
}
```

The extra new-lines in the previous code snippet are ignored. I could have written the following:

```
cout << "My name is " << pName << "\n";
```

but I thought the three separate lines looked nicer.

In the previous examples, all the objects being inserted are of the same type, `char*`; different types, however, can be strung together as well. This is shown in the following example:

```
void outSSNum(long ssNumber)
{
   cout << "Social Security Number ="
        << ssNumber
        << '\n';
}
```

Here you see the advantage of streams over `printf()`. Nothing about the output line, other than the object itself, tells the compiler the types of the objects to be printed. Compare this with the equivalent `printf()`-based function:

```
void outSSNum(long ssNumber)
{
   printf("Social Security Number = %ld\n",
          ssNumber);
}
```

The `%ld` tells `printf()` that `ssNumber` is a `long`. If this information is not correct, `printf()` will not generate the proper output. With the stream output solution, this type of error is not possible.

Give It a Try

Stream I/O is a feature you can ignore for a while, if you absolutely insist. However, I think you should give it a try. You already bought the book.

In Chapter 23, I revisit stream I/O. There you find that stream I/O can do a lot more for you, and you may be more tempted to try it. After you do a little C++ programming using streams, feel free to return to your old `printf()` ways, if you really want to.

Rewriting BUDGET as a C++ Program: BUDGET2.CPP

You can see how the features you have studied in Part II look by applying them to the BUDGET program. In this version, I did the following:

- Changed comments to the new style
- Overloaded the functions `init()` and `process()` to highlight the similarities between the checking and savings account versions
- Used referential arguments to avoid pointer types
- Converted `init()` to an inline function because of its small size
- Declared variables near their point of use
- Converted my I/O to stream I/O
- Replaced `#defines` with `const` variables

Although this is a C++ program (if you don't believe it, just try compiling it with your old C compiler), not much has changed philosophically. This is not an object-oriented program in any sense of the word.

```
//BUDGET2.CPP - Budget program in the "C++ as a better C"
//              version.

#include <iostream.h>

//the maximum number of accounts you can have
const int maxAccounts = 10;

//Checking - this describes checking accounts
struct Checking
{
   unsigned accountNumber;
   float    balance;
} chkAcnts[maxAccounts];

//Savings - you can probably figure this one out
```

```
struct Savings
{
   unsigned accountNumber;
   float    balance;
   int      noWithdrawals;
} svgAcnts[maxAccounts];

//prototype declarations
void process(Checking &checking);      //Note 1
void process(Savings &savings);

//inline functions
//init(Checking) - initialize a checking account
inline void init(Checking &checking)   //Note 2
{
   cout << "Enter account number:";
   cin  >> checking.accountNumber;
   checking.balance = 0.0;
}

//init(Savings) - initialize a savings account
inline void init(Savings  &savings)
{
   cout << "Enter account number:";
   cin  >> savings.accountNumber;
   savings.balance = 0.0;
   savings.noWithdrawals = 0;
}

//main - accumulate the initial input and output totals
int main()
{
   //loop until someone enters an 'X' or 'x'
   int noChkAccounts = 0;    //count the number of accounts
   int noSvgAccounts = 0;
   char     accountType;     //S or C

   unsigned keepLooping = 1;
   while (keepLooping)
   {
      cout << "Enter S for Savings, "
              "C for Checking, X for exit\n";
      cin  >> accountType;
```

(continued)

(continued)

```
      switch (accountType)
      {
         case 'c':
         case 'C':
            if (noChkAccounts < maxAccounts)
            {
               init(chkAcnts[noChkAccounts]);
               process(chkAcnts[noChkAccounts]);
               noChkAccounts++;
            }
            else
            {
               cout << "No more room for checking accounts\n";
            }
            break;

         case 's':
         case 'S':
            if (noSvgAccounts < maxAccounts)
            {
               init(svgAcnts[noSvgAccounts]);
               process(svgAcnts[noSvgAccounts]);
               noSvgAccounts++;
            }
            else
            {
               cout << "No more room for savings accounts\n";
            }
            break;

         case 'x':
         case 'X':
            keepLooping = 0;
            break;

         default:
            cout << "I didn't get that.\n";
      }
   }

   //now present totals
   float chkTotal = 0;        //total of all checking accounts
```

```
    cout << "Checking accounts:\n";
    for (int i = 0; i < noChkAccounts; i++)  //Note 3
    {
       cout << "Account " << chkAcnts[i].accountNumber
            << " = "      << chkAcnts[i].balance
            << "\n";
       chkTotal += chkAcnts[i].balance;
    }
    float svgTotal = 0;       //total of all savings accounts
    cout << "Savings accounts:\n";
    for (i = 0; i < noSvgAccounts; i++)      //Note 4
    {
       cout << "Account "              << svgAcnts[i].accountNumber
            << " = "                   << svgAcnts[i].balance
            << " (no. withdrawals = " << svgAcnts[i].noWithdrawals
            << ")\n";
       svgTotal += svgAcnts[i].balance;
    }

    float total = chkTotal + svgTotal;
    cout << "Total for checking accounts = " << chkTotal << "\n";
    cout << "Total for savings accounts  = " << svgTotal << "\n";
    cout << "Total worth                 = " << total << "\n";
    return 0;
}

//process(Checking) - input the data for a checking account
void process(Checking &checking)
{
    cout << "Enter positive number for deposit,\n"
            "negative for check, 0 to terminate";

    float transaction;
    do
    {
       cout << ":";
       cin  >> transaction;

       //is it a deposit?
       if (transaction > 0)
       {
          checking.balance += transaction;
       }
```

(continued)

(continued)

```
      //how about withdrawal?
      if (transaction < 0)
      {
         //withdrawal
         transaction = -transaction;
         if (checking.balance < transaction)   //Note 5
         {
            cout << "Insufficient funds: balance "
                 << checking.balance
                 << ", check "
                 << transaction
                 << "\n";
         }
         else
         {
            checking.balance -= transaction;

            //if balance falls too low, charge service fee
            if (checking.balance < 500.00F)
            {
               checking.balance -= 0.20F;
            }
         }
      }
   } while (transaction != 0);
}

//process(Savings) - input the data for a savings account
void process(Savings &savings)
{
   cout << "Enter positive number for deposit,\n"
           "negative for withdrawal, 0 to terminate";

   float transaction;
   do
   {
      cout << ":";
      cin  >> transaction;

      //is this a deposit?
      if (transaction > 0)
      {
         savings.balance += transaction;
      }
```

```
        //is it a withdrawal?
        if (transaction < 0)
        {
            transaction = -transaction;
            if (savings.balance < transaction)
            {
                cout << "Insufficient funds: balance "
                     << savings.balance
                     << ", withdrawal "
                     << transaction
                     << "\n";
            }
            else
            {
                if (++savings.noWithdrawals > 1)
                {
                    savings.balance -= 5.00F;
                }
                savings.balance -= transaction;
            }
        }
    } while (transaction != 0);
}
```

If you give this program the same test data as you gave the C version in Part I, the output appears almost the same:

```
Enter S for Savings, C for Checking, X for exit
S
Enter account number:123
Enter positive number for deposit,
negative for withdrawal, 0 to terminate:200
:-50
:-50
:0
Enter S for Savings, C for Checking, X for exit
C
Enter account number:234
Enter positive number for deposit,
negative for check, 0 to terminate:200
:-25
:-20
:0
Enter S for Savings, C for Checking, X for exit
X
```

(continued)

(continued)

```
Checking accounts:
Account 234 = 154.600006
Savings accounts:
Account 123 = 95 (no. withdrawals = 2)
Total for checking accounts = 154.600006
Total for savings accounts  = 95
Total worth                 = 249.600006
```

Notice first that all the comments have changed. (Whoopee. But really, the new comment style grows on you.)

Also, the names of the functions `processSavings()` and `processChecking()` have been changed to simply `process()`, with the distinction made by the argument types. (See the `Note 1` comment in the code.) In addition, the argument is now a reference to the object rather than a pointer to the object.

The `init()` functions (`Note 2`) have been not only renamed but also inlined. These are the nice short types of functions that bear inlining (even though there's no performance reason to do so).

The references to `printf()` and `scanf()` have been replaced by their iostream equivalents, which require inclusion of the `iostream.h` include file instead of `stdio.h`. Note that in the BUDGET program in Part I, I used fancy `printf()` controls to reduce the number of significant digits after the decimal point to two (for the cents). I didn't do that with iostreams, because you haven't yet seen how to format stream output. For now, you have to put up with all those extra digits. (Depending on the details of your compiler, you might not see all those trailing digits. Whether or not you see them, there's nothing you can do to change it for now.)

Making declarations at the point of use makes it easier to associate a variable's type with its use. This is especially obvious in places such as the `for` loop (`Note 3`). Notice, however, that after I declare `i` in the first `for` loop, I do not have to (nor am I allowed to) redeclare it in the second `for` loop (`Note 4`).

The arguments to the two `process()` functions are now referential. This means that the . operator is used instead of the -> operator throughout the functions (`Note 5`). These functions could have been declared as follows:

```
void process(Checking checking);
```

Declaring the functions like the preceding line would have also allowed me to use the . notation. However, passing by value would have resulted in a common error that is difficult to find. When checking is passed by value, a copy of the original `Checking` object — not the original — is passed to the function. The function goes about merrily changing the copy, which is thrown away when the function returns, leaving the original unchanged. (Don't believe it? Just remove `&` in the argument checking in both the prototype and the function, and recompile the program.)

Part III
Wading In: Introduction to Classes

The 5th Wave By Rich Tennant

"CAREFUL, SUNDANCE, THIS ONE'S BEEN LOCKED UP AND FORCED TO BETA-TEST POORLY DOCUMENTED SOFTWARE PRODUCTS ALLLL WEEK AND HE'S ITCHING FOR A FIGHT."

In this part . . .

So far, C++ still looks basically like C — a slightly improved C maybe, but C nonetheless. If that were all there were to it, C++ certainly would not have generated as much interest as it has (and my editors would not have agreed to let me write this neat book).

The feature that differentiates C++ from C is C++'s support for object-oriented programming. *Object-oriented* is about the most hyped term in the computer world, next to *the Internet*. Computer languages, editors, and databases all claim to be object-oriented, sometimes with justification but most of the time without.

What is it about being object-oriented that makes it so desired around the world? Read on to find out.

Chapter 7

Object-Oriented Programming

In This Chapter

- Making nachos
- Overview of object-oriented programming
- Introduction to abstraction and classification
- Why is object-oriented programming important?

Okay, you've waited long enough. What, exactly, is object-oriented programming? Object-oriented programming, or OOP as those in the know prefer to call it, relies on two principles you learned before you ever got out of Pampers: abstraction and classification. To explain, let me tell you a little story.

Abstraction and Microwave Ovens

Sometimes when my son and I are watching football, I whip up a terribly unhealthy batch of nachos. I dump some chips on a plate, throw on some beans, cheese, and lots of jalapeños, and nuke the whole mess in the microwave oven for 5 minutes.

To use my microwave, I open the door, throw the stuff in, and punch a few buttons on the front. After a few minutes, the nachos are done. (I try not to stand in front of the microwave while it's working lest my eyes start glowing in the dark.)

Now think for a minute about all the things I don't do to use my microwave:

- I don't rewire or change anything inside the microwave to get it to work. The microwave has an interface — the front panel with all the buttons and the little time display — that lets me do everything I need.
- I don't have to reprogram the software used to drive the little processor inside my microwave, even if I cooked a different dish the last time I used the microwave.

- I don't look inside the case of my microwave.
- Even if I were a microwave designer and knew all about the inner workings of a microwave, including its software, I would still use it to heat my nachos without thinking about all that stuff.

These are not profound observations. You can think about only so much at one time. To reduce the number of things that you must deal with, you work at a certain level of detail. In object-oriented (OO) computerese, the level of detail at which you are working is called the *level of abstraction*. To introduce another OO term while I have the chance, I *abstract away* the details of the microwave's internals.

When I'm working on nachos, I view my microwave oven as a box. (As I'm trying to knock out a snack, I can't worry about the innards of the microwave oven and still follow the Cowboys on the tube.) As long as I use the microwave only through its interface (the keypad), there should be nothing I can do to cause the microwave to enter an inconsistent state and crash or, worse, turn my nachos into a blackened, flaming mass.

Functional nachos

Suppose I were to ask my son to write an algorithm for how Dad makes nachos. After he understood what I wanted, he would probably write "open a can of beans, grate some cheese, cut the jalapeños," and so on. When it came to the part about microwaving the concoction, he would write something like "cook in the microwave for 5 minutes."

That description is straightforward and complete. But it's not the way a functional programmer would code a program to make nachos. Functional programmers live in a world devoid of objects such as microwave ovens and other appliances. They tend to worry about flow charts with their myriad functional paths. In a functional solution to the nachos problem, the flow of control would pass through my finger to the front panel and then to the internals of the microwave. Pretty soon, flow would be wiggling around through complex logic paths about how long to turn on the microwave tube and whether to sound the "come and get it" tone.

In a world like this, it's difficult to think in terms of levels of abstraction. There are no objects, no abstractions behind which to hide inherent complexity.

Object-oriented nachos

In an object-oriented approach to making nachos, I would first identify the types of objects in the problem: chips, beans, cheese, and an oven. Then I would begin the task of modeling these objects in software, without regard to the details of how they will be used in the final program.

While I am doing this, I'm said to be working (and thinking) at the level of the basic objects. I need to think about making a useful oven, but I don't have to think about the logical process of making nachos yet. After all, the microwave designers didn't think about the specific problem of my making a snack. Rather, they set about the problem of designing and building a useful microwave.

After the objects I need have been successfully coded and tested, I can ratchet up to the next level of abstraction. I can start thinking at the nacho-making level, rather than the microwave-making level. At this point, I can pretty much translate my son's instructions directly into C++ code.

Classification and Microwave Ovens

Critical to the concept of abstraction is that of classification. If I were to ask my son, "What's a microwave?" he would probably say, "It's an oven that. . . ." If I then asked, "What's an oven?" he might reply, "It's a kitchen appliance that. . . ." (If I then asked "What's a kitchen appliance?" he would probably say, "Why are you asking so many stupid questions?")

The answers my son gave in my example questioning stem from his understanding of our particular microwave as an example of the type of things called microwave ovens. In addition, my son sees microwave ovens as just a special type of oven, which is in turn a special type of kitchen appliance.

REMEMBER

In object-oriented computerese, my microwave is an *instance* of the *class* microwave. The class microwave is a subclass of the class oven, and the class oven is a subclass of the class kitchen appliances.

Humans classify. Everything about our world is ordered into taxonomies. We do this to reduce the number of things we have to remember. Take, for example, the first time you saw a Saturn automobile. The advertisement called the Saturn "revolutionary, the likes of which have never been seen." But you and I know that that just isn't so. I like the looks of the Saturn, but hey, it's a car. As such, it shares all of (or at least most of) the properties of other cars. It has a steering wheel, seats, a motor, brakes, and so on. I bet I could even drive one without help.

I don't have to clutter my limited storage with all the things that a Saturn has in common with other cars. All I have to remember is "a Saturn is a car that . . ." and tack on those few things that are unique to a Saturn. I can go further. Cars are a subclass of wheeled vehicles, of which there are other members, such as trucks and pickups. Maybe wheeled vehicles are a subclass of vehicles, which include boats and planes. And on and on and on.

Why Classify?

True to form, one of the important questions I ask in this book is "Why?" Why do we want to classify? It sounds like a lot of trouble. (Besides, I've been programming the functional way for so long. Why do I need to change now?)

It may seem easier to design and build a microwave oven specifically for this one problem, rather than build a separate, more generic oven object. Suppose, for example, that I want to build a microwave to cook nachos and nachos only. There would be no need to put a front panel on it, other than a START button. I always cook nachos the same amount of time. I could dispense with all that DEFROST and TEMP COOK nonsense. It would need to hold only one flat little plate. Three cubic feet of space would be wasted on nachos.

For that matter, I can dispense with the concept of "microwave oven" altogether. All I really need is the guts of the oven. Then, in the recipe, I put the instructions to make it work: "Put nachos in the box. Connect the red wire to the black wire. Notice a slight hum. Try not to stand too close if you intend to have children." Stuff like that.

But the functional approach has some problems:

- **Too complex.** I don't want the details of oven building mixed into the details of nacho building. If I can't define the objects and pull them out of the morass of details to deal with separately, I must deal with all the complexities of the problem at the same time.
- **Not flexible.** Someday I may need to replace the microwave oven with some other type of oven. I should be able to do so as long as its interface is the same. Without being clearly delineated and developed separately, it becomes impossible to cleanly remove an object type and replace it with another.
- **Not reusable.** Ovens are used to make lots of different dishes. I don't want to create a new oven every time I encounter a new recipe. Having solved a problem once, it would be nice to be able to reuse the solution in future programs.

Chapter 8
Adding Class to C++

In This Chapter

- Transforming a structure into a class
- Declaring and defining member functions
- Accessing member functions
- Overloading member functions

C structures enable you to group related data elements into a single entity. For example, in the BUDGET program at the end of Part I, you were able to create a structure `Savings` with the following information:

```
struct Savings
{
   unsigned accountNumber;
   float  balance;
};
```

Every instance of `Savings` contains the same two data elements:

```
void fn(void)
{
   Savings a;
   Savings b;
   a.accountNumber = 1;  /*this is not the same as...*/
   b.accountNumber = 2;  /*...this one*/
}
```

The two `accountNumber`s are different because they belong to different objects (`a` and `b`).

TIP

Note that the keyword `struct` is no longer necessary in the declarations of `a` and `b`. (It's allowed, but nobody includes it.) Thus, you say `Savings a` in C++, not `struct Savings a` as in C.

As nice as C structures may be, however, they are limited to data elements. The C++ class does not have this restriction. A class can have both data and function members:

```
class Savings
{
  public:
   unsigned accountNumber;
   float    balance;

   unsigned deposit(unsigned amount)
   {
      balance += amount;
      return balance;
   }
};
```

Here, the function `deposit()` is a member of the class `Savings` just like the two data members.

Why Add Classes to C++?

Remember that your goal is to create a software analog to real-world objects, such as microwaves and savings accounts. Real-world objects certainly have data-type properties, such as time, account numbers, and balances. This makes a C `struct` a good starting point. But real-world objects can also do things. Ovens cook. Savings accounts accumulate interest. CDs charge a substantial penalty for early withdrawal. However, a C `struct` does not have such active properties.

How Do I Add Classes to C++?

To demonstrate classes, start by defining a class `Student`. One possible representation of such a class follows:

```
class Student
{
  public:
   int   semesterHours;  //hours earned toward graduation
   float gpa;
   float addCourse(int hours, float grade); //add a...
                    //completed...course to the record
};
```

You can see that this class declaration looks very much like a structure declaration. In fact, this declaration looks exactly like the declaration of a `struct`, except

- It substitutes the keyword `class` for `struct`.
- It adds the keyword `public`.
- It declares a member function along with the data members.

The `class` keyword is a new keyword in C++ used in place of `struct` to differentiate a class from a structure. Other than that, the syntax of `class` and `struct` are the same. (I'll skip the `public` keyword for now.)

The function `addCourse(int, float)` is called a member function of the class `Student`. In principle, it's a property of the class like the data members `semesterHours` and `gpa`.

Functions defined in a class are called *member functions*. Their data buddies are called *data members*. Together, they're both known as members of the class. There isn't a name for functions or data that are not members of a class, but I'll refer to them as *non-members*. All the functions you wrote in C were non-member functions because they didn't belong to any class.

For historical reasons, member functions are also called *methods*. This term has an obtuse meaning in other object-oriented languages, but no meaning in C++. Nevertheless, it has gained some popularity in OO circles because it's easier to say than "member function." (The fact that it sounds more impressive probably doesn't hurt either.) So, if your friends start spouting off at a dinner party about "methods of the class," just replace *methods* with *member functions* and reparse anything they say. Because the term *method* has little relevance to C++, I won't use it here.

The full name of the function `addCourse(int, float)` is `Student::addCourse(int, float)`. The class name in front indicates that the function is a member of the class `Student`. (The class name is added to the extended name of the function like arguments are added to an overloaded function name.) You could have other functions called `addCourse()` that are members of other classes, such as `Teacher::addCourse(int, float)` or even `Golf::addCourse()`. A function `addCourse(int, float)` without any class name is a conventional non-member function.

Data members are not any different than member functions with respect to extended names. Outside a structure, it is not sufficient to refer to `semesterHours` by itself. The data member `semesterHours` makes sense only in the context of the class `Student`. The extended name for `semesterHours` is `Student::semesterHours`.

The `::` is called the *scope resolution operator* because it indicates to which class a member belongs. You can use the `::` operator with a non-member function as well by using a null structure name. The non-member function `addCourse`, for example, can be referred to as `::addCourse(int, float)`, if you prefer.

The operator is optional except when two functions of the same name exist. For example:

```
float addCourse(int hours, float grade)
{
   return hours * grade;
}

class Student
{
  public:
   int   semesterHours;  //hours earned toward graduation
   float gpa;

   //add a completed course to the record
   float addCourse(int hours, float grade)
   {
      //...whatever stuff...
      addCourse(hours, grade);//call global function(?)
      //...more stuff...
   }
};
```

Here, I really want the member function `Student::addCourse()` to call the non-member function `::addCourse()`. Without the `::` operator, however, a call to `addCourse()` from `Student` refers to `Student::addCourse()`. This results in the function calling itself. Adding the `::` operator to the front directs the call to the global version, as desired:

```
class Student
{
  public:
   int   semesterHours;  //hours earned toward graduation
   float gpa;

   //add a completed course to the record
   float addCourse(int hours, float grade)
   {
```

```
        //...whatever stuff...
        ::addCourse(hours, grade);//call global function
        //...more stuff...
    }
};
```

The extended name of a function includes not only the arguments, as shown in Part II, but also the class name to which the function belongs.

Defining a Member Function in the Class

A member function can be defined either in the class or separately. When defined in the class definition, the function looks like the following in STUDENT.H:

```
class Student
{
  public:
   int   semesterHours;  //hours earned toward graduation
   float gpa;

   //add a completed course to the record
   float addCourse(int hours, float grade)
   {
      float weightedGPA;

      weightedGPA = semesterHours * gpa;

      //now add in the new course
      semesterHours += hours;
      weightedGPA += grade * hours;
      gpa = weightedGPA / semesterHours;
      return gpa;
   }
};
```

Member functions defined in the class default to inline (unless they have been specifically outlined because they contain a loop or by a compiler switch). Mostly, this is because a member function defined in the class is usually very small, and small functions are prime candidates for inlining.

There is another good, but more technical, reason to inline member functions defined within a class. Remember that C structures are normally defined in include files, which are then included in the .C source files that need them. Such include files should not contain data or functions because these files are compiled multiple times. Including an inline function is okay, however, because it (like a macro) expands in place in the source file. The same applies to C++ classes. By defaulting member functions defined in classes inline, the preceding problem is avoided.

Keeping a Member Function After Class

For larger functions, putting the code directly in the class definition can lead to some very large, unwieldy class definitions. To prevent this, C++ lets you define member functions somewhere else.

When written outside the class definition, the `Student` example looks like the following in `STUDENT.H`:

```
class Student
{
  public:
    int   semesterHours;  //hours earned toward graduation
    float gpa;

    //add a completed course to the record
    float addCourse(int hours, float grade);
};
```

The actual code appears in `STUDENT.CPP`:

```
#include "student.h"
float Student::addCourse(int hours, float grade)
{
    float weightedGPA;

    weightedGPA = semesterHours * gpa;

    //now add in the new course
    semesterHours += hours;
    weightedGPA += grade * hours;
    gpa = weightedGPA / semesterHours;
    return gpa;
}
```

Here you see that the class definition contains nothing more than a prototype declaration for the function `addCourse()`. The actual function definition appears separately.

The member function prototype declaration in the structure is analogous to any other prototype declaration and, like all prototype declarations, is required.

Notice that when the function was among its `Student` buddies in the class, it wasn't necessary to include the class name with the function name — the class name was assumed. When the function is by itself, the fully extended name is required. It's just like at my home. My wife calls me by only my first name (provided I'm not in the doghouse). Among the family, the last name is assumed. Outside the family (and my circle of acquaintances), others call me by my full name.

I have flagged the preceding structure and member function definitions as being in separate `.H` and `.CPP` files. They don't have to be, but it's a good idea. Other functions that want to use `Student` need to include the structure definitions but need to link with only the stuff in the `.CPP` file.

Calling a Member Function

Before you look at how to call a member function, refresh your memory as to how to reference a data member. In the following, you use an object of class `Student`, which was defined previously:

```
#include "student.h"
Student s;
void fn(void)
{
    //access one of the data members of s
    s.semesterHours = 10;
    s.gpa           = 3.0;
}
```

You must specify an object along with the member name. In other words, the following makes no sense:

```
#include "student.h"
Student s;
void fn(void)
```

(continued)

(continued)

```
{
   //access one of the data members of s
   //neither of these is legal
   semesterHours = 10;    //member of what object of what
                          //class?
   Student::semesterHours = 10; //okay, I know the class but
                          //I still don't know the object
}
```

Member functions are invoked with an object just like data members, as follows:

```
Student s;
void fn()
{
   //all of the following reference an object
   s.semesterHours = 10;
   s.gpa           = 3.0;
   s.addCourse(3, 4.0);  //call the member function
}
```

Calling a member function without an object makes no more sense than referencing a data member without an object. The syntax for calling a member function looks like a cross between the syntax for accessing a data member and the syntax for calling a conventional function.

Calling a member function with a pointer?

The same parallel for the objects themselves can be drawn for pointers to objects. The following references a data member of an object with a pointer:

```
#include "student.h"

void someFn(Student *pS)
{
   pS->semesterHours = 10;
   pS->gpa           = 3.0;
   pS->addCourse(3, 4.0);  //call the member function
}
```

```
Student s;
int main()
{
   someFn(&s);
   return 0;
}
```

Calling a member function with a reference to an object appears identical to the simple case of using the object itself. Remember, when passing or returning a reference as an argument to a function, C++ passes only the address of the object. In using a reference, however, C++ dereferences the address automatically, as the following example shows:

```
#include "Student.h"

//same as before, but this time using references
void someFn(Student &refS)
{
   refS.semesterHours = 10;
   refS.gpa           = 3.0;
   refS.addCourse(3, 4.0);  //call the member function
}

Student s;
int main()
{
   someFn(s);
   return 0;
}
```

Accessing members from a member function

I can see it clearly: You repeat to yourself, "Member functions must be invoked with an object. Referencing a data member without an object makes no sense." Just about the time you've accepted this, you look at the member function `Student::addCourse()` and BAMMO, it strikes you: This function is accessing class members without reference to an object!

Okay, which is it, can you or can't you? Believe me, you can't. When you reference a member of `Student` from `addCourse()`, that reference is against the `Student` object with which the call to `addCourse()` was made. Huh? Go back to the example:

```
#include "student.h"
float Student::addCourse(int hours, float grade)
{
   float weightedGPA;
   weightedGPA = semesterHours * gpa;

   //now add in the new course
   semesterHours += hours;
   weightedGPA += hours * grade;
   gpa = weightedGPA / semesterHours;
   return gpa;
}

Student s;
Student t;
int main()
{
   s.addCourse(3, 4.0);  //here's an A+
   t.addCourse(3, 2.5);  //give this guy a C
   return 0;
}
```

When `addCourse()` is invoked with the object `s`, all of the otherwise unqualified member references in `addCourse()` refer to `s`. Thus, `semesterHours` refers to `s.semesterHours`, and `gpa` refers to `s.gpa`. But in the next line of `main()`, when `addCourse()` is invoked with the `Student t`, these same references refer to `t.semesterHours` and `t.gpa` instead.

The object with which the member function was invoked is the "current" object, and all unqualified references to class members refer to this object. Put another way, unqualified references to class members made from a member function are always against the current object.

How does the member function know what the current object is? It's not magic — the address of the object is passed to the member function as an implicit and hidden first argument. In other words, the following conversion is taking place:

`s.addCourse(3, 2.5)` is like `Student::addCourse(&s, 3, 2.5)`

(Note that you can't actually use the syntax on the right; this line just shows you the way C++ interprets the call on the left.)

Inside the function, this implicit pointer to the current object has a name, in case you need to refer to it. It is called `this`, as in "Which object? *this* object." Get it? The type of `this` is always a pointer to an object of the appropriate class.

Anytime a member function refers to another member of the same class without providing an object explicitly, C++ assumes `this`. You also can refer to this explicitly, if you like. You could have written `Student::addCourse()` as follows:

```
#include "student.h"
float Student::addCourse(int hours, float grade)
{
   float weightedGPA;
   weightedGPA = this->semesterHours * this->gpa;

   //now add in the new course
   this->semesterHours += hours;
   weightedGPA += hours * grade;
   this->gpa = weightedGPA / this->semesterHours;
   return this->gpa;
}
```

Whether you explicitly include `this`, as in the preceding example, or leave it implicit, as you did before, the effect is the same.

Overloading Member Functions

Member functions can be overloaded in the same way that conventional functions are overloaded. Remember, however, that the class name is part of the extended name. Thus, the following functions are all legal:

```
class Student
{
  public:
   //grade - return the current grade point average
   float grade();

   //grade - set the grade and return previous value
   float grade(float newGPA);

   //...data members and stuff...
};
class Slope
{
  public:
   //grade - return the percentage grade of the slope
   float grade();
```

(continued)

(continued)

```
    //...stuff goes here too...
};

//grade - return the letter equivalent of a numerical grade
char grade(float value);

int main()
{
    Student s;
    s.grade(3.5);           //Student::grade(float)
    float v = s.grade();    //Student::grade()
    char c = grade(v);      //::grade(float)
    Slope o;
    float m = o.grade();    //Slope::grade()
    return 0;
}
```

Each call made from `main()` is noted in the comments with the extended name of the function called.

When calling overloaded functions, not only the arguments of the function but also the type of the object (if any) with which the function is invoked are used to disambiguate the call. (The term *disambiguate* is object-oriented talk for "decide at compile time which overloaded function to call.")

In the example, the first two calls to the member functions `Student::grade(float)` and `Student::grade()` are differentiated by their argument lists. The third call has no object, so it unambiguously denotes the non-member function `grade(float)`. Because the final call is made with an object of type `Slope`, it must refer to the member function `Slope::grade()`.

Chapter 9

Do Not Disturb: Protected Members

In This Chapter

- Declaring members protected
- Accessing protected members from within the class
- Accessing protected members from outside the class

In Chapter 8, I ask you to ignore the public keyword, with a campaign promise that I would return to it really soon. Let me make good on that promise now. (If you haven't read Chapter 8, you might want to take a look at it now.)

Protected Members

The members of a class can be marked protected, which makes them inaccessible outside the class. The alternative is to make the members public. Public members are accessible to all.

Why do I need them?

To understand the role of protected, think about the goals of object-oriented programming:

- Protect the internals of the class from outside functions. Suppose you had a plan to build a software microwave (or whatever), provide it with a simple interface to the outside world, and then put a box around it to keep others from messing with the insides. The protected keyword is that box.

- Make the class responsible for maintaining its internal state. It's not fair to ask the class to be responsible if others can reach in and manipulate its internals (any more than it was fair to ask a microwave designer to be responsible for the consequences of me mucking with a microwave's internal wiring).
- Limit the interface of the class to the outside world. It's easier to learn and use a class that has a limited interface (the public members). Protected members are hidden from the user and need not be learned. The interface becomes the class; this is called *abstraction* (see Chapter 8).
- Reduce the level of interconnection between the class and other code. By limiting interconnection, you can more easily replace one class with another, or use the class in other programs.

Now, I know what you functional types out there are saying: "You don't need some fancy feature to do all that. Just make a rule that says certain members are publicly accessible and others are not."

Although that is true in theory, it doesn't work. People start out with all kinds of good intentions, but as long as the language doesn't at least discourage direct access of protected members, these good intentions get crushed under the pressure to get the product out the door.

How do they work?

Adding the keyword `public` to a class makes subsequent members public, which means that they are accessible by non-member functions. Adding the keyword `protected` makes subsequent members of the class protected, which means they are not accessible by non-members of the class. You can switch between public and protected as often as you like.

Suppose you have a class named `Student`. In this example, the following capabilities are all that a fully functional, upstanding `Student` needs (notice the absence of `spendMoney()` and `drinkBeer()` — this is a highly stylized student):

`addCourse(int hours, float grade)` — add a course

`grade()` — return the current grade point average

`hours()` — return the number of hours earned toward graduation

The remaining members of `Student` can be declared protected to keep other functions' prying opcodes out of `Student`'s business.

```
class Student
{
  public:
   //grade - return the current grade point average
   float grade()
   {
      return gpa;
   }
   //hours - return the number of semester hours
   int hours()
   {
      return semesterHours;
   }
   //addCourse - add another course to the student's record
   float addCourse(int hours, float grade);

  //the following members are off-limits to others
  protected:
   int   semesterHours;  //hours earned toward graduation
   float gpa;            //grade point average
};
```

Now the members `semesterHours` and `gpa` are accessible only to other members of `Student`. Thus, the following doesn't work:

```
Student s;
int main()
{
   //raise my grade (don't make it too high; otherwise, no
   //one would believe it)
   s.gpa = 3.5;      //<- generates compiler error
   float gpa = s.grade(); //<- this public function reads
                     //a copy of the value, but you can't
                     //change it from here
   return 0;
}
```

The application's attempt to change the value of `gpa` is flagged with a compiler error.

TIP

It's considered good form not to rely on the default and specify either public or private at the beginning of the class. Most of the time, people start with the public members, because these make up the interface of the class. Protected members are saved until later.

Class members can be protected from access by non-member functions also by declaring them private. In fact, private is the default for classes (that is, classes start out in private mode). The difference between protected and private first becomes apparent in the presence of inheritance, which is covered in Chapter 17. For a detailed discussion of private, see Chapter 20.

Tell Me Again Why I Should Use Protected Members

Now that you know a little more about how to use protected members in an actual class, I replay the arguments for using protected members.

The class can protect its internal state

Making the `gpa` member protected precludes the application from setting the grade point average to some arbitrary value. The application can add courses, but it can't change the grade point average.

If the application has a legitimate need to set the grade point average directly, the class can provide a member function for that purpose, as follows:

```
class Student
{
  public:
   //same as before
   float grade()
   {
      return gpa;
   }

   //here we allow the grade to be changed
   float grade(float newGPA)
   {
      float oldGPA = gpa;
      //only if the new value is valid
      if (newGPA > 0 && newGPA <= 4.0)
```

```
        {
            gpa = newGPA;
        }
        return oldGPA;
    }

    //...other stuff is the same including the data members:
  protected:
    int   semesterHours;  //hours earned toward graduation
    float gpa;
};
```

The addition of the member function `grade(float)` allows the application to set the `gpa`. Notice, however, that the class still hasn't given up control completely. The application can't set `gpa` to any old value; only a `gpa` in the legal range of values (from 0 through 4.0) is accepted.

Thus, `Student` has provided access to an internal data member without abdicating its responsibility to make sure that the internal state of the class is valid.

It's easier to use a class with a limited interface

A class provides a limited interface. To use a class, all you need (or want) to know are its public members, what they do, and what their arguments are. This can drastically reduce the number of things you need to learn — and remember — to use the class.

As conditions change or as bugs are found, you want to be able to change the internal workings of a class. When you have hidden the internal workings of the class, changes to those details are less likely to require changes in the external application code.

What Are Friends for Anyway?

Occasionally, you want a non-member function to have access to the protected members of a class. You can do this by naming that function a friend of the class using the keyword friend.

Why do I need friends? (I am a rock, I am an island)

Sometimes an external function requires direct access to a data member. Without some type of friend mechanism, the programmer would be forced to declare the member public. This would give everyone else access to the one function as well.

It's like having a neighbor check on your house during your vacation. Giving non-family members the key to your house is not normally a good idea, but it beats the alternative of leaving the house unlocked.

How do they work?

The friend declaration appears in the class that contains the protected member. The friend declaration is like a prototype declaration in that it includes the extended name and the return type. In the following example, the function `initialize()` can now access anything it wants in `Student`:

```
class Student
{
   friend void initialize(Student*);
  public:
   //same public members as before...

  protected:
   int   semesterHours;  //hours earned toward graduation
   float gpa;
};

//the following function is a friend of Student
//so it can access the protected members
void initialize(Student *pS)
{
    pS->gpa = 0;               //this is now legal...
    pS->semesterHours = 0;     //...when it wasn't before
}
```

A single function can be declared to be a friend of two classes at the same time. Although this can be convenient, it tends to bind the two classes together. This binding of classes is normally considered bad because it makes one class dependent on the other. If the two classes naturally belong together, however, it's not all bad. For example:

```
class Student;      //forward declaration
class Teacher
{
    friend void registration();
  protected:
    int      noStudents;
    Student *pList[100];
  public:
    void assignGrades();
};

class Student
{
    friend void registration();
  public:
    //same public members as before...

  protected:
    Teacher *pT;
    int   semesterHours;  //hours earned toward graduation
    float gpa;
};
```

In this example, the function `registration()` can reach into both the `Student` and `Teacher` classes to tie them together at registration time, without being a member function of either one.

Notice that the first line in the example declares the class `Student` but none of its members. Remember, this is called a forward declaration and just defines the name of the class so that other classes, such as `Teacher`, can refer to it. Forward references are necessary when two classes refer to each other.

A member function of one class may be declared a friend of another class. For example:

```
class Teacher
{
    //...other members as well...
  public:
    void assignGrades();
};
```

(continued)

(continued)

```
class Student
{
    friend void Teacher::assignGrades();
  public:
    //same public members as before...
  protected:
    int   semesterHours;  //hours earned toward graduation
    float gpa;
};
void Teacher::assignGrades()
{
    //can access protected members of Teacher from here
}
```

Unlike in the non-member example, the member function `assignGrades()` must be declared before the class `Student` can declare it to be a friend.

An entire class can be named a friend of another. This has the effect of making every member function of the class a friend. For example:

```
class Student;      //forward declaration
class Teacher
{
  protected:
    int      noStudents;
    Student *pList[100];
  public:
    void assignGrades();
};

class Student
{
    friend class Teacher; //make entire class a friend
  public:
    //same public members as before...
  protected:
    int   semesterHours;  //hours earned toward graduation
    float gpa;
};
```

Now any member function of `Teacher` has access to the protected members of `Student`. Declaring one class a friend of the other inseparably binds the two classes together.

Chapter 10

Getting an Object Off to a Good Start: The Constructor

In This Chapter

- Comparing objects and classes
- Creating and destroying objects
- Declaring constructors and destructors
- Invoking constructors and destructors

Like objects in the real world, objects in programs are created and scrapped. If the class is to be responsible for its well-being, it must have some control over this process. As luck would have it (I suppose some preplanning was involved as well), C++ provides just the right mechanism. But first, a discussion of what it means to create an object.

Creating Objects

So far, I've been a little sloppy in my use of the terms *class* and *object*. What is the difference? What is the relationship?

I can create a class `Dog` that describes the relevant properties of man's best friend. At my house, we have two dogs. Thus, my class `Dog` has two instances, Trudie and Scooter.

A *class* describes a type of thing. An *object* is an instance of a class. The class is `Dog`, and the objects are Trudie and Scooter. Each dog has a separate object, but only one class `Dog`, no matter how many dogs I may have.

Objects are created and destroyed, but classes simply exist. My pets Trudie and Scooter might come and go, but the class `Dog` (evolution aside) is perpetual.

Different types of objects are created at different times. Global objects are created when the program first begins execution. Local objects are created when the program encounters their declaration (see Chapter 4).

Under C rules, global objects are initialized to all zeros. Objects declared local to a function have no particular initial value. This is probably not acceptable to classes.

C++ allows the class to define a special member function that is invoked automatically when an object of that class is created. This member function, called the constructor, must initialize the object to some valid initial state. In addition, the class may define a destructor to handle the destruction of the object. These two functions are the topic of this chapter.

Using Constructors

The constructor is a member function that is called automatically with an object when an object of a certain class is created. Its primary job is to initialize the object to a legal initial value for the class.

Why do I need them?

For a C structure, you can initialize an object as part of the declaration. For example:

```
struct Student
{
   int   semesterHours;
   float gpa;
};

void fn()
{
   Student s = {0, 0};
   //...function continues...
}
```

But this doesn't work for a class because the application doesn't have access to the protected members of the class. The following snippet is invalid:

```
class Student
```

```
{
  public:
   //...public members...
  protected:
   int   semesterHours;
   float gpa;
};

void fn()
{
   Student s = {0, 0};   //illegal; data members not      //accessible
   //...function continues...
}
```

In this example, the non-member `fn()` can't write to the protected members `semesterHours` and `gpa`.

You could outfit the class with an initialization function that the application calls as soon as the object is created. Because this initialization function is a member of the class, it would have access to the protected members. This solution appears as follows:

```
class Student
{
  public:
   void init()
   {
      semesterHours = 0;
      gpa = 0.0;
   }
   //...other public members...

  protected:
   int   semesterHours;
   float gpa;
};

void fn()
{
   Student s;        //create the object...
   s.init();         //...then initialize it
   //...function continues...
}
```

The only problem with this solution is that it abrogates the responsibility of the class to look after its own data members. In other words, the class must rely on the application to call the `init()` function. If it does not, the object is full of garbage and who knows what might happen.

What is needed is a way to take the responsibility for calling the `init()` function away from the application code and give it to the compiler. Every time an object is created, the compiler can insert a call to the special init function to initialize it. That's a constructor!

How do they work?

The constructor is a special member function that is called automatically when an object is created. It carries the same name as the class. That way, the compiler knows which member function is the constructor. (The designers of C++ could have made up a different rule, such as: "The constructor must be called `init()`." It wouldn't have made any difference, as long as the compiler could recognize the constructor.)

With a constructor, the class `Student` appears as follows:

```
class Student
{
  public:
   Student()
   {
      semesterHours = 0;
      gpa = 0.0;
   }
   //...other public members...

  protected:
   int   semesterHours;
   float gpa;
};

void fn()
{
   Student s;         //create the object and initialize it
   //...function continues...
}
```

At the point of the declaration of `s`, the compiler inserts a call to the constructor `Student::Student()`.

This simple constructor was written as an inline member function. Constructors can be written also as outline functions. For example:

```
class Student
{
  public:
   Student();
   //...other public members...

  protected:
   int   semesterHours;
   float gpa;
};
Student::Student()
{
   semesterHours = 0;
   gpa = 0.0;
}
void fn()
{
   Student s;       //create the object and initialize it
   //...function continues...
}
int main()
{
   fn();
   return 0;
}
```

I added a small `main()` function here so that you can execute this program. You really should single-step this simple program in your debugger before going any further.

As you single-step through this example, control eventually comes to rest at the `Student s`; declaration. Select `Step Into` or `Trace` one more time and control magically jumps to `Student::Student()`. (If you are using the inline version, be sure to compile with the "Outline inline functions" compiler switch enabled; otherwise the entire constructor is executed as a single statement, and you won't notice the call.) Continue single-stepping through the constructor. When the function has finished, control returns to the statement after the declaration.

Multiple objects can be declared on a single line. Rerun the single-step experiment with `fn()` declared as follows:

```
void fn()
{
   Student s[5];    //create an array of objects
   //...function continues...
}
```

You should see the constructor invoked five times, once for each element in the array.

If you can't get the debugger to work (or you just don't want to bother), add an output statement to the constructor so that you can see output to the screen whenever the constructor is invoked. The effect is not as dramatic, but it is convincing.

The constructor can be invoked only automatically. It cannot be called like a normal member function. That is, you cannot use something like the following to reinitialize a `Student` object:

```
void fn()
{
   Student s;         //initialize the object
   //...other stuff...
   s.Student();       //reinitialize it; this doesn't work
}
```

The constructor has no return type, not even `void`.

If a class contains a data member that is an object of another class, the constructor for that class is called automatically as well. Consider the following example. Output statements have been added so that you can see the order in which the objects are invoked.

```
#include <iostream.h>
class Student
{
  public:
   Student()
   {
      cout << "constructing student\n";
      semesterHours = 0;
      gpa = 0.0;
   }
   //...other public members...

  protected:
   int   semesterHours;
   float gpa;
};
```

```
class Teacher
{
  public:
   Teacher()
   {
      cout << "constructing teacher\n";
   }
};

class TutorPair
{
  public:
   TutorPair()
   {
      cout << "constructing tutor pair\n";
      noMeetings = 0;
   }

  protected:
   Student student;
   Teacher teacher;
   int     noMeetings;
};

int main()
{
   TutorPair tp;
   cout << "back in main\n";
   return 0;
}
```

Executing this program generates the following output:

```
constructing student
constructing teacher
constructing tutor pair
back in main
```

Creating the object `tp` in main invokes the constructor for `TutorPair` automatically. Before control passes into the body of the `TutorPair` constructor, however, the constructors for the two member objects `student` and `teacher` are invoked.

The constructor for `Student` is called first because it is declared first. Then the constructor for `Teacher` is called. After these objects have been constructed, control returns to the open brace and the constructor for `TutorPair` is allowed to construct the remainder of the object.

It would not do for `TutorPair` to be responsible for initializing student and teacher. Each class is responsible for initializing its own objects.

Using the Destructor

Just as objects are created, so are they destroyed (ashes to ashes, dust to dust). If a class can have a constructor to set things up, it should also have a special member function that's called to destruct, or take apart, the object. This member is called the destructor.

Why do I need it?

A class may allocate resources in the constructor; these resources need to be deallocated before the object ceases to exist. For example, if the constructor opens a file, the file needs to be closed before leaving that class or the program itself. Or if the constructor allocates memory from the heap, this memory must be freed before the object goes away. The destructor allows the class to do these cleanup tasks automatically without relying on the application to call the proper member functions.

How does it work?

The destructor member has the same name as the class but with a tilde (~) added to the front. (C++ is being cute again — the tilde is the symbol for NOT in C. Get it? A destructor is a "not constructor.") Like a constructor, the destructor has no return type. For example, the class `Student` with a destructor added appears as follows:

```
class Student
{
  public:
   Student()
   {
      semesterHours = 0;
      gpa = 0.0;
   }
  ~Student()
   {
      //...whatever assets are returned here...
   }
   //...other public members...

  protected:
```

```
    int   semesterHours;
    float gpa;
};
```

The destructor is invoked automatically when an object is destroyed, or in C++ parlance, when an object is *destructed*. That sounds sort of circular ("the destructor is invoked when an object is destructed"), so I've avoided the term until now. You can also say, "when the object goes out of scope." A local object goes out of scope when the function returns. A global or static object goes out of scope when the program terminates.

If more than one object is being destructed, the destructors are invoked in the reverse order in which the constructors were called. This is also true when destructing objects that have class objects as data members. For example, here's the example tutor pair program from Chapter 9, with destructors added:

```
#include <iostream.h>
class Student
{
  public:
    Student()
    {
       cout << "constructing student\n";
       semesterHours = 0;
       gpa = 0.0;
    }
   ~Student()
    {

       cout << "destructing student\n";    }
    //...other public members...

  protected:
    int   semesterHours;
    float gpa;
};

class Teacher
{
  public:
    Teacher()
    {
       cout << "constructing teacher\n";
    }
   ~Teacher()
```

(continued)

(continued)

```
    {
        cout << "destructing teacher\n";
    }
};

class TutorPair
{
  public:
    TutorPair()
    {
        cout << "constructing tutor pair\n";
        noMeetings = 0;
    }
   ~TutorPair()
    {
        cout << "destructing tutor pair\n";
    }

  protected:
    Student s;
    Teacher t;
    int     noMeetings;
};

int main()
{
    TutorPair tp;
    cout << "back in main\n";
    return 0;
}
```

If you execute this program, it generates the following output:

```
constructing student
constructing teacher
constructing tutor pair
back in main
destructing tutor pair
destructing teacher
destructing student
```

The constructor for `TutorPair` is invoked at the declaration of `tp`. The destructor is invoked at the closing brace of `main()`.

Chapter 11

Finding the Classes

In This Chapter

- Defining the role of object-oriented design
- Finding the classes in all that detail
- Attributing properties to classes
- Describing the relationship between classes

It's all very nice that you know how to build a class in C++, but that's not of much use if you don't know where classes fit into a real-world problem. So in this chapter you take a simple problem, solve it using an OO approach, and contrast that with a conventional structured approach. (The structured approach is what you've been doing in C until now.)

Object-Oriented Analysis and Design

The process of writing a program can be divided into three distinct steps: analysis, design, and coding. Some people think programming involves only the last step — coding — but programming includes all three.

Problems start out in the real world, often called the problem domain. Solving a problem at this point is difficult because of all the confusing details of the problem. During the analysis phase, you extract the essential elements of the problem and abstract away the unimportant details. The result of this analysis is a model of the problem. This model is written by and for humans. (One type of model is a block diagram; boxes represent the agents, and arrows connecting the boxes represent the data being passed back and forth.)

During the design phase, the model is manipulated into a proposed solution. This solution may take the form of a flow chart, a PDL (Preliminary Design Language), or even pseudocode. Whatever the form, it looks more like a computer language but is still readable by humans. During the coding phase, the solution is converted to code.

At this point, you're saying either "I don't do all that!" or "This is true even in structured programming." To the first comment I say, "Yes you do, whether you know it or not." Even if you don't put all this stuff on paper, you have to go through these steps (or something like them) to solve any nontrivial programming problem.

To the second comment I say, "You're right." You have to go through these steps in a structured language as well, but the process is more difficult. Here's the argument: One result of analysis is the identification of the essential abstractions (read "classes") of the problem. Because you can't code classes in a structured language, the design and the model are more different in a structured language than they are in an object-oriented language. Another way to say "more different" in this context is "conceptually more distant." (Conceptual distance refers to the length of the mental jump you make to get from one phase of development to the other.)

Increased conceptual distance introduces more errors in the design. It also makes it more difficult to see the abstractions the designer was using when solving the problem, which in turn makes the resulting program more difficult to understand and maintain.

An Example Analysis and Design Problem

To see how object-oriented analysis and design (OOA&D, as those in the know call it) works, solve a problem down to the rough design level. (Generating the code at this point wouldn't add much to your understanding of the problem.)

Your task is to write the tuner controller for the new PaleColor 500 TV set. This controller will be connected to the TV hardware, as shown in Figure 11-1.

The controller takes input from both the infrared sensor (for the remote) and the front panel of the TV. (Did you remember that you can still control most sets without a remote?) The viewer can select either the channel to tune to or NEXT or PREV (for the next or previously stored channel in the channel list). When a channel is selected, the controller sends the frequency to the tuner and then displays the channel by enabling the display character generator for five seconds.

Quick analysis and design: An object-oriented approach

In object-oriented analysis and design, you can perform the following steps:

- Find the classes.
- Describe the classes and the relationships between them.
- Use the classes to structure the program.

Finding the classes is mostly a matter of experience. The programmer starts with a list of candidate classes and then considers which of these are fundamental and which are secondary or derivative.

Candidate classes can be found among the following:

- Tangible or visible things, such as televisions or microwaves
- Roles, such as TV viewer or coach potato
- Events, such as tuning the TV or turning it off
- Interactions, such as the IR communication path between the remote and the TV

For more-complicated programs, programmers must undertake a complete domain analysis. They must immerse themselves in the problem domain, learn the lingo of the domain experts, and study solutions to similar problems (whether computer-based or not), looking for the key abstractions. (They must be sure to take note of which abstractions worked and which did not.)

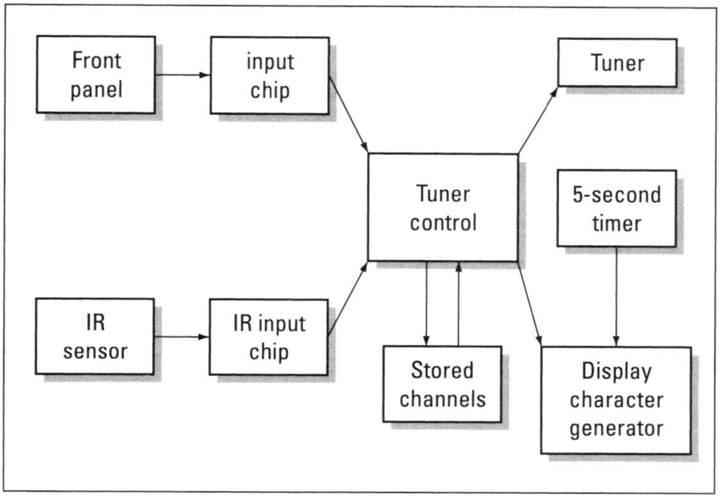

Figure 11-1: The hardware interconnections for the TV tuner controller.

For simple problems, it is often useful to go through a statement of the problem and list the nouns. Here's a list from our TV tuner controller problem:

```
Controller
Input
InfraredSensor
FrontPanel
TV
Viewer
Channel
ChannelList
Tuner
DisplayCharacterGenerator
```

Now that you have a list, you need to figure out which terms might be useful. (The hardware connection diagram might help with this task.) You are building the Controller, so this is a possible class. The nouns Viewer and TV appear to be valid classes also, but at a higher level of abstraction. That is, the Controller is part of the TV, which is used by the Viewer. The remaining nouns might be valid classes, so leave them as candidates for now.

You can describe the classes and their relationships. This is an iterative process, so the two parts to this step — describing the classes and describing their relationships — should be considered simultaneously. In general, the validity of key abstractions doesn't change, but the border between them may move back and forth. That is, a particular capability allocated to one class may be moved to another.

Classes and their relationships can be described in several ways, but most involve expensive CASE tools that you don't have. One approach, however, is clever and simple, and everything you need is available in your kitchen. It is called the Class-Responsibility-Collaboration (CRC) Method (proposed by Ward Cunningham and described in "Think Like an Object," Kent Beck, UNIX Review, October 1991).

The CRC method characterizes each class by the following:

- **Class name.** Select candidate classes as described (or use any other technique you like). Use names that clearly describe the responsibility of each class (that is, don't use wishy-washy names).
- **Responsibilities.** Each class does something. Describe each class, using a short phrase with an active verb. Refine the verb, if necessary, to describe unambiguously what the class does. These verbs eventually become member functions.

- **Collaborators.** Each class relies on other classes, called collaborators, to implement the complete design. By noting the collaborators for each class, you deepen your understanding of the role each class plays. Note also which member functions these collaborators need access to.

Start by writing the class name in the upper-left corner of a 3-by-5 index card. Below this, write the initial responsibility list (use pencil because this will change). Along the right side, note the collaborator classes that the class depends on.

The properties of each class can be jockeyed back and forth until you think you have a good description of the essential abstractions of the problem.

When assigning responsibilities, use terse, strongly worded verbs. Use the same verb in different classes to do the same thing. For example, both class `IRSensor` and `FrontPanel` have the responsibility `read`. Classes that have no responsibilities should be deleted because they don't do anything.

An object-oriented solution to the problem

Using the candidate classes in the preceding section, I came up with the CRC cards shown in Figure 11-2. From this, you can see that `Controller` does not make a very good class. It depends on every class in the system, which indicates that it is probably conceived functionally. In addition, its responsibilities are "do everything." `Controller` incorporates the entire solution. You can let this be the main program, which uses the other classes to solve the problem.

Look at `main()` and one of the classes to get a feel for what the complete solution would look like:

```
DECLARE INPUT OBJECT
LOOP
   DO
      INPUT.READ
   UNTIL INPUT DETECTED
   INPUT.PARSE
   CONVERT CHANNEL TO FREQUENCY
   TUNER.SEND FREQUENCY
   DISPLAYCG.WRITE
ENDLOOP
```

Controller	
	Tuner
	DisplayCG
	Input
	Timer

Input	
read	FrontPanel
parse	IRSensor

FrontPanel	
read	

IRSensor	
read	

Tuner	
tune	

ChannelList	
saveChan	
reset	
getNext	
getPrev	

DisplayCG	
write	Timer

Timer	
setTime	

Figure 11-2: CRC cards for the TV tuner problem.

The `Input` class looks like the following:

```
CONSTRUCTOR:
   DECLARE IRSENSOR
   DECLARE FRONTPANEL
READ:
   DO
      IRSENSOR.READ
      FRONTPANEL.READ
   UNTIL INPUT DETECTED
   RETURN INPUT
PARSE:
   PARSE THE INPUT STREAM
```

(You may be a bit hampered by the fact that you haven't gone very far in the study of constructors. In Part IV, you see how to build the `Input` class so that it works for any number and type of input devices.)

The PDL for `Controller` is simpler than the functional PDL presented previously. You could argue that you got this simplicity by pushing more of the code into functions. (These functions are the member functions of the classes.) This is not completely correct, however.

Consider that details about how data will be read from the IR sensor appear at the highest level of the functional PDL. At this level, how the IR sensor hardware is handled is useless extra informational baggage for the reader. Further, if this hardware changes (which it undoubtedly will as soon as Hyundai starts making a cheaper one), even code at this level will have to be modified.

Consider the object-oriented PDL. You can see that all you are interested in doing is "reading input." The details of the IR sensor, if one is even present, are of no interest at this level. These details, along with details of parsing the input, are left to the `Input` class, where they belong. If the IR sensor hardware changes, you change only the part of the `Input` class that deals with the IR sensor. (C++ helps you here as well, as you see later.) And if you do your job well, those changes will not propagate outside the class.

Trial and Error

As Grady Booch said (I'm such a name-dropper), "The identification of classes and objects is the fundamental issue in object-oriented design; identification involves both discovery and invention" (Grady Booch, Object-Oriented Design with Applications, Benjamin-Cummings, 1991). This last idea is very important. The act of identifying classes teaches you something about the problem — organize your thoughts and figure out the essential abstractions. (Why do you think biology students spend all their time studying taxonomies of plants and animals?)

As you learn, don't be afraid to reevaluate your classes. If necessary, try different classes. If you choose the wrong ones, they will tell you. They will be difficult to envision because they will be difficult to describe. In addition, such classes will have lots of member functions without a clear purpose. Classes with many collaborators are suspicious. A large number of friend functions is another tip-off that something's amiss.

Get the classes right and you'll know it just as fast. They will be easy to visualize and adaptable to changing conditions. There won't be too many member functions, and their purpose will be clear. The clouds will part, and rainbows will shine. Your sex life will improve and your premature balding will reverse itself as if by magic.

A Budget with Class BUDGET3.CPP

Looking at the BUDGET program, it's easy to see what the class candidates are: `Checking` and `Savings`. You may already know that it's a good idea to make data members protected, so a few access functions are necessary in case a non-member function needs the account number or balance.

Like all classes, `Checking` and `Savings` need a constructor to initialize objects to legal values (mostly to a balance of zero). Two additional member functions are also necessary: `deposit()` and `withdrawal()`. You need some way to associate an account number with the object, so I have introduced a member function called `init()`.

Finally, I added one other member function called `display()` to display the current object. This is not a requirement, but it is common to let the object display itself rather than rely on an external function to do it. (Those other functions would need knowledge of the class's internals to know how to display it properly, and that's something you want to avoid.)

Here is the resulting program:

```
//BUDGET3.CPP - Budget program with real classes for
//              the first time. Transform the
//              C structs into classes. This is starting
//              to look like something.

#include <iostream.h>

//the maximum number of accounts one can have
const int maxAccounts = 10;

//Checking - this describes checking accounts
class Checking                        //Note 1
{
  public:
   Checking()                         //Note 2
   {
accountNumber = 0;
      balance = 0.0F;
   }
```

```
    void init()                          //Note 3
    {
       cout << "Enter account number:";
       cin  >> accountNumber;
    }

    //access functions                   //Note 4
    int accountNo()
    {
       return accountNumber;
    }
    float acntBalance()
    {
       return balance;
    }

    //transaction functions              //Note 5
    void deposit(float amount)
    {
       balance += amount;
    }
    void withdrawal(float amount);

    //display function for displaying self on 'cout'
    void display()                       //Note 6
    {
       cout << "Account " << accountNumber
            << " = "      << balance
            << "\n";
    }

  protected:                             //Note 7
    unsigned accountNumber;
    float    balance;
};
//withdrawal - this member function is too big to
//             be inlined
void Checking::withdrawal(float amount)
{
    if (balance < amount )
    {
       cout << "Insufficient funds: balance " << balance
            << ", check "                     << amount
            << "\n";
    }
```

(continued)

(continued)

```
    else
    {
       balance -= amount;

       //if balance falls too low, charge service fee
       if (balance < 500.00F)
       {
          balance -= 0.20F;
       }
    }
}

//Savings - you can probably figure this one out
class Savings
{
  public:
    Savings()
    {
       accountNumber = 0;
       balance = 0.0F;
       noWithdrawals = 0;
    }
    void init()
    {
       cout << "Enter account number:";
       cin  >> accountNumber;
    }

    //access functions
    int accountNo()
    {
       return accountNumber;
    }
    float acntBalance()
    {
       return balance;
    }
    //transaction functions
    void deposit(float amount)
    {
       balance += amount;
    }
    void withdrawal(float amount);
```

```
    //display function - display self to cout
    void display()
    {
       cout << "Account "              << accountNumber
            << " = "                   << balance
            << " (no. withdrawals = " << noWithdrawals
            << ")\n";
    }

  protected:
    unsigned accountNumber;
    float    balance;
    int      noWithdrawals;
};
void Savings::withdrawal(float amount)
{
    if (balance < amount)
    {
       cout << "Insufficient funds: balance " << balance
            << ", withdrawal "                << amount
            << "\n";
    }
    else
    {
       if (++noWithdrawals > 1)
       {
          balance -= 5.00F;
       }
       balance -= amount;
    }
}

//prototype declarations
void process(Checking &checking);
void process(Savings &savings);

//checking and savings account objects
Checking chkAcnts[maxAccounts];        //Note 8
Savings svgAcnts[maxAccounts];

//main - accumulate the initial input and output totals
int main()
{
    /*loop until someone enters an 'X' or 'x'*/
    int noChkAccounts = 0;    //count the number of accounts
```

(continued)

(continued)

```
int noSvgAccounts = 0;
char      accountType;      //S or C

unsigned keepLooping = 1;
while (keepLooping)
{
   cout << "Enter S for Savings,"
           "C for Checking, X for exit\n";
   cin  >> accountType;

   switch (accountType)
   {
      case 'c':
      case 'C':
         if (noChkAccounts < maxAccounts) {
            chkAcnts[noChkAccounts].init(); //Note 9
            process(chkAcnts[noChkAccounts]);
            noChkAccounts++;
         }
         else
         {
            cout << "No more room for checking accounts\n";
         }
         break;

      case 's':
      case 'S':
         if (noSvgAccounts < maxAccounts)
         {
            svgAcnts[noSvgAccounts].init();
            process(svgAcnts[noSvgAccounts]);
            noSvgAccounts++;
         }
        else
         {
            cout << "No more room for savings accounts\n";
         }
         break;

      case 'x':
      case 'X':
         keepLooping = 0;
         break;

      default:
```

```
            cout << "I didn't get that.\n";
        }
    }

    //now present totals
    float chkTotal = 0;        //total of all checking accounts
    cout << "Checking accounts:\n";
    for (int i = 0; i < noChkAccounts; i++)
    {
        chkAcnts[i].display();          //Note 10
        chkTotal += chkAcnts[i].acntBalance();
    }
    float svgTotal = 0;        //total of all savings accounts
    cout << "Savings accounts:\n";
    for (i = 0; i < noSvgAccounts; i++)
    {
        svgAcnts[i].display();
        svgTotal += svgAcnts[i].acntBalance();
    }

    float total = chkTotal + svgTotal;
    cout << "Total for checking accounts = " << chkTotal << "\n";
    cout << "Total for savings accounts  = " << svgTotal << "\n";
    cout << "Total worth                 = " << total << "\n";
    return 0;
}

//process(Checking) - input the data for a checking account*/
void process(Checking &checking)
{
    cout << "Enter positive number for deposit,\n"
            "negative for check, 0 to terminate";

    float transaction;
    do
    {
        cout << ":";
        cin  >> transaction;

        //deposit
        if (transaction > 0)
        {
            checking.deposit(transaction);
        }
```

(continued)

(continued)

```
      //withdrawal
      if (transaction < 0)
      {
         checking.withdrawal(-transaction);
      }
   } while (transaction != 0);
}
//process(Savings) - input the data for a savings account
void process(Savings &savings)
{
   cout << "Enter positive number for deposit,\n"
           "negative for withdrawal, 0 to terminate";

   float transaction;
   do
   {
      cout << ":";
      cin  >> transaction;

      //deposit
      if (transaction > 0)
      {
         savings.deposit(transaction);
      }

   //withdrawal
      if (transaction < 0)
      {
         savings.withdrawal(-transaction);
      }
   } while (transaction != 0);
}
```

Executing this program with the same input as before generates the same output as the previous version. (If it didn't, I'd be worried.)

```
Enter S for Savings, C for Checking, X for exit
S
Enter account number:123
Enter positive number for deposit,
negative for withdrawal, 0 to terminate:200
:-50
:-50
:0
Enter S for Savings, C for Checking, X for exit
```

```
C
Enter account number:234
Enter positive number for deposit,
negative for check, 0 to terminate:200
:-25
:-20
:0
Enter S for Savings, C for Checking, X for exit
X
Checking accounts:
Account 234 = 154.600006
Savings accounts:
Account 123 = 95 (no. withdrawals = 2)
Total for checking accounts = 154.600006
Total for savings accounts  = 95
Total worth                 = 249.600006
```

Starting with class Checking (`Note 1`), you can see each of the member functions mentioned earlier. The constructor (`Note 2`) zeros out the account number and the balance. Initializing the balance to zero is critical; otherwise, every account would start with a random amount of money in it.

The `init()` member function (`Note 3`) assigns the object an account number. The access functions (`Note 4`) simply return the account number or the balance. The two transaction functions (`Note 5`) implement the deposit and withdrawal rules that apply to checking accounts. Because the `deposit()` function is quite simple, it has been implemented inline. The `withdrawal()` function, however, has been written as an outline function.

The `display()` function (`Note 6`) outputs the important data members to the standard output. The data members have been protected (`Note 7`) to keep prying fingers off.

The class `Savings` is virtually identical to the class `Checking`. `Checking` and `Savings` objects are allocated from a global array and therefore constructed before `main()` starts (at `Note 8`). Function `main()` looks similar, except for the format used to call member functions (`Note 9`) and the fact that data members must be accessed through access functions (`Note 10`).

The `process()` functions are considerably simpler because their class-specific code has been moved into the class.

I encourage you to type this program and single step through it. Nothing else will give you a feel for what's going on faster than seeing the program in action. (Be sure and set the "Outline inline functions" option as explained in Chapter 5 so that you can see the member functions single step.)

Part IV
Warming to the Water: Getting Comfortable with Classes

The 5th Wave

In this part . . .

Part III introduces you to the concept of classes — particularly protected members, member functions, and constructors. In Part IV, I delve further into these concepts and introduce a few more to prepare you for the next big step — inheritance, which Part V covers.

Chapter 12

Making Constructive Arguments

In This Chapter

- Making argumentative constructors
- Overloading the constructor
- Creating objects using constructors
- Invoking member constructors
- Order of construction and destruction

If you looked at Part III, you may have noticed that the constructors did not completely relieve the need for an initialization member function. The constructors had no arguments, so they had no choice but to initialize the object as "empty." In some cases, an initialization function was required to go back and "fill" the object with useful data.

If I could have passed arguments to the constructor, I could have avoided this clumsy two-step process. This chapter shows you how to do just that.

Constructors Outfitted with Arguments

C++ allows the programmer to define a constructor with arguments. For example:

```
#include <iostream.h>
#include <string.h>
class Student
{
   Student(char *pName)
   {
      cout << "constructing student " << pName << "\n";
      strncpy(name, pName, sizeof(name));
      name[sizeof(name) - 1] = '\0';
```

(continued)

(continued)

```
    }
      //...other public members go here
  protected:
    char  name[40];
    int   semesterHours;
    float gpa;
};
```

Why do I need them?

Something as straightforward as adding arguments to the constructor shouldn't require much justification, but let me take a shot at it anyway. First, allowing arguments to constructors is convenient. It's a bit silly to make the programmer construct an empty object and then immediately call an initialization function to store data in it. A constructor with arguments is like one-stop shopping — sort of a full-service constructor.

Another, more important reason to provide arguments to constructors is that an empty object may not make sense. Remember that a constructor's job is to construct a legal object (legal as defined by the class). If an empty object is not legal, the constructor isn't doing its job.

For example, a bank account without an account number is probably not legal. (C++ doesn't care one way or the other, but the bank might get a bit excited.) We could construct a numberless `BankAccount` object and then require that the application use some other member function to initialize the account number before it is used. In fact, this is exactly what we did previously in our BUDGET program. This breaks our rules, however, because it lets information about the bank account class leak into the application.

How do they work?

Conceptually, the idea of adding an argument is simple. A constructor is a member function and member functions can have arguments. Ergo, constructors can have arguments.

Remember, though, that you don't call the constructor like a normal function. Therefore, the only way to pass arguments to the constructor is when the object is created. For example, the following program creates an object `s` of class `Student` by calling the `Student(char*)` constructor. The object `s` is destructed when the function `main()` returns.

```
#include <iostream.h>
#include <string.h>
class Student
{
  public:
   Student(char *pName)
   {
      cout << "constructing student " << pName << "\n";
      strncpy(name, pName, sizeof(name));
      name[sizeof(name) - 1]  = '\0';
      semesterHours = 0;
      gpa = 0.0;
   }
  ~Student()
   {
      cout << "destructing " << name << "\n";
   }

   //...other public members...
  protected:
   char  name[40];
   int   semesterHours;
   float gpa;
};

int main()
{
   Student s("Danny");        //construct little Danny
   return 0;
}                             //now, get rid of him
```

The constructor looks like the constructors shown in Part III except for the addition of the `char*` argument `pName`. The constructor initializes the data members to their empty start-up values, except for the data member `name`, which gets its initial value from `pName`.

The object `s` is created in `main()`. The argument to be passed to the constructor appears in the declaration of `s`, right next to the name of the object. Thus, the student `s` is given the name `Danny` in this declaration. The closed brace invokes the destructor on poor little Danny.

Executing the program generates the following output:

```
constructing student Danny
destructing Danny
```

WARNING!

Many of the constructors in this chapter violate the "functions with more than three lines shouldn't be inlined" rule. I decided to make them inline anyway because I think they're easier for you to read that way.

When outlined, constructors and destructors appear as follows:

```
#include <iostream.h>
#include <string.h>
class Student
{
  public:
   //declarations only
   Student(char *pName);
  ~Student();

   //...other public members...
  protected:
   char  name[40];
   int   semesterHours;
   float gpa;
};

//definitions (notice no return type)
Student::Student(char *pName)
{
   cout << "constructing student " << pName << "\n";
   strncpy(name, pName, sizeof(name));
   name[sizeof(name) - 1]  = '\0';
   semesterHours = 0;
   gpa = 0.0;
}

//check out this destructor declaration
//     - does this look bizarre or what?
Student::~Student()
{
   cout << "destructing " << name << "\n";
}
```

As your experience in C++ grows, you should have no trouble mentally converting from one form to the other.

Overloading the Constructor (Is That Like Placing Too Many Demands on the Carpenter?)

While I am drawing parallels between constructors and other, more normal member functions in this chapter, I can draw one more: Constructors can be overloaded. C++ chooses the proper constructor based on the arguments in the declaration. For example, the class `Student` can have all three constructors shown in the following snippet at the same time:

```
#include <iostream.h>
#include <string.h>
class Student
{
  public:
   Student()
   {
      cout << "constructing student no name\n";
      semesterHours = 0;
      gpa = 0.0;
      name[0] = '\0';
   }
   Student(char *pName)
   {
      cout << "constructing student " << pName << "\n";
      strncpy(name, pName, sizeof(name));
      name[sizeof(name) - 1]  = '\0';
      semesterHours = 0;
      gpa = 0;
   }
   Student(char *pName, int xfrHours, float xfrGPA)
   {
      cout << "constructing student " << pName << "\n";
      strncpy(name, pName, sizeof(name));
      name[sizeof(name) - 1]  = '\0';
      semesterHours = xfrHours;
      gpa = xfrGPA;
   }
  ~Student()
   {
      cout << "destructing student\n";
   }
```

(continued)

(continued)

```
   //...other public members...
  protected:
   char  name[40];
   int   semesterHours;
   float gpa;
};

//the following invokes each constructor in turn
int main()
{
   Student noName;
   Student freshMan("Smell E. Fish");
   Student xfer("Upp R. Classman", 80, 2.5);
   return 0;
}
```

Because the object `noName` appears with no arguments, it is constructed using the constructor `Student::Student()`. This constructor is called the *default,* or *void, constructor.* (I prefer the latter name, but the former is more common, so I use it in this book.) The `freshMan` is constructed using the constructor that has only a `char*` argument, and the `xfer Student` uses the constructor with three arguments.

Notice how similar all three constructors are, particularly the last two. By adding defaults to the last constructor, all three constructors can be combined into one. For example, the following class combines all three constructors into a single, clever constructor:

```
#include <iostream.h>
#include <string.h>
class Student
{
  public:
   Student(char *pName   = "no name",
           int xfrHours = 0,
           float xfrGPA = 0.0)
   {
     cout << "constructing student " << pName << "\n";
     strncpy(name, pName, sizeof(name));
     name[sizeof(name) - 1]  = '\0';
     semesterHours = xfrHours;
     gpa = xfrGPA;
   }
  ~Student()
   {
```

```
        cout << "destructing student\n";
    }

    //...other public members...
  protected:
    char  name[40];
    int   semesterHours;
    float gpa;
};

int main()
{
    Student noName;
    Student freshMan("Smell E. Fish");
    Student xfer("Upp R. Classman", 80, 2.5);
    return 0;
}
```

Now all three objects are constructed using the same constructor; defaults are provided for nonexistent arguments in `noName` and `freshMan`.

In earlier versions of C++, you could not create a default constructor by providing defaults for all the arguments. The default constructor had to be a separate explicit constructor. Although this restriction was lifted in the standard (it seems to have had no good basis), some older compilers may still impose it.

Default Default Constructors

As far as C++ is concerned, every class must have a constructor; otherwise, you can't create any objects of that class. If you don't provide a constructor for your class, C++ should probably just generate an error, but it doesn't. To provide compatibility with existing C code, which knows nothing about constructors, C++ automatically provides a default constructor (sort of a "default default constructor") that sets all the data members of the object to binary zero. Sometimes I call this a "Miranda constructor" — you know, "if you cannot afford a constructor, a constructor will be provided for you."

If your class already has a constructor, C++ doesn't provide the automatic default constructor. (Having tipped your hand that this isn't a C program, C++ doesn't feel obliged to do any extra work to ensure compatibility.)

The result is: If you define a constructor for your class but you also want a default constructor, you must define it yourself.

Some code snippets help demonstrate this. The following is legal:

```
class Student
{
   //...all the same stuff as before but no constructors
};

int main()
{
   Student noName;
   return 0;
}
```

`noName` is declared with no arguments, so C++ invokes the default constructor to construct it. Because the programmer has not already defined any constructors for class `Student`, C++ provides a default constructor that zeros out any data members that `Student` may have.

The following code snippet does not compile properly:

```
class Student
{
  public:
    Student(char *pName);
};

int main()
{
   Student noName;
   return 0;
}
```

The seemingly innocuous addition of the `Student(char*)` constructor precludes C++ from automatically providing a `Student()` constructor with which to build object `noName`. This example generates the following error message from the Microsoft Visual C++ compiler. (The error message from any other compiler would be similar.)

```
'Student' : no appropriate default constructor available
```

The compiler is telling you that it can't find the `Student::Student()` constructor. Adding a default constructor solves the problem:

```
class Student
{
  public:
    Student(char *pName);
    Student();                 //manually provided default constructor
};

int main()
{
   Student noName;             //used to build this object
   return 0;
}
```

This is why C++ programmers earn really big bucks!

Declaration ambiguity

Look again at the way the `Student` objects were declared in the earlier example:

```
Student noName;
Student freshMan("Smell E. Fish");
Student xfer("Upp R. Classman", 80, 2.5);
```

All `Student` objects except `noName` are declared with parentheses surrounding the arguments to the constructor. Why is `noName` declared without parentheses?

To be neat and consistent, you may think you could have declared `noName` as follows:

```
Student noName();
```

Unfortunately, this is allowed, but it does not have the intended effect. Instead of declaring an object `noName` of class `Student` to be constructed with the default constructor, this declares a function that returns an object of class `Student` by value. Surprise! (I think I need a raise.)

The following two declarations demonstrate how similar the new C++ format for declaring an object is to that of declaring a function. (I think this was a mistake, but what do I know?) The only difference is that the function declaration contains types in the parentheses, whereas the object declaration contains objects:

```
Student thisIsAFunc(int);
Student thisIsAnObject(10);
```

If the parentheses are empty, nothing can differentiate between an object and a function. To retain compatibility with C, C++ chose to make a declaration with empty parentheses a function. (A safer alternative would have been to force the keyword `void` in the function case, but that would not have been compatible with existing C programs.)

Constructing Class Members

In the preceding examples, all data members have been of simple types, such as `int` and `float`. With simple types, it's sufficient to assign a value to the variable within the constructor. But what if the class contains data members of a user-defined class? Consider the following example:

```
#include <iostream.h>
#include <string.h>

int nextStudentId = 0;
class StudentId
{
  public:
   StudentId()
   {
      value = ++nextStudentId;
      cout << "Assigning student id " << value << "\n";
   }
  protected:
   int value;
};

class Student
{
  public:
   Student(char *pName  = "no name")
   {
      cout << "Constructing student " << pName << "\n";
      strncpy(name, pName, sizeof(name));
      name[sizeof(name) - 1]  = '\0';
   }
  protected:
   char  name[40];
   StudentId id;
};

int main()
{
   Student s("Randy");
   return 0;
}
```

A student ID is assigned to each student as the `student` object is constructed. In this example, IDs are handed out sequentially using the global variable `nextStudentId`.

This Student class contains a member id of class StudentId. The constructor for Student can't assign a value to this id member because Student does not have access to the protected members of StudentId. You could make Student a friend of StudentId, but that violates the "you take care of your business, I'll take care of mine" philosophy. Somehow you need to invoke the constructor for StudentId when Student is constructed.

C++ does this for you automatically in this case, invoking the default constructor StudentId::StudentId() on id. This occurs after the Student constructor is called but before control passes to the first statement in the constructor. (Single step the preceding program in the debugger to see what I mean. As always, be sure that inline functions are forced outline.) The output from executing this simple program follows:

```
Assigning student id 1
Constructing student Randy
```

Notice that the message from the StudentId constructor appears before the output from the Student constructor.

(By the way, with all these constructors performing output, you may think that constructors must output something. Most constructors don't output a darned thing. Book constructors do because readers usually don't take the good advice provided by authors and single step the programs.)

If the programmer does not provide a constructor, the default constructor provided by C++ automatically invokes the default constructors for any data members. The same is true come harvesting time. The destructor for the class automatically invokes the destructor for any data members that have destructors. The C++ provided destructor does the same.

Okay, this is all great for the default constructor. But what if we wanted to invoke a constructor other than the default? Where do we put the object? To demonstrate, assume that instead of calculating the student ID, it is provided to the Student constructor, which passes the ID to the constructor for class StudentId.

Let me first show you what doesn't work. Consider the following program:

```
#include <iostream.h>
#include <string.h>

class StudentId
{
  public:
   StudentId(int id = 0)
   {
```

(continued)

(continued)

```
        value = id;
        cout << "Assigning student id " << value << "\n";
    }

  protected:
    int value;
};

class Student
{
  public:
    Student(char *pName  = "no name", int ssId = 0)
    {
        cout << "Constructing student " << pName << "\n";
        strncpy(name, pName, sizeof(name));
        name[sizeof(name) - 1]  = '\0';
        //don't try this at home kids. It doesn't work
        StudentId id(ssId);     //construct a student id
    }
  protected:
    char  name[40];
    StudentId id;
};

int main()
{
    Student s("Randy", 1234);
    cout << "This message from main\n";
    return 0;
}
```

The constructor for `StudentId` has been changed to accept a value externally (the default value is necessary to get the example to compile, for reasons that will become clear shortly). Within the constructor for `Student`, the programmer (that's me) has (cleverly) attempted to construct a `StudentId` object named `id`.

If you look at the output from this program, you notice a problem:

```
Assigning student id 0
Constructing student Randy
Assigning student id 1234
Destructing id 1234
This message from main
Destructing id 0
```

The first problem is that the constructor for `StudentId` appears tc be invoked twice, once with zero and a second time with the expected 1234. Then we notice that the 1234 object is destructed before the output string in `main()`. Apparently the `StudentId` object is destructed within the `Student` constructor itself.

The explanation for this rather bizarre behavior is clear. The data member `id` already exists by the time the body of the constructor is entered. Rather than constructing the existing data member `id`, the declaration prcvided in the constructor creates a local object of the same name. This local object is destructed upon returning from the constructor.

Somehow you need a different mechanism to indicate "construct the existing member; don't create a new one." This mechanism needs to appear before the open brace, before the data members are declared. For this, C++ defined a new construct, as follows:

```
class Student
{
  public:
   Student(char *pName  = "no name", int ssId = 0) : id(ssId)
   {
     cout << "Constructing student " << pName << "\n";
     strncpy(name, pName, sizeof(name));
     name[sizeof(name) - 1]  = '\0';
   }
  protected:
   char  name[40];
   StudentId id;
};
```

Notice in particular the first line of the constructor. Here's something you may not have seen before. The `:` means that what follows are calls to the constructors of data members of the current class. To the C++ compiler, this line reads: "Construct the member `id` using the argument `ssId` of the `Student` constructor. Whatever data members are not called out in this fashion are constructed using the default constructor."

This new program generates the expected result:

```
Assigning student id 1234
Constructing student Randy
This message from main
Destructing id 1234
```

The : syntax must also be used to assign values to `const` or reference type members. Consider the following silly class:

```
class SillyClass
{
  public:
   SillyClass(int& i) : ten(10), refI(i)
   {
   }
  protected:
   const int ten;
   int& refI;
};

int main()
{
     int i;
     SillyClass sc(i);
   return 0;
}
```

After the constructor for `SillyClass` has been entered, the data members `ten` and `refI` have already been created. This is analogous to declaring a `const` or reference variable in a function. Such variables must be assigned a value when declared.

In fact, any data member can be declared using the preceding syntax, but `const` and reference variables must be declared in this way.

Order of Construction

When there are multiple objects, all with constructors, the programmer usually doesn't care about the order in which things are built. If one or more of the constructors has side effects, however, the order can make a difference.

The rules for the order of construction are as follows:

- Local and static objects are constructed in the order in which their declarations are invoked.
- Static objects are constructed only once.
- All global objects are constructed before `main()`.
- Global objects are constructed in no particular order.

- Members are constructed in the order in which they are declared in the class.
- Destructors are invoked in the reverse order from constructors.

Consider each of these rules in turn.

Local objects are constructed in order

Local objects are constructed in the order in which the program encounters their declaration. Normally this is the same as the order in which the objects appear in the function, unless your function jumps around particular declarations. (By the way, jumping around declarations is a bad thing to do. It confuses the reader and the compiler.)

Static objects are constructed only once

Static objects are similar to other local variables, except that they are constructed only once. This is to be expected because they retain their value from one invocation of the function to the next. However, unlike C, which is free to initialize statics when the program begins, C++ must wait until the first time control passes through the static's declaration to perform the construction. Consider the following trivial program:

```
#include <iostream.h>
#include <string.h>
class DoNothing
{
  public:
   DoNothing(int initial)
   {
      cout << "DoNothing constructed with a value of "
           << initial
           << "\n";
   }
};
void fn(int i)
{
   static DoNothing dn(i);
   cout << "In function fn with i = " << i << "\n";
}

int main()
{
```

(continued)

(continued)

```
    fn(10);
    fn(20);
    return 0;
}
```

Executing this program generates the following results:

```
DoNothing constructed with a value of 10
In function fn with i = 10
In function fn with i = 20
```

Notice that the message from the function `fn()` appears twice, but the message from the constructor for `DoNothing` appears only the first time `fn()` is called.

All global objects are constructed *before* `main()`

As mentioned in the review of C in Part I, all global variables go into scope as soon as the program starts. Thus, all global objects are constructed before control is passed to `main()`.

This can cause a real debugging headache. Some debuggers try to execute up to `main()` as soon as the program is loaded and before they hand over control to the user. This makes perfect sense for C because no user code is ready to execute until `main()` is entered. For C++, however, this can be a problem because the constructor code for all global objects has already been executed by the time you get control. If one of them has a fatal bug, you never even get control. In this case, the program appears to die before it even starts!

You can approach this problem in several ways. One is to test each constructor on local objects before using them on globals. If that doesn't solve the problem, you can try adding output statements to the beginning of all suspected constructors. The last output statement you see probably came from the flawed constructor.

Global objects are constructed in no particular order

Figuring out the order of construction of local objects is easy. An order is implied by the flow of control. With globals, no such flow is available to give order. All globals go into scope simultaneously, remember? Okay, you argue, why can't the compiler just start at the top of the file and work its way down the list of global objects? That would work fine for a single file (and I presume that's what most compilers do).

Unfortunately, most programs in the real world consist of several files that are compiled separately and then linked. Because the compiler has no control over the order in which these files are linked, it cannot affect the order in which global objects are constructed from file to file.

Most of the time this is pretty ho-hum stuff. Once in a while, though, it can generate bugs that are extremely difficult to track down. (It happens just often enough to make it worth mentioning in a book.)

Consider the following example:

```
//in Student.H:
class Student
{
  public:
   Student (unsigned id) : studentId(id)
   {
   }
    const unsigned studentId;
};
class Tutor
{
  public:
   Tutor(Student &s)
{
     tutoredId = s.studentId;
   }
  protected:
   unsigned tutoredId;
};


//in FILE1.CPP
//set up a student
Student randy(1234);


//in FILE2.CPP
//assign that student a tutor
Tutor   jenny(randy);
```

Here the constructor for `Student` assigns a student ID. The constructor for `Tutor` records the ID of the student to help. The program declares a student `randy` and then assigns that student a tutor `jenny`.

The problem is that you are making the implicit assumption that `randy` gets constructed before `jenny`. Suppose that it was the other way around. Then `jenny` would get constructed with a block of memory that had not yet been turned into a `Student` object and, therefore, had garbage for a student ID.

TIP

The preceding example is not too difficult to figure out and more than a little contrived. Nevertheless, problems deriving from global objects being constructed in no particular order can appear in subtle ways. To avoid this problem, don't allow the constructor for one global object to refer to the contents of another global object.

Members are constructed in the order in which they are declared

Members of a class are constructed according to the order in which they are declared within the class. This is not quite as obvious as it might sound. Consider the following example:

```
class Student
{
  public:
    Student (unsigned id, unsigned age) : sAge(age), sId(id)
    {
    }
    const unsigned sId;
    const unsigned sAge;
};
```

In this example, `sId` is constructed before `sAge` even though it appears second in the constructor's initialization list. The only time you could probably detect any difference in the construction order is if both of these were members of classes that had constructors and these constructors had some mutual side effect.

Destructors are invoked in the reverse order of the constructors

Finally, no matter in what order the constructors kick off, you can be assured that the destructors are invoked in the reverse order. (It's nice to know that at least one rule in C++ has no ifs, ands, or buts.)

Chapter 13

More New and Improved Keywords

In This Chapter

- Using the newest thing in heap maintenance: `new` and `delete`
- Constructing and destructing heap objects
- Allocating and deallocating big arrays from the heap

The heap manipulation tools `malloc()` and `free()` are important tools in the C programmer's toolbox. Although heap manipulation is no less important to the C++ programmer, the English-standard `malloc()` and `free()` tools don't fit on C++ metric bolts.

The `new` *Keywords: Now You're* `free()` *to* `delete malloc()`

C++ provides alternates for the `malloc()` and `free()` Standard C library calls to allocate memory off the heap. The replacement for `malloc()` is called `new`; the replacement for `free()` is `delete`. Both `new` and `delete` are keywords rather than library functions.

Why do I need them?

The malloc() mechanism was great for the purpose of C, but it's unusable from the C++ standpoint for one simple reason: It can't invoke the constructor. Consider the following code snippet:

```
void fn()
{
   Student *pS;     //this doesn't call any constructor
   pS = (Student*)malloc(sizeof Student); //neither does this
   //...party on, dudes...
   free(pS);        //this doesn't call the destructor either
}
```

The declaration of the pointer pS doesn't call the constructor for Student because pS doesn't point to anything.

If the constructor is to be called, it must happen at the malloc() call when memory is first allocated. Unfortunately, however, malloc() is just a function call and doesn't have enough information to call a constructor. (For example, malloc() wouldn't know which constructor to call; there's nothing in the arguments it receives to tell it the class of the block of memory it's trying to allocate.)

You could make the programmer initialize the memory into a Student separately, as follows:

```
void fn()
{
   Student *pS;
   //allocate memory block
   pS = (Student*)malloc(sizeof Student);
   //now initialize it into a Student
   pS->init();
   //...party time...
}
```

Anyone who's stayed awake this far knows what's wrong with this: The class shouldn't rely on the application to remember to do the class's work.

What you need is a new construct that first calls malloc() and then calls the proper constructor on the returned block of memory. Hey, that's exactly what new is. Similarly, delete calls the destructor before calling free() to return the memory to the heap.

How do they work?

In use, the new and delete mechanisms are straightforward. Compare this to the preceding example:

```
void fn()
{
   Student *pS;
   //allocate heap memory and construct it
   pS = new Student;
   //...excellent...
   //put it back and invoke the destructor
   delete pS;
}
```

Notice that casting the pointer returned from new to the proper type is not necessary. new knows the type of the object that it's trying to allocate — it must know in order to invoke the proper constructor. The pointer returned from new always has the type of the argument to the right of new.

Arguments to the constructor are passed by adding them to the class name. Thus spake Zarathustra:

```
void fn()
{
   Student *pS;
   //allocate a student with a name and an id
   pS = new Student("Randy", 1234);
   //...and so on...
}
```

Allocating Arrays

It is possible to allocate arrays of objects off the heap. The following code snippet demonstrates how this is accomplished:

```
void fn(int noOfObjects)
{
   Student *pS;
   pS = new Student[noOfObjects];
   //...dance to the music...
}
```

This allocates an array of `noOfObjects` students. The default constructor is invoked on each object in the array starting with `pS[0]`, progressing to `pS[1]`, and so on. It is not possible to invoke any other constructor when allocating arrays.

A problem arises on the `delete` side because `delete` can't tell the difference between a pointer to a single object and a pointer to an array of objects. An empty pair of brackets tells `delete` that this is an array:

```
void fn(int noOfObjects)
{
    Student *pS;
    pS = new Student[noOfObjects];
    //...dance to the music...
    //delete the array
    delete[] pS;
}
```

The destructor is invoked separately for each object in the array. Without the brackets, only the first object in the array would be destructed and returned to the heap.

This somewhat peculiar syntax came about historically. Originally, the programmer had to indicate how many members in the array to destruct, as shown in the following:

```
void fn(int noOfObjects)
{
    //...just like above
    //delete the array
    delete[noOfObjects] pS;
}
```

The more natural-looking `delete pS[noOfObjects];` would have meant to delete the `noOfObjects`th member of the array.

As C++ developed, people realized that keeping track of the size of the array was a big problem. The array might be allocated in one place in the program and not deallocated for quite some time. To save the programmer the effort, C++ saves the length of the array, but the programmer still has to tell C++ to look for this information — hence the empty brackets. Nowadays, if you include the length of the array in the brackets, most C++ compilers (including Visual C++) ignore the value that you put there and act as if the brackets were empty.

new and delete were introduced to handle class objects, but they can be used also for intrinsic types such as char and int. For example, the following snippet allocates an array of chars:

```
char *someFn(int length)
{
    char *pS = new char[length];
    //who knows what evil lurks in the hearts of men?
    return pS;
}
```

This example is slightly neater than the malloc() syntax because it avoids the cast. In addition, why use two mechanisms if one will do?

Chapter 14

The Copy Copy Copy Constructor

In This Chapter

- Introducing the copy constructor
- Making copies
- Having copies made for you automatically
- Shallow copies versus deep copies
- Avoiding all those copies

One other constructor deserves particular attention. This constructor, known as the copy constructor, is used to make copies of objects.

The Copy Constructor

A copy constructor is a constructor that has the name `X::X(X&)`, where `X` is any class name. That is, it is the constructor of class `X`, which takes as its argument a reference to an object of class `X`. Now I know that this sounds really useless, but just give me a chance to explain why C++ needs such a beastie.

Why do I need it?

Think for a moment about what happens when you call a function like the following:

```
void fn(Student fs)
{
   //...same scenario; different argument...
}
int main()
{
   Student ms;
   fn(ms);
   return 0;
}
```

As you know, a copy of the object ms — and not the object itself — is passed to the function fn(). With C, the procedure is pretty simple: C just makes a binary copy of the object on the stack and passes that to the function.

It isn't that simple in C++. First, it takes a constructor to create an object, even a copy of an existing object. Second, what if you don't want a simple copy of the object? (Ignore the "why?" of this for a little while.) You need to be able to specify how the copy should be constructed.

Thus, the copy constructor is necessary in the preceding example to create a copy of the object ms on the stack during the call of function fn(). (This particular copy constructor would be Student::Student(Student&) — say that three times quickly.)

How does it work?

The best way to understand how the copy constructor works is to see one in action. Consider the following Student class:

```
#include <iostream.h>
#include <string.h>
class Student
{
  public:
   //conventional constructor
   Student(char *pName  = "no name", int ssId = 0)
   {
      cout << "Constructing new student " << pName << "\n";
      strncpy(name, pName, sizeof(name));
      name[sizeof(name) - 1]  = '\0';
      id = ssId;
   }

   //copy constructor
   Student(Student &s)
   {
      cout << "Constructing Copy of " << s.name << "\n";
      strcpy(name, "Copy of ");
      strcat(name, s.name);
      id = s.id;
   }
  ~Student()
   {
      cout << "Destructing " << name << "\n";
   }
  protected:
```

```
   char  name[40];
   int   id;
};

//fn - receives its argument by value
void fn(Student s)
{
   cout << "In function fn()\n";
}

int main()
{
   Student randy("Randy", 1234);
   cout << "Calling fn()\n";
   fn(randy);
   cout << "Returned from fn()\n";
   return 0;
}
```

The output from executing this program follows:

```
Constructing new student Randy
Calling fn()
Constructing Copy of Randy
In function fn()
Destructing Copy of Randy
Returned from fn()
Destructing Randy
```

Starting with `main()`, you can see how this program works. The normal constructor generates the first message. `main()` generates the `calling...` message. C++ calls the copy constructor to make a copy of `randy` to pass to `fn()`, which generates the next line of output. The copy is destructed at the return from `fn()`. The original object, `randy`, is destructed at the end of `main()`.

The copy constructor here is flagged with comments. It looks like a normal constructor except that it takes its input from another object rather than from several separate arguments.

(Notice that this copy constructor does a little bit more than just make a copy of the object; it tacks the phrase `Copy of` to the front of the name. That was for your benefit. Normally, copy constructors should restrict themselves to just making copies. But, if the truth be known, they can do anything they want.)

The Automatic Copy Constructor

Like the default constructor, the copy constructor is important. Important enough that C++ thinks no class should be without one. If you don't provide your own copy constructor, C++ generates one for you. (This is different from the default constructor, which C++ provides unless your class has any constructors defined for it.)

The copy constructor provided by C++ performs a member-by-member copy of each data member. Originally, the copy constructor that C++ provided performed a bitwise copy. The difference is that a member-by-member copy invokes any copy constructors that might exist for the members of the class, whereas a bitwise copy does not. You can see the effects of this difference in the following example:

```
#include <iostream.h>
#include <string.h>

class Student
{
  public:
   Student(char *pName   = "no name")
   {
      cout << "Constructing new student " << pName << "\n";
      strncpy(name, pName, sizeof(name));
      name[sizeof(name) - 1]  = '\0';
   }
   Student(Student &s)
   {
      cout << "Constructing Copy of " << s.name << "\n";
      strcpy(name, "Copy of ");
      strcat(name, s.name);
   }
  ~Student()
   {
      cout << "Destructing " << name << "\n";
   }
  protected:
   char  name[40];
};


class Tutor
```

```
{
  public:
   Tutor(Student &s) : student(s) //invoke copy
                                   //constructor
   {                               //on member student
       cout << "Constructing tutor\n";
    }
  protected:
   Student student;
};

void fn(Tutor tutor)
{
   cout << "In function fn()\n";
}
int main()
{
   Student randy("Randy");
   Tutor tutor(randy);
   cout << "Calling fn()\n";
   fn(tutor);
   cout << "Returned from fn()\n";
   return 0;
}
```

Executing this program generates the following output:

```
Constructing new student Randy
Constructing Copy of Randy
Constructing tutor
Calling fn()
Constructing Copy of Copy of Randy
In function fn()
Destructing Copy of Copy of Randy
Returned from fn()
Destructing Copy of Randy
Destructing Randy
```

Constructing the object `randy` invokes the `Student` constructor, which outputs the first line.

The object `tutor` is created by invoking the constructor `Tutor(Student&)`. This constructor initializes the data member `Tutor::student` by invoking the copy constructor for `Student` explicitly. This generates the next line of output.

The call to function `fn()` requires a copy of `tutor` to be created. Because I did not provide a copy constructor for `Tutor`, the default copy constructor (provided by C++) copies each member. This invokes the copy constructor for class `Student` to copy the data member `tutor.student`.

Shallow Copies versus Deep Copies

Performing a member-by-member copy seems the obvious thing to do in a copy constructor. Other than adding the capability to tack silly things such as `Copy of` to the front of students' names, when would you ever want to do anything but a member-by-member copy?

Consider what happens if the constructor allocates an asset such as memory off the heap. If the copy constructor simply makes a copy of that asset without allocating its own, you end up with a troublesome situation: two objects thinking they have exclusive access to the same asset. This becomes nastier when the destructor is invoked for both objects and they both try to put the same asset back. To make this more concrete, consider the following example class:

```
#include <iostream.h>
#include <string.h>
class Person
{
  public:
   Person(char *pN)
   {
      cout << "Constructing " << pN << "\n";
      pName = new char[strlen(pN) + 1];
      if (pName != 0)
      {
          strcpy(pName, pN);
        }
   }
  ~Person()
   {
      cout << "Destructing " << pName << "\n";
      //let's wipe out the name just for the heck of it
      pName[0] = '\0';
      delete pName;
   }
  protected:
   char *pName;
};
```

```
int main()
{
    Person p1("Randy");
    Person p2 = p1;         //invoke the copy constructor...
    return 0;               //...equivalent to Person p2(p1);
}
```

Here, the constructor for `Person` allocates memory off the heap to store the person's name, rather than put up with some arbitrary limit imposed by a fixed-length array. The destructor dutifully puts this heap memory back as it should. The main program simply creates one person, `p1`, and then makes a copy of that person, `p2`.

When you execute this program, you get only one constructor output message. That's not too surprising, because C++ provided the copy constructor used to build `p2` and it performs no output. As `p1` and `p2` go out of scope, you don't receive the two output messages that you might have expected.

If you are single-stepping the program under a debugger such as Visual C++, you should see the expected `Destructing Randy` message when the first object is destructed. Instead of a second destructor message, however, you get some type of error message. In the case of Microsoft Visual C++, you get a window like that shown in Figure 14-1.

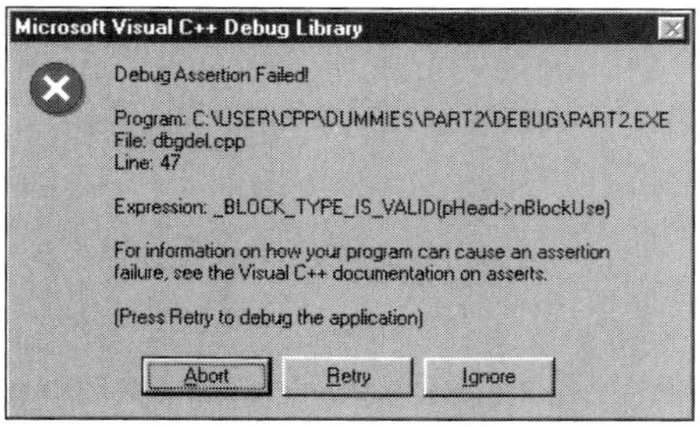

Figure 14-1: Error window opened by the Visual C++ debugger when executing the preceding program in debug mode.

The constructor is called once and allocates a block of memory off the heap to hold the person's name. The copy constructor provided by C++ copies that address into the new object without allocating a new block.

When the objects are destructed, the destructor for p2 gets at the block first. This destructor clears out the name and then releases the block. When p1 comes along, the memory has been released and the name has been wiped out already. This explains the error message (the message is a bit obscure, but if you look into dbgdel.cpp, one of the functions that makes up the Visual C++ standard C++ library, you see that this function is making sure that the pointer you handed it refers to a block of heap memory that is still in use). The problem is shown in Figure 14-2. The object p1 is copied into the new object p2, but the assets are not. Thus, p1 and p2 end up pointing to the same assets (in this case, heap memory). This is known as a shallow copy because it just "skims the surface," copying the members themselves.

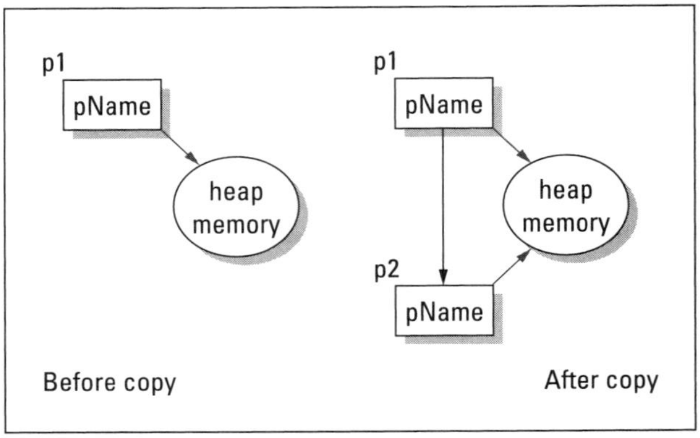

Figure 14-2: Shallow copy of p1 to p2.

What you need to fix the problem shown in Figure 14-2 is a copy constructor that allocates its own assets to the new object. Add one of these to Person and see how it looks. The following shows an appropriate copy constructor for class Person:

```
class Person
{
  public:
    //copy constructor allocates a new heap block
    Person(Person &p)
    {
        cout << "Copying " << p.pName << " into its own➥ block\n";
        pName = new char[strlen(p.pName) + 1];
        if (pName != 0)
        {
            strcpy(pName, p.pName);
```

```
        }
    }
    //...everything else the same...
}
//...same here as well...
```

Here you see that the copy constructor allocates its own memory block for the name and then copies the contents of the source object name into this new name block. See Figure 14-3. Deep copy is so named because it reaches down and copies all the assets. (Okay, the analogy is pretty strained, but that's what they call it.)

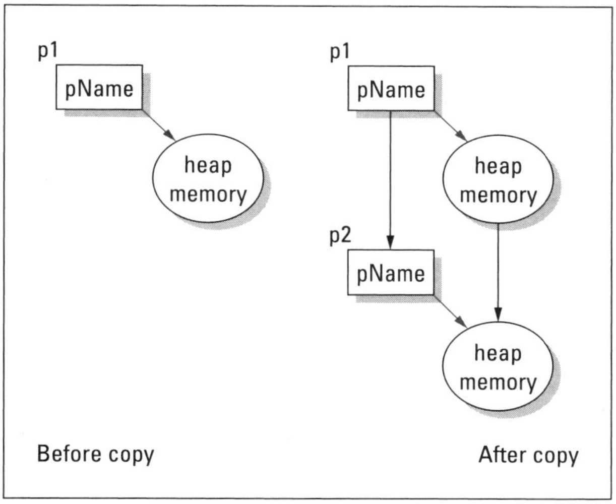

Figure 14-3: Deep copy of p1 to p2.

The output from this program is as follows:

```
Constructing Randy
Copying Randy into its own block
Destructing Randy
Destructing Randy
```

TIP

Heap memory is not the only asset that requires a deep copy constructor, but it is the most common. Open files, ports, and allocated hardware (such as printers) also require deep copies. These are the same types of assets that destructors must return. Thus, a general rule is that if your class requires a destructor to deallocate assets, it also requires a copy constructor.

It's a Long Way to Temporaries

Copies are generated when objects are passed by value. Copies are created under other conditions as well, such as when objects are returned by value. Consider the following example:

```
Student fn();                    //returns object by value
int main()
{
    Student s;
    s = fn();                    //call to fn() creates temporary
    //how long does the temporary returned by fn()...
    //...last?
    return 0;
}
```

The function `fn()` returns an object by value. Eventually, the returned object is copied to `s`, but where does it reside until then?

C++ creates a temporary object into which it stuffs the returned object. (Temporaries are created in other ways as well.) "Okay," you say. "C++ creates the temporary, but how does it know when to destruct the temporary?" (How clever you are for asking just the right question.) In this example, it doesn't make much difference because you'll be through with the temporary when the copy constructor copies it into `s`. But what if `s` were defined as a reference:

```
int main()
{
    Student &refS = fn();
    //...now what?...
    return 0;
}
```

Now it makes a big difference how long temporaries live because `refS` exists for the entire function. Temporaries created by the compiler are valid throughout the extended expression in which they were created and no further. In the following function, I mark the point at which the temporary is no longer valid:

```
Student fn1();
int fn2(Student&);
int main()
{
```

```
    int x;
    //create a Student object by calling fn1(). Pass that
    //object to the function fn2(). fn2() returns an integer
    //that is used in some silly calculation. All this time,
    //the temporary returned from fn1() is valid.
    x = 3 * fn2(fn1()) + 10;
    //the temporary returned from fn1() is now no longer valid
    //...other stuff...
    return 0;
}
```

This makes the reference example invalid, because the object may go away before refS does, leaving refS referring to a non-object.

It may have occurred to you that all this copying of objects hither and yon can be a bit time-consuming. What if you don't want to make copies of everything? The most straightforward solution is to pass objects to functions and return objects from functions by reference. This knocks out the majority of cases.

But what if you're still not convinced that C++ isn't out there craftily constructing temporaries that you know nothing about? Or what if your class allocates unique assets that you don't want copied? What do you do then?

You can simply add an output statement to your copy constructor. The presence of this message warns you that a copy has just been made. Another approach is to declare the copy constructor protected, as follows:

```
class Student
{
  protected:
   Student(Student&s){}
  public:
   //...everything else normal...
};
```

This precludes any external functions, including C++, from constructing a copy of your Student objects. (This does not affect the capability of member functions to create copies.)

The fact that the copy constructor is used to create temporaries and copies on the stack answers one pesky detail that may have occurred to you. Namely, consider the following program:

```
class Student
{
  public:
    Student()
    {
            // ...whatever...
    }
    Student(Student s)
    {
            // ...whatever...
    }
};
void fn(Student fs)
{
}
int main()
{
    Student ms;
    fn(ms);
    return 0;
}
```

Why is it that the copy constructor for the class `Student` isn't declared `Student::Student(Student)`? In fact, under the Microsoft Visual C++ compiler such a declaration isn't even legal. The compiler complains with the error message

```
'Student' : illegal copy constructor: first parameter must not be a 'Student'
```

Why must the argument to the constructor be referential? Consider carefully the program. When `main()` calls the function `fn()`, the C++ compiler uses the copy constructor to create a copy of the `Student` object on the stack. However, the copy constructor itself requires an object of class `Student`. No problem, the compiler can invoke the copy constructor to create a `Student` object for the copy constructor. But, of course, that requires another call to the copy constructor, and so it goes until eventually the compiler collapses in a confused heap of exhaustion.

Chapter 15

Changing an Object's Type

In This Chapter

- Anonymous programming, or creating objects with no names
- How do I convert an object from the class it is to the class I want it to be?
- Using constructors to perform type conversion

Generally, when you create an object, it has a name and a variable associated with it so that you can refer to the object by name. If you have read Chapter 14, however, you saw how C++ used the copy constructor to create objects that have no name. This is not a capability limited to C++.

In this chapter, you see how you can also use any of a class's constructors to create objects without a name. You also see how these nameless objects can act as a sort of type conversion.

Nameless Objects

The programmer creates an object without assigning it a name by invoking the constructor directly. For example:

```
void fn()
{
    //create a nameless object of type Student
    Student("Randy", 1234);
    //...carry on...
}
```

Why do I need them?

Creating a nameless object may seem like a worthless thing to do, but it can be useful. For example, you may be interested in the side effects of the class rather than the object itself. Or you may want to use the object in an expression, as in the following example:

```
class Student
{
  public:
   Student(char *pName);
   Student(Student&);
};
class Course
{
  public:
   void enroll(Student);
   //...other members like before...
};

//enrollStudent - enroll a student with a given name
//                in the specified course
void enrollStudent(Course *pC, char *pName)
{
   pC->enroll(Student(pName)); //create and use object at
                               //once
}
```

Here the function `enrollStudent()` needs a `Student` to pass to the `Course::enroll()` function. I could have first created an object with a name and then passed that object to the `enroll` function. In this case, the function `enrollStudent()` would appear as follows:

```
//enrollStudent - enroll a student with a given name
//                in the specified course
void enrollStudent(Course *pC, char *pName)
{
   Student s(pName);         //this time first create the
                             //object...
   pC->enroll(s);            //...and then use it
}
```

Using a nameless object merely dispenses with the variable. (I know this doesn't sound profound, but stick with me. The next few sections show you that there's more to the story.)

How do they work?

The following are all mechanisms for creating nameless objects:

```
class Student
{
  public:
   Student(char *pName);
   Student(Student&);
};
void fn(Student);
int main()
{
   Student &refS = Student("Randy");
   Student s = Student("Jenny");
   fn(Student("Danny"));
   return 0;
}
```

The first declaration in `main()` generates a reference to a nameless `Student` object. This is no different than declaring an object in the conventional fashion.

The second declaration appears to first construct a nameless object using the `Student(char*)` constructor outlined and then copy that object into the `Student` object `s`. The definition of C++ says that a compiler may do just that, if it wants. However, the standard also says that the compiler may avoid the extraneous nameless object and just construct the `s` object as if it had been declared as follows:

```
int main()
{
   Student s("Jenny");   //alternate for s above
   //...continue as before...
}
```

The third case, the call `fn(Student("Danny"))`, constructs a nameless object for the purpose of passing the object to the function.

Type Conversion Using Constructors

Sometimes, the type of the object the programmer has and the type of the object the programmer needs are not the same. For example, you may want to multiply a `float` by an `int`. You can convert the `int` to a `float` by specifying a cast. (You can also cast a `float` to an `int`.) But this isn't necessary because C++ automatically converts the `int` to a `float` for you.

You don't have to tell C++ how to convert from an `int` to a `float`. C++ already understands how to convert from one intrinsic type to another. It doesn't understand *a priori* how to convert to or from a user-defined type, but you can tell it how.

Consider a constructor such as `Student(char*)`. This constructor takes a `char*` and uses it to produce an object of class `Student`. In a way, this is like a type conversion. In other words, it's as if the constructor `Student(char*)` tells C++ how to convert a `char*` into a `Student`. Well, that's the way C++ sees it.

In other words, the following is legal:

```
class Student
{
  public:
    Student(char*);
    Student(Student&);
};
void fn(Student s);
int main()
{
    fn("Danny");       //what exactly are we calling here?
    return 0;
}
```

Let me direct your attention to the call to `fn()` in `main()`. The programmer is attempting to pass a character string, that is, a `char*`. However, there is no function `fn(char*)`. (If there were, C++ would call that function without any further ado.) Rather than just give up, C++ sees whether it can convert the argument into something that it can use to make the call to some other overloaded function `fn()`.

C++ notices that there is a function `fn(Student)` and that a constructor `Student(char*)` can convert a `char*` into a `Student`. Putting two and two together, C++ uses `char*` to construct a `Student` object with which to make the call.

C++ treats the call to `fn()` as if it had been written as follows:

```
//...all this stuff stays the same...
int main()
{
   fn(Student("Danny"));  //call to constructor made explicit
   return 0;
}
```

Except for the comment, this call to `fn()` looks like the call in the seemingly useless example at the beginning of the chapter. I told you it had a purpose.

C++ has used the constructor to convert an object from one type to another. It will attempt to do this anytime it can. The limitations are as follows:

- C++ must use constructors with only a single argument (or with all arguments defaulted except for one). This is a syntactical problem more than a technical problem.
- If ambiguities arise, C++ throws up its electronic hands and gives up.

The following code snippet demonstrates how ambiguities can arise:

```
class Student
{
  public:
   Student(char *pName  = "no name");
   Student(Student&);
};
class Teacher
{
  public:
   Teacher(char *pName  = "no name");
   Teacher(Teacher&);
};
void addCourse(Student&s);
void addCourse(Teacher&t);

int main()
{
   addCourse("Prof. Dingleberry");
   return 0;
}
```

Here you can see that C++ could convert the `char*` to a `Student` and call `addCourse(Student)`. Or it could convert the `char*` to a `Teacher` to call `addCourse(Teacher)`. With no way to resolve the ambiguity, C++ has no choice but to generate an error.

To correct the ambiguity, you must add an explicit call to the intended constructor:

```
int main()
{
    addCourse(Teacher("Prof. Dingleberry"));
    return 0;
}
```

Consider how similar the preceding call to the constructor is to a cast. Here you have cast `char*` into `Teacher`. The similarity is more than superficial. C++ considers this to be a new format for specifying a cast. This new format can be used for intrinsic casts, plus the old format can be used for constructor conversions, as shown in the following:

```
void fn(int *pI)
{
    float x = 10.5;
    int i = int(x);        //same as i = (int)x;
    addCourse(Teacher("Prof. Dingleberry")); //new format
    addCourse((Teacher)"Prof. Dingleberry"); //same as above
    char *pC = (char*)pI;  //older format must be used when
                           //casting pointers
}
```

Some people prefer the newer format because it looks like the format for invoking the constructor. Others prefer the older, more familiar format. Note, however, that you must use the older format when casting from one pointer type to another due to the syntactical confusion that `*` by itself would cause.

If you play with these examples long enough, you'll notice that they don't work if `fn()` is declared `fn(Student&)` rather than `fn(Student)`. This is because the type of a string such as "Prof. Dingleberry" is not `char*` but `const char*`. When left to its own devices, C++ implicitly converts a `const char*` into a `const Student` object so as not to lose the `const`-ness. Now the problem arises that a `const Student` object can't be passed by reference to a function declared to accept a `Student` object because the function might change the object passed to it.

One solution would be to change the declaration of `fn()` to `fn(const Student&)`. The problem with this solution, however, is that `fn()` could not then pass the `const Student` object to any functions (including member functions) that don't specifically promise not to change their argument. Redeclaring the function arguments to be `const` in all the right places can become quite complicated, especially because I haven't discussed `const` member functions. (That's a topic I cover in *More C++ For Dummies*.)

A simpler, if not quite as efficient, solution is to declare `fn()` to accept its argument by value rather than by reference. It is legal to pass a `const Student` object to `fn(Student)` by value because `fn()` can't change the `const` object in the calling function.

A better solution is to not rely on implicit conversions. The expression `Student("Prof. Dingleberry")` creates a non-`const Student` object. C++ figures that you must know what you're doing — if you had wanted a `const` object, you could have said `const Student("Prof. Dingleberry")`. Thus, the call `fn(Student("Prof. Dingleberry"))` is allowed even if `fn()` is declared `fn(Student&)`. Relying on implicit object conversions is not good programming style anyway.

Chapter 16

Static Members: Can Fabric Softener Help?

In This Chapter

- How do I declare static member data?
- What about static member functions?
- Why can't my static member function call my other member functions?

Turn your attention away from constructors for a moment. The data members discussed in the previous chapters have all been on a "per object" basis. For example, each student has his or her own name.

You can also declare a member to be shared by all objects of a class by declaring that member static. The term *static* applies to both data members and member functions, although the meaning is slightly different. This chapter describes these differences, beginning with static data members.

Static Data Members

Data members are made common to all objects of a class by declaring them *static*. Such members are called *static data members*.

Why do I need them?

Most properties are properties of the object. Using the well-worn (one might say, threadbare) student example from earlier in this book, properties such as name, ID number, and courses are specific to the individual student. However, some properties are shared by all students — for example, the number of students currently enrolled, the highest grade of all students, or a pointer to the first student in a linked list.

Storing this type of class information in global variables is possible. The problem is that global variables are "outside" the class. I would like to bring this type of class information inside the class boundaries, where it can be protected. This is the idea behind static members.

You sometimes hear static members referred to as *class members* because they are shared by all objects in the class. Normal members are referred to as *instance members,* or *object members.*

How do they work?

A static data member is one that has been declared with the `static` storage class. For example:

```
class Student
{
  public:
   Student(char *pName  = "no name")
   {
      strcpy(name, pName);
      noOfStudents++;
   }
  ~Student()
   {
      noOfStudents--;
   }
   int number()
   {
      return noOfStudents;
   }
  protected:
   static int noOfStudents;
   char name[40];
};
Student s1;
Student s2;
```

The data member `noOfStudents` is not part of either `s1` or `s2`. That is, for every object of class `Student`, there is a separate `name`, but there is only one `noOfStudents`, which all `Student`s must share. If you used an assembly language debugger to look into `s1` or `s2`, you would see space allocated only for `name` and not for `noOfStudents`.

"Well then," you ask, "if the space for noOfStudents is not allocated in any of the objects of class Student, where is it allocated?" The answer is, "It isn't." You have to specifically allocate space for it, as follows:

```
int Student::noOfStudents = 0;
```

This somewhat peculiar-looking syntax allocates space for the static data member and initializes it to zero. Static data members can be initialized only at the file level (that is, they can't be initialized from within a function).

That's because all static data members must be initialized before any constructors can be executed, and the constructors for global variables execute before main() is called. See how this all fits?

The name of the class is required for any member when it appears outside its class boundaries.

Referencing static data members

The access rules for static members are the same as the access rules for normal members. From within the class, static members are referenced like any other class member. Public static members can be referenced from outside the class as well. Both types of reference are shown in the following code snippet:

```
class Student
{
  public:
   Student()
   {
      noOfStudents++;      //reference from inside the class
      //...other stuff...
   }

   static int noOfStudents;
   //...other stuff like before...
};
void fn(Student &s1, Student &s2)
{
   //reference public static
   cout << "No of students "
        << s1.noOfStudents //reference from outside the class
        << "\n";
}
```

In `fn()`, `noOfStudents` is referenced using the object `s1`. But `s1` and `s2` share the same member `noOfStudents` — how did I know to choose `s1`? Why didn't I use `s2` instead? It doesn't make any difference. You can reference a static member using any object of that class. For example:

```
//...class defined the same as before...
void fn(Student &s1, Student &s2)
{
   //the following produce identical results
   cout << "No of students " << s1.noOfStudents << "\n";
   cout << "No of students " << s2.noOfStudents << "\n";
}
```

In fact, you don't need an object at all. You can use the class name directly instead, if you prefer, as in the following:

```
//...class defined the same as before...
void fn(Student &s1, Student &s2)
{
   //the following produce identical results
   cout << "No of students "
        << Student::noOfStudents
        << "\n";
}
```

If you use an object name, C++ uses only the class of the object.

The object used to reference a static member is not evaluated even if it's an expression. For example, consider the following case:

```
class Student
{
  public:
   static int noOfStudents;
   Student& nextStudent();
   //...other stuff the same...
};
void fn(Student &s)
{
   cout << s.nextStudent().noOfStudents << "\n"
}
```

The member function `nextStudent()` is not actually called. All C++ needs to access `noOfStudents` is the return type, and it can get that without bothering to evaluate the expression. This is true even if `nextStudent()`

should do other things, such as wash windows or shine your shoes. None of those things will get done. Although the example is obscure, it does happen. That's what you get for trying to cram too much stuff into one expression.

Uses for static data members

You have probably umpteen uses for static data members, but let me touch on three common ones. First, you can use static members to keep count of the number of objects floating about. In the `Student` class, for example, the count is initialized to zero, the constructor increments it, and the destructor decrements it. Remember, however, that this count reflects the number of `Student` objects (including any temporaries) and not necessarily the number of students.

A closely related use for a static member is as a flag to indicate whether a particular action has occurred. For example, a class `Radio` may need to initialize hardware before sending the first `tune` command but not before subsequent `tune`s. A flag indicating that this is the first `tune` is just the ticket.

What is `this` about, anyway?

I mention `this` a few times throughout this book, but look at it again just for grins. `this` is a pointer to the "current" object. It's used when no other object name is specified. In a normal member function, `this` is the implied first argument to the function. For example:

```
class SC
{
  public:
          void nFn(int a); //like
   SC::nFn(SC *this, int a)
   static void sFn(int a); //like
   SC::sFn(int a)
};
void fn(SC &s)
{
   s.nFn(10); //—converts to—> SC::nFn(&s,
   10);
   s.sFn(10); //—converts to—> SC::sFn(10);
}
```

That is, the function `nFn()` is interpreted almost as if it were declared `void SC::nFn(SC *this, int a)`. The call to `nFn()` is converted by the compiler as shown, with the address of `s` passed as the first argument. (You can't actually write the call this way; this is only what the compiler is doing.)

Within the function, `SC::nFn()` references to other non-static members automatically use the `this` argument as the pointer to the current object. When `SC::sFn()` was called, no object address was passed. Thus, it has no `this` pointer to use when referencing non-static functions. This is why we say that a static member function is not associated with any current object.

Finally, a very common use for static members is to contain the pointer to the first member of a linked list.

Static Member Functions

Like static data members, static member functions are associated with a class and not with any particular object of that class. This means that like a reference to a static data member, a reference to a static member function does not require an object. If an object is present, only its type is used.

Thus, both calls to the static member function `number()` in the following example are legal:

```
#include <iostream.h>
#include <string.h>
class Student
{
  public:
    static int number()
    {
       return noOfStudents;
    }
    //...other stuff the same...
  protected:
    char name[40];
    static int noOfStudents;
};
int Student::noOfStudents = 0;
int main()
{
    Student s;
    cout << s.number() << "\n";
    cout << Student::number() << "\n";
    return 0;
}
```

Notice how the static member function can access the static data member. A static member function is not directly associated with any object, however, so it does not have default access to any non-static members. Thus, the following would not be legal:

```
class Student
{
  public:
   //the following is not legal
   static char *sName()
   {
      return name;       //which name? there is no object
   }
   //...other stuff the same...
  protected:
   char name[40];
   static int noOfStudents;
};
```

That is not to say that static member functions have no access to non-static data members. Consider the following useful function:

```
#include <iostream.h>
#include <string.h>
class Student
{
  public:
   //same constructor and destructor as earlier
   Student(char *pName);
  ~Student();

   //findName - return student w/specified name
   static Student *findName(char *pName);
  protected:
   static Student *pFirst;
   Student *pNext;
   char name[40];
};
Student* Student::pFirst = 0;
//findName - return the Student with the specified name.
//           Return zero if no match.
Student* Student::findName(char *pName)
{
   //loop thru the linked list...
   for (Student *pS = pFirst; pS; pS = pS->pNext)
   {
      //...if we find the specified name...
      if (strcmp(pS->name, pName) == 0)
      {
```

(continued)

(continued)

```
            //...then return the object's address
            return pS;
        }
    }
    //...otherwise, return a zero (item not found)
    return (Student*)0;
}

int main()
{
    Student s1("Randy");
    Student s2("Jenny");
    Student s3("Kinsey");
    Student *pS = Student::findName("Jenny");
    return 0;
}
```

The function `findName()` has access to `pFirst` because it's shared by all objects. Being a member of class `Student`, `findName()` has access also to `name`, but the call must specify the object to use (that is, whose name). No default object is associated with a static member function. Calling the static member function with an object doesn't help. For example:

```
//...same as before...
int main()
{
    Student s1("Randy");
    Student s2("Jenny");
    Student s3("Kinsey");
    Student *pS = s1.findName("Jenny");
    return 0;
}
```

The `s1` is not evaluated and not passed to `findName()`. Only its class is used to decide which `findName()` to call.

Maintaining a More Reasonable Budget: BUDGET4.CPP

Adding some of the features presented in Part IV jazzes up the budget program, creating a more attractive result. I've added the following

- More reasonable constructors to build accounts
- `new` and `delete` to avoid any limitations on the number of accounts
- Static members to retain class information

Without further ado, here is the program that you've all come to know and love:

```
//BUDGET4.CPP - Budget program with expanded constructors,
//              new (and improved) heap management, and
//              static members. The Checking and Savings
//              classes should have a destructor to remove
//              the object from the list, but the destructors
//              aren't included to save space.

#include <iostream.h>
#include <stdlib.h>

//Checking - this describes checking accounts
class Checking
{
  protected:
   Checking(Checking &c)
   {
      cout << "No creating funds\n";
   }

  public:                               //Note 1
   Checking(unsigned accNo, float initialBalance = 0.0F);
```

(continued)

(continued)

```
  //access functions
  int accountNo()
  {
     return accountNumber;
  }
  float acntBalance()
  {
     return balance;
  }
  static Checking *first()
  {
     return pFirst;
  }
  Checking *next()
  {
     return pNext;
  }
  static int noAccounts()
  {
     return count;
  }

  //transaction functions
  void deposit(float amount)
  {
     balance += amount;
  }
  void withdrawal(float amount);

  //display function for displaying self on 'cout'
  void display()
  {
     cout << "Account " << accountNumber
          << " = "      << balance
          << "\n";
  }

protected:
  //keep accounts in a linked list so there's no limit
  static Checking *pFirst;            //Note 2
         Checking *pNext;
  static int count;         //number of accounts
```

```
   unsigned   accountNumber;
   float      balance;
};

//allocate space for statics
Checking *Checking::pFirst = 0;         //Note 3
int       Checking::count  = 0;

//define constructor
Checking::Checking(unsigned accNo, float initialBalance)
{
   accountNumber = accNo;
   balance = initialBalance;

   //add this to end of list and count it
   count++;
   if (pFirst == 0)                    //Note 4
   {
      pFirst = this;      //empty list; make it first
   }
   else                   //list not empty; look for last
   {
      for (Checking *pC = pFirst; pC->pNext; pC = pC->pNext)
      {                   //do nothing (we're just looking...
      }                   //...for the last element in the list)
      pC->pNext = this;   //tack us onto end
   }
   pNext = 0;             //we're always last
}

//withdrawal - now the withdrawal function
void Checking::withdrawal(float amount)
{
   if (balance < amount )
   {
      cout << "Insufficient funds: balance " << balance
           << ", check "                     << amount
           << "\n";
   }
   else
   {
      balance -= amount;
      //if balance falls too low, charge service fee
```

(continued)

(continued)

```
      if (balance < 500.00F)
      {
         balance -= 0.20F;
      }
   }
}

//Savings - you can probably figure this one out
class Savings
{
  protected:
   Savings(Savings &s)
   {
      cout << "No creating funds\n";
   }

  public:
   Savings(unsigned accNo, float initialBalance = 0.0);

   //access functions
   int accountNo()
   {
      return accountNumber;
   }
   float acntBalance()
   {
      return balance;
   }
   static Savings *first()
   {
      return pFirst;
   }
   Savings *next()
   {
      return pNext;
   }
   static int noAccounts()
   {
      return count;
   }
   //transaction functions
   void deposit(float amount)
```

```
    {
       balance += amount;
    }
    void withdrawal(float amount);

    //display function - display self to cout
    void display()
    {
       cout << "Account "              << accountNumber
            << " = "                   << balance
            << " (no. withdrawals = " << noWithdrawals
            << ")\n";
    }

  protected:
    //keep savings accounts in linked list as well
    static Savings *pFirst;
           Savings *pNext;

    static int count;           //number of accounts
    unsigned   accountNumber;
    float      balance;
    int        noWithdrawals;
};

//allocate space for statics
Savings *Savings::pFirst = 0;
int      Savings::count  = 0;

//define constructor
Savings::Savings(unsigned accNo, float initialBalance)
{
   accountNumber = accNo;
   balance = initialBalance;
   noWithdrawals = 0;

   //add this to end of list and count it
   count++;
   if (pFirst == 0)
   {
      pFirst = this;          //empty list; make it first
   }
   else                       //list not empty; look for last
```

(continued)

(continued)

```
   {
      for (Savings *pS = pFirst; pS->pNext; pS = pS->pNext)
      {
      }
      pS->pNext = this;       //make last point to us
   }
   pNext = 0;                 //and we point to nothing
}

//withdrawal - perform a Savings withdrawal
void Savings::withdrawal(float amount)
{
   if (balance < amount)
   {
      cout << "Insufficient funds: balance " << balance
           << ", withdrawal "                << amount
           << "\n";
   }
   else
   {
      if (++noWithdrawals > 1)
      {
         balance -= 5.00F;
      }
      balance -= amount;
   }
}

//prototype declarations
unsigned getAccntNo();
void process(Checking &checking);
void process(Savings &savings);
void outOfMemory();

//main - accumulate the initial input and output totals
int main()
{
   /*loop until someone enters an 'X' or 'x'*/
   Checking *pC;
   Savings  *pS;
   char     accountType;     //S or C
```

```
unsigned keepLooping = 1;
while (keepLooping)
{
   cout << "Enter S for Savings, "
           "C for Checking, X for exit\n";
   cin  >> accountType;

   switch (accountType)
   {
      case 'c':
      case 'C':                          //Note 5
         pC = new Checking(getAccntNo());
         if (pC == 0)
         {
            outOfMemory();
         }
         process(*pC);
         break;

      case 's':
      case 'S':                          //Note 5
         pS = new Savings(getAccntNo());
         if (pS == 0)
         {
            outOfMemory();
         }
         process(*pS);
         break;

      case 'x':
      case 'X':
         keepLooping = 0;
         break;

      default:
         cout << "I didn't get that.\n";
   }
}

//now present totals
float chkTotal = 0.0F;
float svgTotal = 0.0F;
cout << "Checking accounts:\n";      //Note 6
```

(continued)

(continued)

```
   for (pC = Checking::first(); pC; pC = pC->next())
   {
      pC->display();
      chkTotal += pC->acntBalance();
   }
   cout << "Savings accounts:\n";       //Note 6
   for (pS = Savings::first(); pS; pS = pS->next())
   {
      pS->display();
      svgTotal += pS->acntBalance();
   }

   float total = chkTotal + svgTotal;
   cout << "Total for checking accounts = " << chkTotal << "\n";
   cout << "Total for savings accounts  = " << svgTotal << "\n";
   cout << "Total worth                 = " << total << "\n";
   return 0;
}

//getAccntNo - return the account number entered
unsigned getAccntNo()
{
   unsigned accntNo;
   cout << "Enter account number:";
   cin  >> accntNo;
   return accntNo;
}

//process(Checking) - input the data for a checking account*/
void process(Checking &checking)
{
   cout << "Enter positive number for deposit,\n"
           "negative for check, 0 to terminate";

   float transaction;
   do
   {
      cout << ":";
      cin  >> transaction;

      //deposit
      if (transaction > 0.0F)
      {
```

```
         checking.deposit(transaction);
      }

      //withdrawal
      if (transaction < 0.0F)
      {
         checking.withdrawal(-transaction);
      }
   } while (transaction != 0.0F);
}

//process(Savings) - input the data for a savings account
void process(Savings &savings)
{
   cout << "Enter positive number for deposit,\n"
           "negative for withdrawal, 0 to terminate";

   float transaction;
   do
   {
      cout << ":";
      cin  >> transaction;

      //deposit
      if (transaction > 0.0F)
      {
         savings.deposit(transaction);
      }

      //withdrawal
      if (transaction < 0.0F)
      {
         savings.withdrawal(-transaction);
      }
   } while (transaction != 0.0F);
}
//outOfMemory - generate out of memory message and quit
void outOfMemory()
{
   cout << "Out of memory\n";
   abort();
}
```

A substantial part of this program is the same as BUDGET3.CPP. (How can you improve an old workhorse like that?) Notice, however, the addition of a more meaningful constructor to `Checking` (`Note 1`). In addition, the elements `pFirst` and `pNext` (`Note 2`) allow for the savings account members to be stored in a linked list rather than in an array.

A linked list does not suffer the array's restriction of limiting the number of accounts to a predeclared number. `pFirst` is static because it points to the first member in the list and is a property of the class. `pNext` is not static because it points to the next member in the list as seen from each object. The space for `pFirst` and the other static, `count`, are allocated outside the class (`Note 3`). The class `Savings` has the same additions as `Checking`.

The constructor for `Checking` must now add the current object to the linked list. It does this by looping to the end of the list and then adding the current object, `this` (`Note 4`). (Tacking `this` onto the front is easier, but it makes all the objects appear in reverse order in the list, which is inconvenient.) The constructor for `Savings` is virtually identical to that for `Checking`. No destructors are provided because objects are not dynamically destructed in this application.

In the main program, new accounts are created by invoking `new` with the new constructors (`Note 5`). `new` first allocates memory off the heap and then passes that memory to the constructor, which adds it to the linked list.

One final change is in the way the program moves through the list of accounts (`Note 6`). When the accounts were maintained in an array, initializing a pointer to the first account and then incrementing the pointer through the array was sufficient.

With a linked list, the program starts with the first element (that is, the element pointed to by `pFirst`) and then links through the list. On each iteration through the loop, the program moves from the current object to the next object (as pointed to by `pNext`). Because both `pFirst` and `pNext` are protected, access functions are used to retrieve these values. The loop is exhausted when the address of the next object is zero. (Iterating through a linked list reminds me of Tarzan's favorite method of travel. He starts out at his tree house and swings from one vine to the next. When he runs out of vines and falls to the ground, he, like the loop, is finished.)

Part V

Plunging In: Inheritance

The 5th Wave By Rich Tennant

In this part . . .

In the discussions of object-oriented philosophy in Part III, two main features of real-world solutions are seemingly not shared by functional programming solutions.

The first is the capability to treat objects separately. I present the example of a microwave oven to whip up a snack. The microwave oven provides an interface (the front panel) that I use to control the oven, without worrying about its internal workings. This is true even if I know all about how the darn things work (which I don't).

A second aspect to real-world solutions is the capability to categorize like objects, recognizing and exploiting their similarities. If my recipe calls for an oven of any type, I should be okay because a microwave is an oven.

I already presented the mechanism that C++ uses to implement the first feature, the class. To support the second aspect of object-oriented programming, C++ uses a concept known as inheritance, which extends classes. Inheritance is the topic of Part V.

Chapter 17

Inheritance (How Do I Get Mine?)

In This Chapter

- Defining inheritance
- Inheriting a base class
- Constructing the base class
- Exploring meaningful relationships: the IS_A versus the HAS_A relationship

In this chapter, I discuss *inheritance,* which is the capability of one class of things to inherit capabilities or properties from another class. For example, I am a human (except when I first wake up in the morning). I inherit from the class `Human` certain properties, such as my ability to converse (more or less) intelligently and my dependence on air, water, and carbohydrate-based nourishment. These properties are not unique to humans. The class `Human` inherited the dependencies on air, water, and nourishment from the class `Mammal`, of which it is a member.

The capability to pass down properties is a powerful one. It allows you to describe things in an economical way. For example, when my son asks, "What's a duck?" I can say, "It's a bird that goes quack." Despite what you may think, that answer conveys a considerable amount of information to him. He knows what a bird is, and now he knows all those same things about a duck plus the duck's additional property of "quackness." (Refer to Chapter 7 for a further discussion of this and other profound observations.)

Object-oriented languages express this inheritance relationship by allowing one class to inherit from another. Thus, OO languages can generate a model that is closer to the real world (remember that real-world stuff!) than the model generated by languages that do not support inheritance.

C++ allows one class to inherit another class as follows:

```
class Student
{
};
class GraduateStudent : public Student
{
};
```

Here, a GraduateStudent inherits all the members of Student. Thus, a GraduateStudent IS_A Student. Of course, GraduateStudent may also contain members unique to a GraduateStudent.

Why Do I Need Inheritance?

Inheritance was introduced into C++ for several reasons. Of course, the major reason is the capability to express the inheritance relationship. (I'll return to that in a moment.) A minor reason is to reduce the amount of typing. Suppose you have a class Student, and you are asked to add a new class called GraduateStudent. Inheritance can drastically reduce the number of things you have to put in the class. All you really need in the class GraduateStudent are things that describe the differences between students and graduate students.

A more important, related issue is that major buzzword of the '90s — reuse. Software scientists have realized for some time that it doesn't make much sense to start from scratch with each new project, rebuilding the same software components.

Compare the situation in software to other industries. How many car manufacturers start from ore to build a car? And even if they did, how many would start completely over from ore with the next model? Practitioners in other industries have found that it makes more sense to start from screws, bolts, nuts, and even larger off-the-shelf components such as motors and compressors.

Unfortunately, except for very small functions, like those found in the Standard C library, it's rare to find much reuse of software components. One problem is that it's virtually impossible to find a component from an earlier program that does exactly what you want. Generally, these components require "tweaking."

A rule to remember, "If you open it, you've broken it." In other words, if you have to modify a function or class to adapt it to a new application, you need to retest everything, not just the parts you add. Changes can introduce bugs anywhere in existing code. ("The one who last touched it is the one who gets to fix it.")

Inheritance allows existing classes to be adapted to new applications without the need for modification. The existing class is inherited into a new subclass that contains any necessary additions and modifications.

This carries with it a third benefit. Suppose you inherit from some existing class. Later you find that the base class has a bug that must be corrected. If you have modified the class to reuse it, you must manually check for, correct, and retest the bug in each application separately. If you have inherited the class without changes, you can probably adopt the fixed base class without further ado.

This IS_Amazing

To make sense out of our surroundings, humans build extensive taxonomies. Fido is a special case of dog, which is a special case of canine, which is a special case of mammal, and so it goes. This shapes our understanding of the world.

To use another example, a student is a (special type of) person. Having said this, I already know a lot of things about students (American students, anyway). I know they have social security numbers, they watch too much TV, and they daydream about living in the south during the winter and in the north during the summer. I know all these things because these are properties of all people.

In C++, this practice of assuming the properties of a parent class is called *inheritance*. The class `Student` inherits from the class `Person`. Also, that `Person` is a *base class* of `Student` and `Student` is a *subclass* of `Person`. Finally, you can say that a `Student` IS_A `Person` (using all caps is a common way of expressing this unique relationship — I didn't make it up). C++ shares this terminology with other object-oriented languages.

Notice that although `Student` IS_A `Person`, the reverse is not true. A `Person` is not a `Student`. (A statement like this always refers to the general case. It could be that a particular `Person` is, in fact, a `Student`.) A lot of people who are members of class `Person` are not members of class `Student`. In addition, class `Student` has properties it does not share with class `Person`. For example, `Student` has a grade point average, but `Person` does not.

The inheritance property is transitive as well. For example, if I define a new class `GraduateStudent` as a subclass of `Student`, `GraduateStudent` must also be `Person`. It has to be that way: If a `GraduateStudent` IS_A `Student` and a `Student` IS_A `Person`, a `GraduateStudent` IS_A `Person`.

How Does Inheritance Work?

Here's the `GraduateStudent` example again. Fill it out with a few example members:

```
#include <string.h>
class Advisor
{
};

class Student
{
  public:
   Student(char *pName = "no name")
   {
     strncpy(name, pName, sizeof(name));
        average = 0.0;
         semesterHours = 0;
  }
   void addCourse(int hours, float grade)
   {
      average = (semesterHours * average + grade);
      semesterHours += hours;
      average = average / semesterHours;
   }
   int  hours( ) { return semesterHours;}
   float gpa( )  { return average;}

  protected:
   char  name[40];
   int   semesterHours;
   float average;
};

class GraduateStudent : public Student
{
  public:
   int qualifier( ) { return qualifierGrade;};
  protected:
   Advisor advisor;
   int qualifierGrade;
};
```

```
int main( )
{
    Student llu("Lo Lee Undergrad");
    GraduateStudent gs;
    llu.addCourse(3, 2.5);
    gs.addCourse(3, 3.0);
    return 0;
}
```

The class `Student` has been defined in a conventional fashion. The object `llu` is just like the other `Student` objects. The colon followed by `public Student` declares class `GraduateStudent` to be a subclass of `Student`.

The appearance of the keyword `public` implies that there is probably `protected` inheritance as well. All right, it's true. But I want to hold off discussing this type of inheritance until Part VI.

The object `gs`, as a member of a subclass of `Student`, can do anything that `llu` can do. It has `name`, `semesterHours`, and `average` data members and the `addCourse( )` member function. After all, `gs` quite literally IS_A `Student` — it's just a little bit more than a `Student`. (If you are reading this book cover to cover, you'll get tired of me reciting this "IS_A" stuff before the book is over.)

Consider the following scenario:

```
void fn(Student &s)
{
    //whatever fn it wants to have
}
int main( )
{
    GraduateStudent gs;
    fn(gs);
    return 0;
}
```

Notice that the function `fn( )` expects to receive as its argument an object of class `Student`. The call from `main( )` passes it an object of class `GraduateStudent`. However, this is fine because once again (all together now) "a `GraduateStudent` IS_A `Student`."

Basically, the same condition arises when invoking a member function of `Student` with a `GraduateStudent` object. For example:

```
int main( )
{
   GraduateStudent gs;
   gs.addCourse(3, 2.5); //calls Student::addCourse( )
   return 0;
}
```

Constructing a Subclass

Even though a subclass has access to the protected members of the base class and could initialize them, it would be nice if the base class constructed itself. In fact, this is what happens. Before control passes beyond the open brace of the constructor for `GraduateStudent`, control passes to the default constructor of `Student` (because no other constructor was indicated). If `Student` were based on another class, such as `Person`, the constructor for that class would be invoked before the `Student` constructor got control. Like a skyscraper, the object is constructed starting at the basement class and working its way up the class structure one story at a time.

Just as with member objects, you sometimes need to be able to pass arguments to the base class constructor. You handle this in almost the same way as with member objects, as the following example shows:

```
class GraduateStudent : public Student
{
  public:
   GraduateStudent(char *pName = "no name",
                   Advisor &adv) : Student(pName),
                                   advisor(adv)
   {
      qualifierGrade = 0;
   }
   //...remainder as before...
};
void fn(Advisor &advisor)
{
   GraduateStudent gs("Yen Kay Doodle", advisor);
   //...whatever this function does...
}
```

Here the constructor for GraduateStudent invokes the Student constructor, passing it the argument pName. The base class is constructed before any member objects; thus, the constructor for Student is called before the constructor for Advisor. After the constructor for Advisor is called for advisor, the constructor for GraduateStudent gets a shot at it.

Following the rule that destructors are invoked in the reverse order of the constructors, the destructor for GraduateStudent is given control first. After it's given its last full measure of devotion, control passes to the destructor for Advisor and then to the destructor for Student. If Student were based on a class Person, the destructor for Person would get control after Student.

This is logical. The blob of memory is first converted to a Student object. Then it is the job of the GraduateStudent constructor to complete its transformation into a GraduateStudent. The destructor simply reverses the process.

The HAS_A Relationship

Notice that the class GraduateStudent includes the members of class Student and Advisor, but in a different way. By defining a data member of class Advisor, you know that a Student has all the data members of an Advisor within it, yet you say that a GraduateStudent HAS_A Advisor. What's the difference between this and inheritance?

Use a car as an example. You could logically define a car as being a subclass of vehicle, and so it inherits the properties of other vehicles. At the same time, a car has a motor. If you buy a car, you can logically assume that you are buying a motor as well. (Unless you went to the used-car lot where I got my last junk heap.)

If some friends asked you to show up at a rally on Saturday with your vehicle of choice and you came in your car, they wouldn't complain because a car IS_A vehicle. But if you appeared on foot carrying a motor, your friends would have reason to be upset because a motor is not a vehicle. A motor is missing certain critical properties that vehicles share. It's even missing properties that cars share, such as electric clocks that don't work.

From a programming standpoint, the HAS_A relationship is just as straightforward. Consider the following:

```
class Vehicle
{
};
class Motor
{
};
class Car : public Vehicle
{
  public:
   Motor motor;
};
void VehicleFn(Vehicle &v);
void motorFn(Motor &m);
int main( )
{
   Car c;
   VehicleFn(c);    //this is allowed
   motorFn(c);      //this is not allowed
   motorFn(c.motor);//this is, however
   return 0;
}
```

The call `VehicleFn(c)` is allowed because `c` IS_A `Vehicle`. The call `motorFn(c)` is not because `c` is not a `Motor`, even though it contains a `Motor`. If what was intended was to pass the `motor` portion of `c` to the function, this must be expressed explicitly, as in the call `motorFn(c.motor)`.

One further distinction: The class `Car` has access to the protected members of `Vehicle`, but not to the protected members of `Motor`.

Chapter 18

Virtual Member Functions: Are They for Real?

In This Chapter

- Overloading member functions in a subclass
- Polymorphism (alias late binding)
- I prefer to have my binding finished early. What's wrong with that?
- Are polymorphic nachos really safe?
- Special considerations with polymorphism

It has always been possible to overload a member function in one class with a member function from another class. With inheritance, however, you can overload a base class member function with a member function in a subclass as well. Consider, for example, the following simple code snippet:

```
class Student
{
  public:
   //...all as it was before...
   float calcTuition();
};
class GraduateStudent : public Student
{
  public:
   float calcTuition();
};

int main()
{
   Student s;
   GraduateStudent gs;
   s.calcTuition();        //calls Student::calcTuition()
```

(continued)

(continued)

```
   gs.calcTuition();        //calls
                            //GraduateStudent::calcTuition()
   return 0;
}
```

As with any overloading situation, when the programmer refers to `calcTuition()`, C++ has to decide which `calcTuition()` is intended. Normally the class is sufficient to resolve the call, and this example is no different. The call `s.calcTuition()` refers to `Student::calcTuition()` because `s` is declared locally as a `Student`, whereas `gs.calcTuition()` refers to `GraduateStudent::calcTuition()`.

But what if the exact class of the object can't be determined at compile time? To demonstrate how this can occur, change the preceding program in a seemingly trivial way:

```
class Student
{
  public:
   //...all as it was before...
   float calcTuition() {
      return 0;
   }
};
class GraduateStudent : public Student
{
  public:
   float calcTuition()
   {
      return 0;
   }
};

void fn(Student &x)
{
   x.calcTuition();      //to which calcTuition() does this
                         //refer?
}
int main()
{
   Student s;
   GraduateStudent gs;
   fn(s);
   fn(gs);
   return 0;
}
```

Instead of calling `calcTuition()` directly, the call is now made through an intermediate function, `fn()`. Depending on how `fn()` is called, `x` can be a `Student` or a `GraduateStudent`. (Remember from Chapter 17? A `GraduateStudent` IS_A `Student`.)

You would like `x.calcTuition()` to call `Student::calcTuition()` when `x` is a `Student` but call `GraduateStudent::calcTuition()` when `x` is a `GraduateStudent`. This is a capability you've probably never seen in a language and certainly haven't seen in C.

Normally, the compiler decides which function a call refers to at compile time. Even when the function is overloaded, which means C++ must use the arguments to help disambiguate the call, the decision is still made at compile time. In the case described here, however, a decision cannot be made until run time, when the actual type of the object can be determined.

The capability to decide at run time which of several overloaded member functions to call based on the actual type is called *polymorphism,* or late binding. The term *polymorphism* comes from *poly* (meaning multiple), *morph* (meaning change), and *ism* (meaning unintelligible Greek word). C++ supports polymorphism. (This is not very surprising by now; I wouldn't be spending all this time talking about polymorphism if C++ didn't support it.) Deciding which overloaded member functions to call at compile time is called early binding because that sounds like the opposite of late binding.

TIP

The type that you've been accustomed to until now is called the declared type. Another name for the actual type is the run-time type. Remember function `fn()` from the previous example? The run-time type of `x` is `Student` when `fn()` is called with `s` and `GraduateStudent` when `fn()` is called with `gs`. The declared type of `x` is always `Student`, however, because that's what the declaration in `fn()` says.

TECHNICAL STUFF

Polymorphism and late binding are not quite identical terms. Polymorphism refers to the capability of the call to decide between possible actions at run time. Late binding is the mechanism C++ uses to implement polymorphism. Other object-oriented languages may use different techniques. This book is limited to discussing C++ (and a bit of C), however, so I use the terms polymorphism and late binding synonymously.

Why Do I Need Polymorphism?

Polymorphism is key to the power of object-oriented programming. It's so important that languages that don't support polymorphism cannot advertise themselves as OO languages. (I think it's an FDA regulation somewhere — you can't label a language OO if it doesn't support polymorphism.) Languages that support classes but not polymorphism are called object-based languages. Ada is an example of such a language.

Without polymorphism, inheritance has little meaning. Let me spring yet another example on you to show why. Suppose that I had written this really boffo program that used some class called, well, `Student`. After months of design, coding, and testing, I release this application to rave reviews from colleagues and critics alike. (There's even talk of starting a new Nobel Prize category for software, but I modestly brush such talk aside.)

Time passes and my boss asks me to add to this program the capability to handle graduate students who are similar but not identical to normal students. (They don't have quite the same attention span.) Deep within the program, `someFunction()` calls the `calcTuition()` member function as follows:

```
void someFunction(Student &s)
{
   //...whatever it might do...
   s.calcTuition();
   //...continues on...
}
```

If C++ did not support late binding, I would need to edit `someFunction()` to something like the following to add class `GraduateStudent` :

```
#define STUDENT 1
#define GRADUATESTUDENT 2
void someFunction(Student &s)
{
   //...whatever it might do...
   //add some member type that indicates
   //the actual type of the object
   switch (s.type)
   {
      STUDENT:
         s.Student::calcTuition();
         break;
      GRADUATESTUDENT:
         s.GraduateStudent::calcTuition();
         break;
   }
   //...continues on...
}
```

I would add the member type to the class, which I would then set to `STUDENT` in the constructor for `Student` and to `GRADUATESTUDENT` in the constructor for `GraduateStudent`. The value of type would refer to the run-time type of `s`. I would then add the test in the preceding code snippet to call the proper member function depending on the value of this member.

That doesn't seem so bad, except for three things. First, this is only one function. Suppose `calcTuition()` is called from a lot of places and suppose that `calcTuition()` is not the only difference between the two classes. The chances are not good that I will find all the places that need to be changed.

Second, I must edit (read "break") code that was debugged, checked in, and working, introducing further opportunities for screwing up. Edits can be time-consuming and boring, which usually makes my attention drift. Any one of my edits may be wrong or may not fit in with the existing code. Who knows?

Finally, after I've finished editing, redebugging, and retesting everything, I now have two versions to keep track of (unless I can drop support for the original version). This means two sources to edit when bugs are found (perish the thought) and some type of accounting system to keep them straight.

Then what happens when my boss wants yet another class added? (My boss is like that.) Not only do I get to repeat the process, but I'll have three copies to keep track of.

With polymorphism, there's a good chance that all I need to do is add the new subclass and recompile. I may need to modify the base class itself, but at least it's all in one place. Modifications to the application should be minimal to none.

This is yet another reason to leave data members protected and access them through public member functions. Data members cannot be polymorphically overloaded by a subclass, whereas a member function can.

At some philosophical level there's an even more important reason for polymorphism. Remember in Chapter 7 how I made nachos in the oven? In this sense, I was acting as the late binder. The recipe read: Heat the nachos in the oven. It didn't read: If the type of oven is a microwave, do this; if the type of oven is conventional, do that; if the type of oven is convection, do this other thing. The recipe (the code) relied on me (the late binder) to decide what the action (member function) heat means when applied to the oven (the particular instance of class `Oven`) or any of its variations (subclasses), such as a microwave oven (`Microwave`). This is the way people think, and designing a language along these lines allows the software model to more accurately describe what people are thinking.

How Does Polymorphism Work?

You may be surprised that the default for C++ is early binding. The reason is simple. Polymorphism adds a small amount of overhead both in terms of data storage and code needed to perform the call. The founders of C++ were concerned that any additional overhead they introduced would be used as a reason not to adopt C++ as the system's language of choice, so they made the more efficient early binding the default.

To indicate polymorphism, the programmer must flag the member function with the C++ keyword virtual, as follows:

```
#include <iostream.h>
class Base
{
  public:
   virtual void fn()
   {
      cout << "In Base class\n";
   }
};
class SubClass : public Base
{
  public:
   virtual void fn()
   {
      cout << "In SubClass\n";
   }
};

void test(Base &b)
{
   b.fn();          //this call bound late
}
int main()

{
   Base bc;
   SubClass sc;
   cout << "Calling test(bc)\n";
   test(bc);
   cout << "Calling test(sc)\n";
   test(sc);
   return 0;
}
```

The keyword virtual is what tells C++ that `fn()` is a polymorphic member function. That is to say, declaring `fn()` virtual means that calls to it will be bound late if there is any doubt as to the run-time type of the object with which `fn()` is called.

In the example snippet, `fn()` is called through the intermediate function `test()`. When `test()` is passed a `Base` class object, `b.fn()` calls `Base::fn()`. But when `test()` is passed a `SubClass` object, the same call invokes `SubClass::fn()`. (You really have to single step this in the debugger to believe it.)

Executing the program generates the following output:

```
Calling test(bc)
In Base class
Calling test(sc)
In SubClass
```

TIP

You need to declare the function virtual only in the base class. The "virtualness" is carried down to the subclass automatically. In this book, however, I follow the coding standard of declaring the function virtual everywhere (virtually).

Making Nachos the Polymorphic Way

Okay, now that you've seen some of the nitty-gritty details of declaring a virtual function, return to the nacho example and see what it looks like in code. Consider the following code snippet:

```
#include <dos.h>              //needed for sleep()

class Stuff{};
class Nachos : public Stuff {};

//Oven - implements a conventional oven

class Oven
{
  public:
   virtual void cook(Nachos &nachos);

   //support functions that we need
```

(continued)

(continued)

```
    void turnOn();              //apply current
    void turnOff();             //turn off current
    void insert(Stuff &s);      //put stuff in oven
    void remove(Stuff &s);      //pull stuff out

  protected:
    float temp;
};

void Oven::cook(Nachos &nachos)
{
    //preheat oven
    turnOn();
    while (temp < 350)
    {
    }

    //now put nachos in for 15 minutes
    insert(nachos);
    sleep(15 * 60);

    //get them out and turn the oven off
    remove(nachos);
    turnOff();
}

class Microwave : public Oven {
  public:
    virtual void cook(Nachos &nachos);
    void rotateStuff(Stuff &s);
};
void Microwave::cook(Nachos &nachos)
{
    //no preheating necessary - temperature irrelevant
    //put nachos in first
    insert(nachos);
    turnOn();

    //only cook for a minute (rotate in the middle)
    sleep(30);
    rotateStuff(nachos);
    sleep(30);
    //turn the oven off first (lest your hair fall out)
    turnOff();
```

```
    remove(nachos);
}

Nachos makeNachos(Oven &oven)
{
    //get all the stuff together
    //and assemble the parts
    Nachos n;

    //now (here comes the critical part), cook it
    //(given whatever kind of oven you have)
    oven.cook(n);

    //return the results
    return n;
}
```

Here you see the class `Nachos`, which is declared as a subclass of `Stuff` (meaning all the stuff you can cook). The class `Oven` is outfitted with the common functions `turnOn()`, `turnOff()`, `insert()`, and `remove()`. (The last two refer to the insertion and extraction of stuff from the oven.) In addition, the class `Oven` has a member function `cook(Nachos&)`, which has been declared virtual.

The function `cook(Nachos&)` has been declared virtual because it is implemented differently in the subclass `Microwave`, which inherits from the class `Oven`. The implementation of `Oven::cook(Nachos&)` preheats the oven to a temperature of 350 degrees, puts the nachos in, and cooks them for 15 minutes. It then removes said nachos before turning off the oven. The implementation of `Microwave::cook(Nachos&)`, by comparison, puts the nachos in, turns the power on for 30 seconds, rotates the nachos, and then waits another 30 seconds before turning the oven off and removing the nachos.

This is fine and dandy, but it is all just a buildup for the really interesting part. The function `makeNachos()` is passed an `Oven` of some type. Given that `oven`, it assembles all the parts into an object `n` and then cooks them by calling `oven.cook()`. Exactly which function is used, function `Oven::cook()` or function `Microwave::cook()`, depends on the real-time type of oven. The function `makeNachos()` has no idea — and doesn't want to know — what the run-time type of oven is.

Why is polymorphism such a good idea? First, it allows the maker of ovens — and not the cooker of nachos — to worry about the details of how ovens work. Our division of labor lays such details at the oven programmer's feet.

Second, polymorphism can greatly simplify the code. Look how simple `makeNachos()` appears without any of the oven details. (I realize that it wouldn't be too complicated even with the details, but remember that polymorphism works for real-world problems with their attendant complexity.) The nacho functions can concentrate on nacho details. Finally, the result is extensible. When a new subclass `ConvectionOven` comes along with a new member function `ConvectionOven::cook(Nachos&)`, we do not need to change one iota of `makeNachos()` to incorporate the new function. Polymorphism automatically includes the new function and calls it when necessary.

This is heady stuff. Reflect on what this means. Polymorphism is the key that unlocks the power of inheritance.

When Is a Virtual Function Not?

Just because you think that a particular function call is bound late doesn't mean it is. C++ generates no indication at compile time of which calls it thinks are bound early and late.

The most critical thing to watch for is that all the member functions in question be declared identically, including the return type. If not declared with the same arguments in the subclasses, the member functions are not overloaded polymorphically, whether or not they are declared virtual. For example, change the previous function so that the arguments don't match exactly, and then rerun the program:

```
#include <iostream.h>
class Base
{
  public:
   virtual void fn(int x)
   {
      cout << "In Base class, int x = " << x << "\n";
   }
};
class SubClass : public Base
{
  public:
   virtual void fn(float x)
   {
      cout << "In SubClass, float x = " << x << "\n";
```

```
    }
};

void test(Base &b)
{
    int i = 1;
    b.fn(i);          //this call not bound late
    float f = 2.0F;
    b.fn(f);          //neither is this one
}

int main()
{
    Base bc;
    SubClass sc;
    cout << "Calling test(bc)\n";
    test(bc);
    cout << "Calling test(sc)\n";
    test(sc);
    return 0;
}
```

The only difference between this program and the one before it is that `fn()` in `Base` is declared as `fn(int)`, whereas the `SubClass` version is declared `fn(float)`. No error is generated because this program is legal. The results, however, show no sign of polymorphism:

```
Calling test(bc)
In Base class, int x = 1
In Base class, int x = 2
Calling test(sc)
In Base class, int x = 1
In Base class, int x = 2
```

Because the first call passes an `int`, it's not surprising that the compiler calls `fn(int)` with both `bc` and `sc`. It is a little surprising that the float in the second call is converted to an `int` and that the same `Base::fn(int)` is called the second time in `test()`. This happens because the object `b` passed to `test()` is declared as an object of class `Base`. Without polymorphism, calls to `b.fn()` in `test()` refer to `Base::fn(int)`.

If the arguments don't match exactly, there is no late binding.

One exception to the preceding identical declaration rule is that if the member function in the base class returns a pointer or reference to a base class object, an overloaded member function in a subclass may return a pointer or reference to an object of the subclass. In other words, the following is allowed:

```
class Base
{
  public:
   Base* aFn();
};

class Subclass : public Base
{
  public:
   Subclass* aFn();
};
```

In practice this is quite natural. If a function is dealing with `Subclass` objects, it seems natural that it should continue to deal with `Subclass` objects.

Virtual Considerations

Static member functions cannot be declared virtual. Because static member functions are not called with an object, there is no run-time object to have a type.

Specifying the class name in the call forces the call to bind early. For example, the following call is to `Base::fn()` because that's what the programmer indicated, even if `fn()` is declared virtual:

```
void test(Base &b)
{
   b.Base::fn();         //this call is not bound late
}
```

A virtual function cannot be inlined. To expand a function inline, the compiler must know which function is intended at compile time. Thus, although the example member functions so far have been declared in the class, all of them have been outline functions.

Constructors cannot be virtual because there is no (completed) object to use to determine the type. At the time the constructor is called, the memory that the object occupies is just an amorphous mass. It's only after the constructor has finished that the object is a member of the class in good standing.

By comparison, the destructor normally should be declared virtual. If not, you run the risk of improperly destructing the object, as in the following circumstance:

```
class Base
{
  public:
   ~Base();
};
class SubClass : public Base
{
  public:
   ~SubClass();
};
void finishWithObject(Base *pHeapObject)
{
   //...work with object...
   //now return it to the heap
   delete pHeapObject;  //this calls ~Base() no matter
}                       //what the run-time type of
                        //pHeapObject is
```

If the pointer passed to `finishWithObject()` really points to a `SubClass`, the `SubClass` destructor is not invoked properly. Declaring the destructor virtual solves the problem.

So when would you not want to declare the destructor virtual? There's only one case. Virtual functions introduce a "little" overhead. Let me be more specific. When the programmer defines the first virtual function in a class, C++ adds an additional, hidden pointer — not one pointer per virtual function, just one pointer if the class has any virtual functions. A class that has no virtual functions (and does not inherit any virtual functions from base classes) does not have this pointer.

Now, one pointer doesn't sound like much, and it isn't unless the following two conditions are true:

- The class doesn't have many data members (so that one pointer represents a lot compared to what's there already).
- You intend to create a lot of objects of this class (otherwise, the overhead doesn't make any difference).

If these two conditions are both met and your class doesn't already have any virtual member functions, you might not want to declare the destructor virtual.

WARNING!

You should always declare the destructor virtual. If you don't declare the destructor virtual, document it!

Chapter 19

Class Factoring and Abstract Classes

In This Chapter

- Factoring common properties into a base class
- Using abstract classes to hold factored information
- Declaring abstract classes
- Using dynamic typing

Although inheritance can be used to extend existing classes to new applications, it also affords the programmer the ability to combine common features from different classes in a process known as *factoring*.

Factoring

To see how factoring works, look back at the two classes used in the BUDGET examples appearing at the end of each Part, `Checking` and `Savings`. These are shown graphically in Figure 19-1.

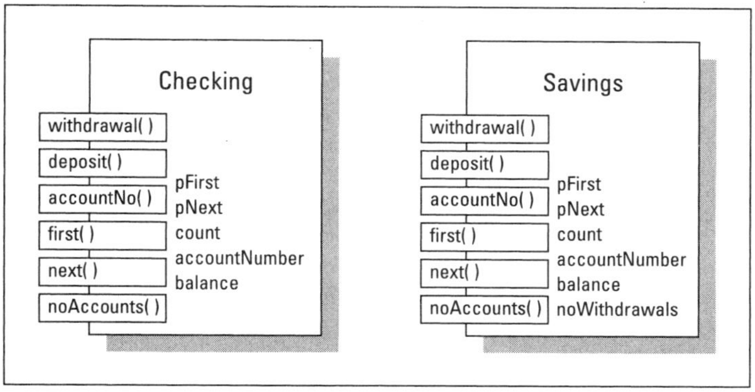

Figure 19-1: Independent classes `Checking` and `Savings`.

To read this figure and the other figures, remember the following:

- The big box is the class, with the class name at the top.
- The names in boxes are member functions.
- The names not in boxes are data members.
- The names that extend partway out of the boxes are publicly accessible members; those that do not are protected.
- A thick arrow represents the IS_A relationship.
- A thin arrow represents the HAS_A relationship.

You can see in Figure 19-1 that the `Checking` and `Savings` classes have a lot in common. Because they aren't identical, however, they must remain as separate classes. (In a real-life bank application, the two classes would be a good deal more different than in this simplistic example.) Still, there should be a way to avoid this repetition.

You could have one of these classes inherit from the other. `Savings` has the extra members, so letting it inherit from `Checking` makes sense, as shown in Figure 19-2. The class is completed with the addition of data member `noWithdrawals` and the virtual overloading of member function `withdrawal()`.

Although letting classes inherit from each other is labor saving, it's not completely satisfying. The main problem is that it, like the weight listed on my driver's license, misrepresents the truth. This inheritance relationship implies that a `Savings` account is a special type of `Checking` account, which is not the case.

"So what?" you say. "Inheriting works and it saves effort." True, but my reservations are more than stylistic trivialities. Such misrepresentations are confusing to the programmer, both today's and tomorrow's. Someday, a programmer unfamiliar with this program will have to read and understand what the code is doing. Misleading tricks are difficult to reconcile and understand.

In addition, such misrepresentations can lead to problems down the road. Suppose, for example, that the bank changes its policies with respect to checking accounts. Say it decides to charge a service fee on checking accounts only if the minimum balance dips below a given value during the month.

A change like this can be easily handled with minimal changes to the class `Checking`. You'll have to add a new data member to the class `Checking`; call it `minimumBalance`.

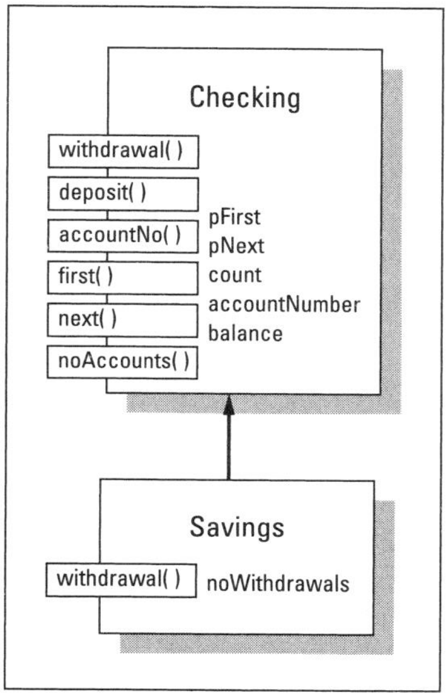

Figure 19-2: `Savings` implemented as a subclass of `Checking`.

But now you have a problem. Because `Savings` inherits from `Checking`, `Savings` gets this new data member as well. It has no use for this member because the minimum balance does not affect savings accounts. One extra data member may not be a big deal, but it does add confusion.

Changes like this accumulate. Today it's an extra data member, tomorrow it's a changed member function. Eventually, the `Savings` account class is carrying a lot of extra baggage that is applicable only to `Checking` accounts.

How can you avoid these problems? The solution is to base both classes on a new class built specially for this purpose; call it `Account`. This class embodies all the features that a savings account and a checking account have in common, as shown in Figure 19-3. (The implementation of this is shown in BUDGET5.CPP at the end of Part V.)

How does building a new account solve the problems? First, creating a new account is a more accurate description of the real world (whatever that is). In your concept of things (or at least in my concept of things), there really is something known as an account. Savings accounts and checking accounts are specializations of this more fundamental concept.

In addition, the class `Savings` is insulated from changes to the class `Checking` (and vice versa). If the bank institutes a fundamental change to all accounts, you can modify `Account` and all subclasses will automatically inherit the change. But if the bank changes its policy only for checking accounts, you just update the checking accounts. The savings accounts remain insulated from the change.

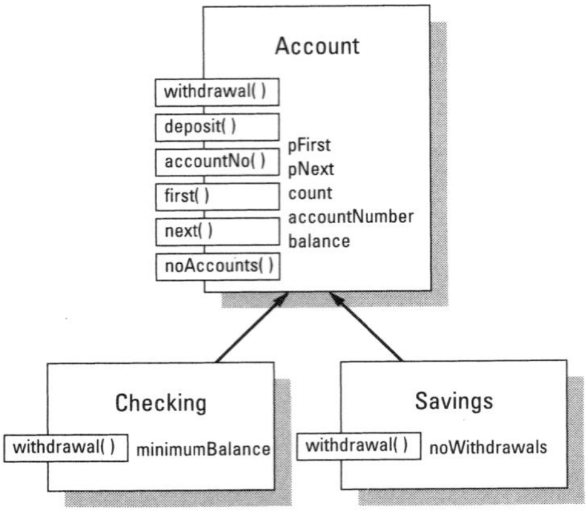

Figure 19-3: Basing `Checking` and `Savings` on a common `Account` class.

This process of culling out common properties from similar classes is called *factoring*. This is an important feature of object-oriented languages for the reasons described so far plus one more: reduction in redundancy.

In software, as in tummies, needless bulk is bad. The more code you generate, the more you have to debug. It's not worth staying up nights generating clever code just to save a few lines here or there — that type of cleverness usually boomerangs. But factoring out redundancy through inheritance can legitimately reduce the programming effort.

WARNING!

Factoring is legitimate only if the inheritance relationship corresponds to reality. Factoring together a class `Mouse` and `Joystick` because they're both hardware pointing devices is legitimate. Factoring together a class `Mouse` and `Display` because they both make low-level operating system calls is not.

Factoring can and usually does result in multiple levels of abstraction. For example, a program written for a more developed bank may have a class structure such as that shown in Figure 19-4.

Here you see that another class has been inserted between `Checking` and `Savings` and the most general class, `Account`. This class, called `Conventional`, incorporates features common to conventional accounts. Other account types, such as stock market accounts, are also foreseen.

Such multitiered class structures are common and desirable as long as the relationships they express correspond to reality. Note, however, that no one correct class hierarchy exists for any given set of classes.

Suppose that the bank allows account holders to access checking and stock market accounts remotely. Withdrawals from other account types can be made only at the bank. Although the class structure in Figure 19-4 seems natural, that shown in Figure 19-5 is also justifiable given this information. The programmer must decide which class structure best fits the data and leads to the cleanest, most natural implementation.

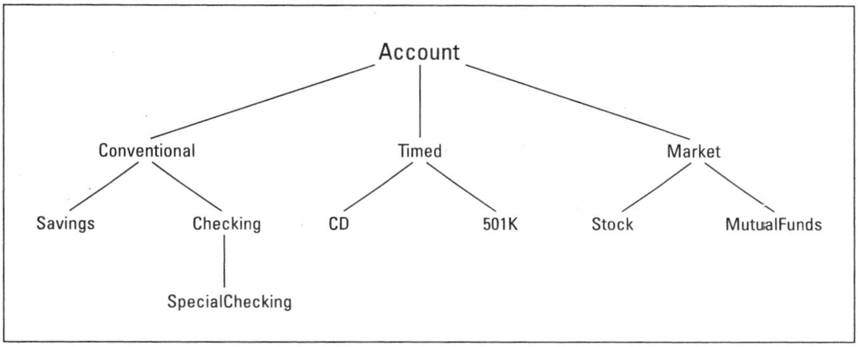

Figure 19-4: A more developed bank account hierarchy.

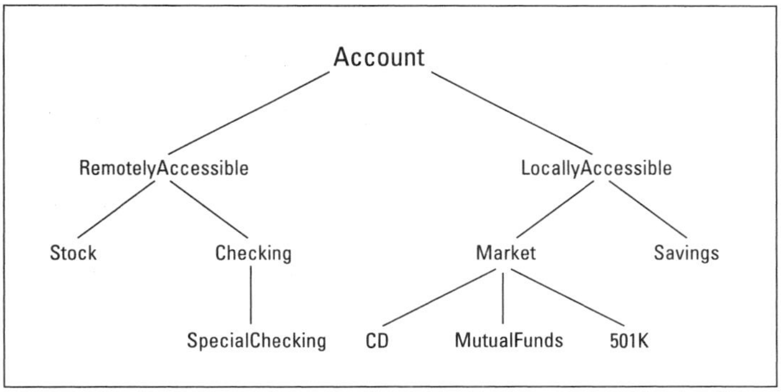

Figure 19-5: Alternate class hierarchy to the one in Figure 19-4.

Implementing Abstract Classes

As intellectually satisfying as factoring is, it introduces a problem of its own. Return one more time to the bank account classes, specifically the common base class `Account`. Think for a minute about how you might go about defining the different member functions defined in `Account`.

Most `Account` member functions are no problem because both account types implement them in the same way. `withdrawal()` is different, however. The rules for withdrawing from a `Savings` account are different than those for withdrawing from a Checking account. Thus, you may expect Savings::withdrawal() to be implemented differently than Checking::withdrawal(). But the question I want to ask is, how do you implement Account::withdrawal()?

"No problem," you say. "Just go to your banker and ask, 'What are the rules for making a withdrawal from an account?'" The reply is, "What type of account? Savings or checking?" "From an account," you say. "Just an account." Blank look. (One might say a "blank bank book" . . . then again, maybe not.)

The problem is that the question doesn't make sense. There's no such thing as "just an account." All accounts (in this example) are either checking accounts or savings accounts. The concept of an account is an abstract one that factors out properties common to the two concrete classes. It is incomplete, however, because it lacks the critical property withdrawal(). (After you get further into the details, you find other properties that a simple account lacks.)

Let me borrow an example from the animal kingdom. You can observe the different species of warm-blooded, baby-bearing animals and conclude that there is a concept Mammal. You can derive classes from mammal, such as canine, feline, and hominid. It is impossible, however, to find anywhere on earth a pure mammal, that is, a mammal that isn't a member of some species. Mammal is a high-level concept that man has created — no instances of mammal exist.

You don't want the programmer to create an object of class Account or class Mammal because you wouldn't know what to do with it. To address this problem, C++ allows the programmer to declare a class that cannot be instanced with an object. The only use for such a class is that it can be inherited. Such a class is called an abstract class.

How do they work?

An *abstract class* is a class with one or more pure virtual functions. A pure virtual function is a virtual member function that is marked as having no implementation because no one knows how to implement it. For example, no one knows how to perform a withdrawal() in class Account. The concept doesn't make sense. However, you can't just not include a definition of withdrawal() because C++ assumes that you forgot to define the function and gives you a link error stating that the function is missing (and presumed forgotten).

The syntax for declaring a function pure virtual — and letting C++ know that the function has no definition — is demonstrated in the following class `Account`:

```
//Account - this class is an abstract class
class Account
{
  protected:
   Account(Account &c);
  public:
   Account(unsigned accNo, float initialBalance = 0.0F);
   //access functions
   unsigned int accountNo( );
   float acntBalance( );
   static Account *first( );
   Account *next( );
   static int noAccounts( );
   //transaction functions
   void deposit(float amount);

   //the following is a pure virtual function
   virtual void withdrawal(float amount) = 0;
  protected:
   //keep accounts in a linked list so there's no limit
   static Account *pFirst;
          Account *pNext;
   static int count;          //number of accounts
   unsigned   accountNumber;
   float      balance;
};
```

The `= 0` after the declaration of `withdrawal()` indicates that the programmer does not intend to define this function. The declaration is a placeholder for the subclasses. The subclasses of `Account` are expected to overload this function with a concrete function.

I think this notation is silly, and I don't like it any more than you do. But it's here to stay, so you just have to learn to live with it. There is a reason, if not exactly a justification, for this notation. Every virtual function must have an entry in a special table. This entry contains the address of the function. The entry for a pure virtual function is zero.

An abstract class cannot be instanced with an object; that is, you can't make an object out of an abstract class. For example, the following declaration is not legal:

```
void fn( )
{
   //declare an account with 100 dollars
   Account acnt(1234, 100.00);//this is not legal
   acnt.withdrawal(50);       //what would you expect this
                              //to do?
}
```

If the declaration were allowed, the resulting object would be incomplete, lacking in some capability. For example, what should the preceding call do? Remember, there is no `Account::withdrawal()`.

Abstract classes serve as base classes for other classes. An `Account` contains all the properties associated with a generic bank account. You can create other types of bank accounts by inheriting from `Account`, but they cannot be instanced with an object.

Making an honest class out of an abstract class

The subclass of an abstract class remains abstract until all pure virtual functions have been overloaded. The class `Savings` is not abstract because it overloads the pure virtual function `withdrawal()` with a perfectly good definition. An object of class `Savings` knows how to perform `withdrawal()` when called on to do so. The same is true of class `Checking`: The class is not virtual, because the function `withdrawal()` overloads the pure virtual function in the base class.

A subclass of an abstract class can remain abstract, however. Consider the following classes:

```
class Display
{
  public:
   virtual void initialize( ) = 0;
   virtual void write(char *pString) = 0;
};

class SVGA : public Display
{
   //overload both member functions with "real" functions
   virtual void initialize( );
   virtual void write(char *pString);
};
```

```
class HWVGA : public Display
{
   //overload the only function we know how to at this point
   virtual void write(char *pString);
};

class ThreedVGA : public HWVGA
{
   virtual void initialize( );
};

void fn( )
{
   SVGA mc;
   VGA vga;
   //...what the function chooses to do from here...
}
```

The class `Display`, intended to represent video PC displays, has two pure virtual functions: `initialize()` and `write()`. You cannot implement either function for adapters in general. The different types of video cards do not initialize or write in the same way.

One of the subclasses, `SVGA`, is not abstract. This is a particular type of video adapter that the programmer knows how to program. Therefore, the class `SVGA` has overloaded both `initialize()` and `write()` appropriately for this adapter.

`HWVGA`, another one of the subclasses, is also not abstract. Here again, the programmer knows how to program the hardware accelerated VGA adapter. In this case, however, a level of abstraction is between the generic `Display` and the specific case of the `ThreedVGA` display, which represents the special 3-D hardware display cards.

For this discussion, assume that all hardware accelerated VGA cards are written to in the same way but that each must be initialized in its own way. (This isn't necessarily true, but assume it is.) To express the common write property, introduce the class `HWVGA` to implement the `write()` function (along with any other properties that all `HWVGA` have in common). Do not overload the member function `initialize()`, however, because the different `HWVGA`s do not have this property in common.

Therefore, even though the function `write()` has been overloaded, the class `HWVGA` is still abstract because the `initialize()` function has yet to be overloaded.

Because `ThreedVGA` inherits from `HWVGA`, it has to overload only the one missing member function, `initialize()`, to complete the definition of `Display` adapter. The function `fn()` is therefore free to instance and use a `ThreedVGA` object.

Overloading the last pure virtual function with a normal member function makes the class complete (that is, non-abstract). Only non-abstract classes can be instanced with an object.

Originally, every pure virtual function in a subclass had to be overloaded, even if the function was overloaded with another pure virtual function. Eventually, the people that count realized that this was as silly as it sounds and dropped the requirement. Older compilers may still require it though.

Passing abstract classes

Because you can't instance an abstract class, it may sound odd that it is possible to declare a pointer or a reference to an abstract class. With polymorphism, however, this isn't as crazy as it sounds. Consider the following code snippet:

```
void fn(Account *pAccount);   //this is legal
void otherFn( )
{
   Savings s;
   Checking c;

   //this is legitimate because Savings IS_A Account
   fn(&s);
   //same here
   fn(&c);
}
```

Here, `pAccount` is declared as a pointer to an `Account`. However, it is understood that when the function is called, it will be passed the address of some non-abstract subclass object such as `Savings` or `Checking`.

All objects received by `fn()` will be of either class `Savings` or class `Checking` (or some future non-abstract subclass of `Account`). The function is assured that you will never pass an actual object of class `Account`, because you could never create one to pass in the first place.

Why do I need pure virtual functions?

If `withdrawal()` can't be defined, why not leave it out? Why not define the function in `Savings` and `Checking` and keep it out of `Account`? In many object-oriented languages, you can do just that. But C++ wants to be able to check that you really know what you're doing.

Like ANSI C, C++ is a strongly typed language. When you refer to a member function, C++ insists that you prove that the member function exists in the class you specified. This avoids unfortunate run-time surprises when a referenced member function turns out to be missing.

Make the following minor changes to `Account` to demonstrate the problem:

```
class Account
{
   //just like before but without withdrawal( ) declared
};
class Savings : public Account
{
  public:
   virtual void withdrawal(float amnt);
};

void fn(Account *pAcc)
{
   //withdraw some money
   pAcc->withdrawal(100.00F);  //this call is not allowed
                              //withdrawal( ) is not a member
                              //of class Account
};
int main( )
{
Savings s;   //open an account
   fn(&s);
   //...continues on...
}
```

Suppose that you open a savings account `s`. You then pass the address of that account to the function `fn()`, which attempts to make a withdrawal. Because the function `withdrawal()` is not a member of `Account`, however, the compiler generates an error.

See how pure virtual functions correct the problem. Here's the same situation with `Account` declared as an abstract class:

```
class Account
{
    public:
     //just like preceding
   //declare withdrawal pure virtual
   virtual void withdrawal(float amnt) = 0;
};
class Savings : public Account
{
    public:
   virtual void withdrawal(float amnt);
};

void fn(Account *pAcc)
{
   //withdraw some money
   pAcc->withdrawal(100.00F);  //now it works
};
int main( )
{
   Savings s;   //open an account
   fn(&s);
   //...same as before...
}
```

The situation is the same except the class `Account` includes a member function `withdrawal()`. Now when the compiler checks to see whether `pAcc->withdrawal()` is defined, it sees the definition of `Account::withdrawal()` just as it expects. The compiler is happy. You are happy.

The pure virtual function is a placeholder in the base class for the subclass to overload with its own implementation. Without that placeholder in the base class, there is no overloading.

Determining the Run-Time Type

With all this IS_A and IS_NOT_A going on, keeping straight who REALLY_IS_A and who isn't is sometimes difficult. Consider the following function:

```
void fn(Account &account)
{
   //...whatever processing...
   //is this account a Savings or Checking account?
}
```

The declaration says that `fn()` is designed to accept any type of account, be it a savings account or a checking account. Fine. But what if the function decides it wants to know the run-time type of the account it's dealing with? How can it do that?

Believe it or not, this is a contentious issue among OO types. The first answer to the question, and the one that I most agree with, is "It shouldn't!" If the function includes code to check for a particular type, it may be ruining the extensibility inherent in inheritance with late binding.

Suppose that a function `runtimeType()` returned the run-time type of an object. Now consider how it might be used:

```
void fn(Account &account)
{
   //process closing accounts
   //use a switch based on dynamic type
   switch(runtimeType(account))
   {
     case SAVINGS:
        //close savings account
        break;
     case CHECKING:
        //close checking account
        break;
   }
}
```

Here the function accepts an `Account`. But when it's time to process the closing of the different account types, the function decides to branch, depending on the run-time type returned by `runtimeType()`.

The preceding program executes fine, but the wide-awake reader sees the problem. Sooner or later, the requirements change and a new class will be added — for example, `NewSavings`. Now the programmer must remember to go back to `fn()` — and to all the other places where a branch is made based on the value returned from `runtimeType()` — and edit it to add the new case. This is functional programming in OO clothing.

Anytime you find yourself writing an `if` or a `switch` statement based on the run-time type of an object, stop and see whether you can't find another, more extensible solution to the problem.

Run-time type identification

If you're determined to know the run-time type, read on. C++ provides a mechanism called Run-Time Type Identification (RTTI).

RTTI introduces some overhead, so it must be specifically enabled in most compilers (including the Visual C++ compiler). The default is usually off. RTTI is both a difficult and controversial feature, so some C++ compilers still do not support it. In addition, RTTI works only for classes with one or more virtual functions.

RTTI works like this:

```
class Account
{
  public:
    Account(int accNo, float initialBalance);
    virtual void deposit(float amount);
    virtual void withdrawal(float amount);
    // addAccount - add current account to the account list
    void addAccount();
    // getNext - get the next account from the account list;
    //           if pPrev == 0, return first;
    //           return 0 when no more left in list
    static Account* getNext(Account *pPrev);
};

class Checking : public Account
{
  public:
    Checking(int accNo, float initialBalance = 0.0F);
};

class Savings : public Account
{
  public:
    Savings(int accNo, float initialBalance = 0.0F);
    // addInterest - calculate the interest for one time
    //               period and add it back in
    void addInterest();
};

// accInterest - loop thru the accounts. For each Savings
//               account you find, calculate the interest and add it back in
//
void accInterest()
{
    // loop thru the Accounts
    Account* pA = (Account*)0;
    while(pA = Account::getNext(pA))
    {
```

```
        // only process Savings accounts
        // make a type-safe downcast:
        Savings* pS = dynamic_cast<Savings*>(pA);
        // if pS is non-zero then this really was a Savings
        if (pS)
        {
            // so add the interest in
            pS->addInterest();
        }
    }
}
```

Here you see the same `Savings` and `Checking` subclasses of the base class `Account`. In this example, all accounts are kept in a common account database. Accounts are added to the list with the `Account::addAccount()` member function. The list of accounts can be traversed using the `Account::getNext()` member function.

The point of interest is the `accInterest()` function, which accumulates interest in the `Savings` accounts contained in the list. This function must be able to differentiate between `Savings` and `Checking` accounts because the `Checking` class has no `addInterest()` member function. (Presumably `Checking` accounts don't accumulate interest.) `accInterest()` starts by getting a pointer to the next `Account` using `getNext()`. It then asks C++ whether the object pointed to by `pA` IS_REALLY_A `Savings` account using the RTTI `dynamic_cast<>()` operator.

`dynamic_cast<S*>(B* pB)` checks to see whether `pB` is really of type `S*`. If it is, the operator returns a `pB` cast into an `S*`. If not, the operator returns a zero. After calling `getNext()`, all you can be assured of is that `pA` points to some type of `Account*`. If the result of `dynamic_cast<Savings*>(pA)` returns a nonzero, you also know that `pA` really pointed to a `Savings` object (or some subclass of `Savings`).

Casting from a base class to the subclass is called a downcast because you move down the inheritance hierarchy. Be careful about performing downcasts unless you are absolutely sure that the object really is what you say it is. If you have any doubt, use an RTTI `dynamic_cast`.

Avoiding RTTI

How could I have avoided the stigma of embarrassing RTTI downcasts? Easily. The reason that `accInterest()` had to differentiate between `Savings` and `Checking` was that the member function `addInterest()` did not exist at the `Account()` level. "But," you say, "checking accounts don't accumulate interest!" Okay, so assign them a do-nothing function:

```
class Account
{
  public:
    Account(int accNo, float initialBalance);
    virtual void deposit(float amount);
    virtual void withdrawal(float amount);
    // addInterest - the default addInterest does nothing
    virtual void addInterest()
    {
    }

    // addAccount - add current account to the account list
    void addAccount();
    // getNext - get the next account from the account list;
    //           if pPrev == 0, return first;
    //           return 0 when no more left in list
    static Account* getNext(Account *pPrev);
};

class Checking : public Account
{
  public:
    Checking(int accNo, float initialBalance = 0.0F) ;
};

class Savings : public Account
{
  public:
    Savings(int accNo, float initialBalance = 0.0F);
    // addInterest - calculate the interest for one time
    //               period and add it back in
    void addInterest();
};

// accInterest - loop thru the accounts. For each Savings
//               account you find, calculate the interest and
//                             add it back in
void accInterest()
{
    // loop thru the Accounts
    Account* pA = (Account*)0;
    while(pA = Account::getNext(pA))
    {
        // so add the interest in
        pA->addInterest();
    }
}
```

Now the default `Account::addInterest()` member function does nothing. Its presence, however, provides a placeholder for subclasses to override. The subclass `Savings` overrides this function with a real `addInterest()` function. Now `accInterest()` does not need to differentiate between different types of accounts. It can simply sit back, call `pA->addInterest()`, and let polymorphism do the driving. This solution is both easier to read and extensible because `accInterest()` does not need to know anything about the `Account` class hierarchy.

Using Inheritance to Rationalize the Budget: BUDGET5.CPP

The addition of classes created quite a bit of change from BUDGET2 to BUDGET3. By comparison, the changes from version 3 to 4 were more cosmetic. Here, you notice quite a change as you add inheritance to create BUDGET5. I think you'll like the results.

In this version, you add the following:

- Use of inheritance to highlight the similarities between checking and savings accounts and to avoid redundancy
- Use of virtual member functions to increase readability and expandability
- Creation of a pure virtual class to capture the commonalities between checking and savings accounts

Until now, you were forced to maintain the two classes `Checking` and `Savings` as separate entities. Although you were painfully aware of the similarities between the two, you were unable to express that relationship.

Now, with the help of the new OO superhero inheritance and its sidekick polymorphism, you can rationalize these two classes into a single class `Account`, which captures the commonalities between these two classes. The result is a much smaller and simpler program:

```
//BUDGET5.CPP - Budget program with inheritance and
//              late binding (aka, polymorphism).  Notice
//              how much smaller the program is now that the
//              redundancy has been removed.  A single
//              function can now handle both checking and
//              savings accounts (and any other accounts that
//              you might invent in the future).

#include <iostream.h>
#include <stdlib.h>
#include <ctype.h>
```

```
//Account - this abstract class incorporates properties
//          common to both account types: Checking and
//          Savings. However, it's missing the concept
//          withdrawal(), which is different between the two
class Account
{
  protected:
   Account(Account &c)
   {
      cout << "No creating funds\n";
   }

  public:
   Account(unsigned accNo, float initialBalance = 0.0F);
   //access functions
   int accountNo()
   {
      return accountNumber;
   }
   float acntBalance()
   {
      return balance;
   }
   static Account *first()
   {
      return pFirst;
   }
   Account *next()
   {
      return pNext;
   }
   static int noAccounts()
   {
      return count;
   }

   //transaction functions
   void deposit(float amount)
   {
      balance += amount;
   }                                  //Note 1
   virtual void withdrawal(float amount) = 0;
   //display function for displaying self on 'cout'
   void display()
```

(continued)

(continued)

```
   {
      cout << "Account " << accountNumber
           << " = "      << balance
           << "\n";
   }

  protected:
   //keep accounts in a linked list so there's no limit
   static Account *pFirst;              //Note 2
          Account *pNext;
   static int count;          //number of accounts
   unsigned   accountNumber;
   float      balance;
};

//allocate space for statics
Account  *Account::pFirst = 0;
int        Account::count  = 0;
Account::Account(unsigned accNo, float initialBalance)
{
   accountNumber = accNo;
   balance = initialBalance;

   //add this to end of list and count it
   count++;
   if (pFirst == 0)
   {
      pFirst = this;      //empty list; make it first
   }
   else                   //list not empty; look for last
   {
     for (Account *pA = pFirst; pA->pNext; pA = pA->pNext)
      {
      }
      pA->pNext = this;   //tack us onto end
   }
   pNext = 0;             //we're always last
}

//Checking - this class contains properties unique to
//           checking accounts.  Not much left, is there?
class Checking : public Account
{
  public:
   //here the constructor is defined inline
```

```
   Checking(unsigned accNo, float initialBalance = 0.0F) :
       Account(accNo, initialBalance)        //Note 3
   {
   }

   //overload pure virtual functions
   virtual void withdrawal(float amount);    //Note 4
};

void Checking::withdrawal(float amount)      //Note 5
{
   if (balance < amount )
   {
      cout << "Insufficient funds: balance " << balance
           << ", check "                     << amount
           << "\n";
   }
   else
   {
      balance -= amount;
      //if balance falls too low, charge service fee
      if (balance < 500.00F)
      {
         balance -= 0.20F;
      }
   }
}


//Savings - same story as Checking except that it also
//          has a unique data member
class Savings : public Account
{
  public:
   //here the constructor is defined as a separate function
   //just to show you the difference
   Savings(unsigned accNo, float initialBalance = 0.0F);
   //transaction functions
   virtual void withdrawal(float amount);
  protected:
   int        noWithdrawals;
};
                                            //Note 6
Savings::Savings(unsigned accNo, float initialBalance) :
   Account(accNo, initialBalance)
```

(continued)

(continued)

```
{
   noWithdrawals = 0;
}
void Savings::withdrawal(float amount)
{
   if (balance < amount)
   {
      cout << "Insufficient funds: balance " << balance
           << ", withdrawal "                << amount
           << "\n";
   }
   else
   {
      if (++noWithdrawals > 1)
      {
         balance -= 5.00F;
      }
      balance -= amount;
   }
}

//prototype declarations
unsigned getAccntNo();
void process(Account &account);        //Note 7
void outOfMemory();

//main - accumulate the initial input and output totals
int main()
{
   /*loop until someone enters 'X' or 'x'*/
   Account *pA;                         //Note 8
   char     accountType;     //S or C

   unsigned keepLooping = 1;
   while (keepLooping)
   {
      cout << "Enter S for Savings, "
              "C for Checking, X for exit\n";
      cin  >> accountType;
      switch (accountType)
      {
         case 'c':
         case 'C':
            pA = new Checking(getAccntNo());//Note 9
            if (pA == 0)
```

```
         {
            outOfMemory();
         }
         process(*pA);
         break;

      case 's':
      case 'S':
         pA = new Savings(getAccntNo()); //Note 9
         if (pA == 0)
         {
            outOfMemory();
         }
         process(*pA);
         break;

      case 'x':
      case 'X':
         keepLooping = 0;
         break;

      default:
         cout << "I didn't get that.\n";
    }
  }

  //now present totals                //Note 10
  float total = 0.0F;
  cout << "Account totals:\n";
  for (pA = Account::first(); pA; pA = pA->next())
  {
     pA->display();
     total += pA->acntBalance();
  }
  cout << "Total worth  = " << total << "\n";
  return 0;
}
//getAccntNo - return the account number entered
unsigned getAccntNo()
{
  unsigned accntNo;
  cout << "Enter account number:";
  cin  >> accntNo;
  return accntNo;
}
```

(continued)

(continued)

```
//process(Account) - input the data for an account
void process(Account &account)
{
   cout << "Enter positive number for deposit,\n"
           "negative for withdrawal, 0 to terminate";
   float transaction;
   do
   {
      cout << ":";
      cin  >> transaction;

      //deposit
      if (transaction > 0)
      {
         account.deposit(transaction);
      }
      //withdrawal
      if (transaction < 0) {
         account.withdrawal(-transaction);  //Note 11
      }
   } while (transaction != 0);
}

//outOfMemory - generate out-of-memory message and quit
void outOfMemory()
{
   cout << "Out of memory\n";
   abort();
}
```

The first batter out of the dugout is now class `Account`. In appearance, it's the same as the earlier classes `Savings` and `Checking`. Because `withdrawal()` is declared pure virtual (see `Note 1`), you know that `Account` is abstract and cannot be instanced.

The first non-abstract class is `Checking`. This class is quite small, consisting of only an empty constructor (`Note 3`) and a `withdrawal()` to overload the pure virtual member function from the base class (`Note 4`). The implementation of `Checking::withdrawal()` appears at `Note 5`.

Class `Savings` is similar, except in this case I implemented the constructor as a non-inline member function to demonstrate the difference (`Note 6`).

Following the class definitions, you can see that you no longer have the function redundancy. The one function `process(Account&)` has replaced both `process(Checking&)` and `process(Savings&)`. See `Note 7`. There is the same reduction in redundancy in `main()`. A single pointer, `pA` (declared at `Note 8`), can point to either a `Checking` account object or a `Savings` account object (`Note 9`).

Skipping ahead to `process()` for a second, you can see that the function is generic. Late binding occurs in the innocuous-looking call to `withdrawal()` (`Note 11`). When the object account refers to a `Checking` account, this call invokes `Checking::withdrawal()`. When account refers to a `Savings` account, this same call ends up at `Savings::withdrawal()`.

After the account objects have been built, they are displayed in the same way as before:

```
Enter S for Savings, C for Checking, X for exit
S
Enter account number:123
Enter positive number for deposit,
negative for withdrawal, 0 to terminate:200
:-50
:-50
:0
Enter S for Savings, C for Checking, X for exit
C
Enter account number:234
Enter positive number for deposit,
negative for withdrawal, 0 to terminate:200
:-25
:-20
:0
Enter S for Savings, C for Checking, X for exit
X
Account totals:
Account 123 = 95
Account 234 = 154.600006
Total worth  = 249.600006
```

BUDGET4 uses the members `pFirst` and `pNext` to keep the account objects in a linked list, thereby removing any artificial limitations that a fixed-sized array might impose. BUDGET5, however, places `pFirst` and `pNext` in the parent class `Account` (`Note 2`). This implies that both `Savings` and `Checking` accounts are linked into the same list, so they are displayed together (`Note 10`). The output reflects this. One of the example problems in the Workout section for Part V (on the CD) is to split these linked lists.

Part VI
Advanced Strokes: Optional Features

The 5th Wave — By Rich Tennant

In this part . . .

As I state in the Introduction, it is not the goal of this book to turn you into a C++ language lawyer. I would be much happier if you came away with a solid understanding of the fundamentals of C++ and object-oriented programming. If you have carefully read and mastered the concepts presented so far, you should have that understanding by now.

The pages before this cover the essential features you need to know to produce a well-written, object-oriented C++ program. C++, however, is a big language (it has a serious case of feature-itis, if you ask me), and I have yet to discuss many features. In Part VI, I present a summary of the additional features that I find most useful, along with my opinion as to when — and when not — to use them.

Chapter 20

Access Control Specifiers

In This Chapter

- Introduction to private members
- A further comparison of `class` and `struct`
- Non-public inheritance
- Guidelines for using private and protected

The capability to hide members of the class from outside functions is an important part of object-oriented programming. So far, however, this access control has been presented as a binary situation: Either you were in the club or you weren't, either you knew the secret handshake or you didn't. C++ provides a little more control than that. In this chapter, I discuss the other aspects of access control.

Really Exclusive Club: Private Members

In addition to protected and public, C++ defines another access control specifier called *private*. Members declared private are like protected members except that they are not accessible from inherited classes.

I point out in Part III why letting a class hide its members from the prying op-codes of outside functions is a good thing. In Part III, the reader has not been exposed to inheritance, so there is only one class. Therefore, in those chapters I don't have to worry about how far the boundary extends.

With the introduction of inheritance, the question becomes, "Are subclasses inside or outside of the fence thrown up by the `protected` keyword?" The answer is inside. A subclass can access the protected members of a base class. The access control specifier private allows you to treat subclass functions as outside that boundary. Class members declared private are not accessible to any subclasses of that class.

`class` versus `struct`

You may be interested to know that a `class` starts out in `private` mode. Thus, I could have coded the `Example` class as follows:

```
class Example
{
    int onlyAccessibleToThisClass;
  public:
    int accessibleToAll;
  protected:
    int accessibleToSubclasses;
};
```

The only difference between keyword `class` and keyword `struct` in C++ is that `struct` starts out in `public` mode. (It does this to retain compatibility with C.) Therefore, I also could have coded the `Example` class as

```
struct Example
{
    int accessibleToAll;
  protected:
    int accessibleToSubclasses;
  private:
    int onlyAccessibleToThisClass;
};
```

C++ even allows the programmer to mix and match the words `class` and `struct`, referring to the same class sometimes as a `class` and sometimes as a `struct`. Don't do it, however. The reader of your code will wonder what you're doing, and you won't have a good explanation.

The general rule is to use `struct` if the structure is C compatible, that is, if it has

- No non-public members
- No member functions
- No base classes (doesn't inherit from anything)

Otherwise, use `class`. In addition, don't rely on the default access mode of `class`. Always specify; it's clearer that way.

When should I use private, and when can I stay with protected?

The arguments for and against declaring members private go something like this: You don't have to look outside the current class to find all the functions that can manipulate a private member. That's good.

On the other hand, forcing subclass functions to access these members through access functions can greatly increase the number of access functions you need. That's bad. But, you say, using that argument, why not just make all members public and dispense with access functions entirely?

When you build a class, you should keep its logic separate from that of the surrounding program as much as possible. That's one of the reasons for data hiding.

Building a class is analogous to the way a carpenter builds a house on a block. Each house has certain well-defined connections to the block, such as electricity, water, sewer, and — the most critical of all — cable.

A subclass is not built as a stand-alone structure. Often, the subclass relies heavily on the class from which it inherits. Such a subclass is more like an extra room attached to an existing structure rather than a stand-alone house. You might like the extra room to be generic, but in practice this is rarely possible. The implementation of the subclass becomes bound to the details of the base class. In this situation, the advantages of data hiding are minimized.

Thus, it boils down to a matter of judgment. If your subclass is of the independent variety, the extra work of private inheritance is rewarded by increased decoupling. If your subclass is more of the "add-on room" variety, the result of private inheritance is just increased complexity.

How do I use private?

The keyword `private` looks and acts just like `protected` and `public`. This is demonstrated in the following `Example` class, which has private, protected, and public members:

```
class Example
{
  public:
   int accessibleToAll;
  protected:
   int accessibleToSubclasses;
  private:
   int onlyAccessibleToThisClass;
};
```

The order of the storage classes is not important. You can put your public members first and your private members last or the other way around. In addition, you can switch between one storage class and another as often as you like.

Secret Wills, or Non-Public Inheritance

The introduction to inheritance in Part V notes that if there is public inheritance, there are probably other modes as well. (It's like my friend says, "If there's artificial intelligence, there's just got to be artificial stupidity.") In fact, two other modes exist: protected inheritance and private inheritance. The differences are highlighted in Table 20-1.

Table 20-1 Access Mode versus Inheritance Type

Inheritance Type	*Public Access Mode*	*Protected Access Mode*	*Private Access Mode*
public	public	protected	private
protected	protected	protected	private
private	private	private	private

In a publicly inherited class, each of the members of the base class retains its same access modes in the subclass. Hence, as shown in Table 20-1, public maps to public, protected to protected, and private to private. (This is what you've seen until now.) In a protectedly inherited class, however, public members become protected in the inherited class; in the table, public maps to protected. Protected and private members are unchanged in the derived class. In a privately inherited class, everything becomes private.

The default for inheritance is private. Again, it's not a good idea to rely on the default. Your code will be easier to read if you always specify the inheritance type.

When Is a Subclass Not?

It is important to note that a privately or protectedly derived class is not a subclass. This is because the non-publicly derived class cannot do all the things that the base class can. Therefore, a non-publicly derived object cannot be used as a replacement for a base class object. Consider the following:

```
class Duck
{
  public:
   void quack();
};
class Mallard : public Duck {};
class LooneyToon: private Duck {};

void fn(Duck &duck)
{
   duck.quack();
}
```

```
int main()
{
    Mallard daisy;
    LooneyToon daffy;
    fn(daisy);        //this is allowed...
    fn(daffy);        //...but this is not
    return 0;
}
```

The function `fn()` expects an object of type `Duck`, but the call `fn(daisy)` is actually passing an object of class `Mallard`. Why is that justified? An object of class `Mallard` IS_A `Duck` because it has all the members of a `Duck`. That is, anything you can ask a `Duck` to do, you can ask a `Mallard` to do.

If you now look at `daffy`, you see that what is true for `daisy` isn't quite true for `daffy`. You cannot pass `daffy` off as a `Duck` because the general public doesn't have access to its ducky functions. In this case, `fn()` can't get `daffy` to `quack()`. That is, `daffy.quack()` is not allowed, not because `daffy` does not have a member function `quack()`, but because that function is not publicly accessible.

REMEMBER

If it don't quack like a duck, it ain't a duck.

When to Declare What

When should you declare members protected and when should you declare them private? My preference is to limit data members as much as possible to private; however, I do give subclasses access to some key data members by making them protected. In addition, I rarely declare member functions private. I seldom, if ever, use anything but public inheritance.

If you find this entire chapter confusing, don't worry. Stick to public and protected members and public inheritance. You generally won't miss the others.

Chapter 21

Overloading Operators

In This Chapter

- Overview of overloading operators in C++
- Discussion of operator format versus function format
- Implementing operators as a member function versus as a non-member function
- The return value from an overloaded operator
- A special case: the cast operator

C++ allows the programmer to define the operators for user-defined C++ types. This is called *operator overloading*. In this chapter, I cover the generic case of operator overloading.

Normally, operator overloading is optional and usually not attempted by beginning C++ programmers. A lot of experienced C++ programmers don't think operator overloading is such a great idea, either. Therefore, if you're feeling a bit overwhelmed, you can skip this chapter and return to it when you feel curious and more at ease. You need to learn how to overload three operators. So that you don't inadvertently skip them as well, they have been granted their own chapters, which immediately follow this one.

The following scenes depict graphic representations of software kludgery. If you begin to feel light-headed as you read this chapter, put the book down and rest. If symptoms persist, proceed immediately to the next chapter.

Operator overloading can introduce errors that are very difficult to find. Be sure that you know how it works before you attempt to use it.

Why Do I Need to Overload Operators?

C++ considers user-defined types to be just as valid as intrinsic types, such as `int` and `char`. Because the operators are defined for the intrinsic types, why not allow them to be defined for user-defined types?

This is a weak argument, but I admit that operator overloading has its uses. Consider a class `USDollar`, for instance, which I will use to represent greenbacks. I will then define what the different operators mean when applied to the class.

Some of the operators make no sense at all when applied to dollars. For example, what would it mean to invert a `USDollar`? Turn it upside down? On the other hand, some operators definitely are applicable. For example, it makes sense to add a `USDollar` to or subtract a `USDollar` from a `USDollar`, the result being a `USDollar`. It also makes sense to multiply or divide a `USDollar` by a `double`. It probably does not make sense to multiply a `USDollar` by a `USDollar`.

Operator overloading can improve readability. Consider the following, first without overloaded operators:

```
//expense - calculate the amount of money paid
//          (including both principle and simple interest)
USDollar expense(USDollar principle, double rate)
{
   //calculate the interest expense
   USDollar interest = principle.interest(rate);
   //now add this to the principle and return the result
   return principle.add(interest);
}
```

With overloaded operators, the same function looks like the following:

```
//expense - calculate the amount of money paid
//          (including both principle and simple interest)
USDollar expense(USDollar principle, double rate)
{
   USDollar interest = principle * rate;
   return principle + interest;
}
```

Before you investigate how to overload an operator, you need to understand the relationship between an operator and a function.

How Does an Operator Function and a Function Operate?

An operator is nothing more than a built-in function with a peculiar syntax. C++ gives each operator a functional name. The functional name of an operator is the operator symbol preceded by the keyword operator and followed by the appropriate argument types. For example, the + operator that adds an `int` to an `int` generating an `int` is called `int operator+(int, int)`.

The programmer can overload all operators — except `.`, `::`, `*` (dereference), and `&` — by overloading their functional name.

The programmer cannot invent new operators nor can the precedence or format of the operators be changed. In addition, the operators cannot be redefined when applied to intrinsic types. Only existing operators can be overloaded for newly defined types.

How Does Operator Overloading Work?

To see operator overloading in action, look at the following, which shows class `USDollar` with an addition operator and an increment operator defined:

```
class USDollar
{
   friend USDollar operator+(USDollar&, USDollar&);
   friend USDollar& operator++(USDollar&);
  public:
   USDollar(unsigned int d, unsigned int c);
  protected:
   unsigned int dollars;
   unsigned int cents;
};

USDollar::USDollar(unsigned int d, unsigned int c)

{
   dollars = d;
   cents = c;
   while (cents >= 100) {
      dollars++;
      cents -= 100;
   }
}

//operator+ - add s1 to s2 and return the result
//             in a new object
USDollar operator+(USDollar& s1, USDollar& s2)
{
```

(continued)

(continued)

```
    unsigned int cents   = s1.cents   + s2.cents;
   unsigned int dollars = s1.dollars + s2.dollars;
   USDollar d(dollars, cents);
   return d;
}

//operator++ - increment the specified argument;
//             change the value of the provided object
USDollar& operator++(USDollar& s)
{
   s.cents++;
   if (s.cents >= 100)
   {
      s.cents -= 100;
      s.dollars++;
   }
   return s;
}

int main()
{
   USDollar d1(1, 60);
   USDollar d2(2, 50);
   USDollar d3(0, 0);
   d3 = d1 + d2;     //straightforward in use
   ++d3;
   return 0;
}
```

The class `USDollar` is defined as having an integer number of dollars and an integer number of cents less than 100. The constructor enforces the latter rule by reducing the number of cents by 100 at a time and increasing the number of dollars appropriately.

Here `operator+()` and `operator++()` have been implemented as conventional non-member functions. As such, they must be declared as friends to be granted access to the protected members.

Because `operator+()` is a binary operator (that is, it has two arguments), you see two arguments to the function (`s1` and `s2`). The `operator+()` takes `s1` and adds it to `s2`. The result of the expression is returned as a `USDollar` object from the function.

Notice that the operator += has nothing to do with the operators + or =. That is, each operator must be overloaded independently.

Notice that nothing forces `operator+(USDollar&, USDollar&)` to perform addition. You could have `operator+()` do anything you like; however, doing anything else besides addition is a REALLY BAD IDEA. People are accustomed to their operators performing in certain ways. They don't like their operators dancing about willy-nilly performing other operations.

The unary operators, such as `operator++()`, take a single argument. `operator++()` increments the cents field. If it goes over 100, it increments the dollar field and zeros out the cents.

Originally you had no way to overload the prefix operator `++x` separately from the postfix version `x++`. Enough programmers complained that the rule was made that `operator++(ClassName)` refers to the prefix operator and `operator++(ClassName, int)` refers to the postfix operator. A zero is always passed as the second argument. The same rule applies to `operator--()`.

If you provide only one `operator++()` or `operator--()`, it is used for both the prefix and postfix versions. The standard for C++ says that a compiler doesn't have to do this, but most do.

In use, the operators appear very natural. What could be simpler than `d3 = d1 + d2` and `++d3`?

A More Detailed Look

Why does `operator+()` return by value, but `operator++()` return by reference? This is not an accident, but a very important difference.

The addition of two objects changes neither object. That is, `a + b` changes neither `a` nor `b`. Thus, `operator+()` must generate a temporary object into which it can store the result of the addition. This is why `operator+()` constructs an object and returns this object by value to the caller.

Specifically, the following would not work:

```
//this doesn't work
USDollar& operator+(USDollar& s1, USDollar& s2)
{
   unsigned int cents = s1.cents + s2.cents;
   unsigned int dollars = s1.dollars + s2.dollars;
   USDollar result(dollars, cents);
   return result;
}
```

Although this compiles without a squeak of complaint, it generates flaky results. The problem is that the returned reference refers to an object, `result`, whose scope is local to the function. Thus, `result` is out of scope by the time it can be used by the calling function.

Why not allocate a block of memory from the heap, as follows?

```
//this sort of works
USDollar& operator+(USDollar& s1, USDollar& s2)
{
   unsigned int cents = s1.cents + s2.cents;
   unsigned int dollars = s1.dollars + s2.dollars;
   return *new USDollar(dollars, cents);
}
```

This would be fine except that no mechanism exists to return the allocated block of memory to the heap. This type of error is called a memory leak and is often very hard to track down. Although this operator works, it slowly drains memory from the heap each time an addition is performed.

Returning by value forces the compiler to generate a temporary object of its own on the caller's stack. The object generated in the function is then copied into the object as part of the return from `operator+()`.

How long does the temporary object returned from `operator+()` hang around? Originally this was vague, but the standards people got together and decided that such a temporary remains valid until the *extended expression* is complete. The extended expression is everything up to the semicolon. For example, consider the following snippet:

```
SomeClass f();
LotsAClass g();
void fn()
{
   int i;
   i = f() + (2 * g());
}
```

The temporary object returned by `f()` remains in existence while `g()` is invoked and while the multiplication is performed. This object becomes invalid at the semicolon. (Chapter 14 has more to say about temporary objects.)

Unlike `operator+()`, `operator++()` does modify its argument. Thus, you don't need to create a temporary or to return by value. The argument provided can be returned to the caller. In fact, the following function, which returns by value, has a subtle bug:

```
//this isn't 100% reliable either
USDollar operator++(USDollar& s)
{
   s.cents++;
   if (s.cents >= 100)
   {
      s.cents -= 100;
      s.dollars++;
   }
   return s;
}
```

By returning `s` by value, the function forces the compiler to generate a copy of the object. Most of the time, this is okay. But what happens with an expression like `++(++a)`? We would expect `a` to be incremented by 2. With the preceding definition, however, `a` is incremented by 1 and then a copy of `a` — not `a` itself — is incremented a second time.

The general rule is: If the operator changes the value of its argument, return the argument by reference; if the operator does not change the value of either argument, create a new object to hold the results and return that object by value. The input arguments can always be referential.

Operators as Member Functions

An operator, in addition to being implemented as a non-member function, can be a nonstatic member function. Implemented in this way, the example `USDollar` class appears as follows:

```
class USDollar
{
  public:
   USDollar(unsigned int d, unsigned int c);
   USDollar& operator++();
   USDollar  operator+(USDollar& s);
  protected:
   unsigned int dollars;
   unsigned int cents;
};


USDollar::USDollar(unsigned int d, unsigned int c)
{
```

(continued)

(continued)

```
    dollars = d;
    cents = c;
    while (cents >= 100)
   {
       dollars++;
       cents -= 100;
    }
}


//operator+ - add s1 to s2 and return the result
//            in a new object
USDollar USDollar::operator+(USDollar& s2)
{
    unsigned int c = cents   + s2.cents;
    unsigned int d = dollars + s2.dollars;
    USDollar t(d, c);
    return t;
}


//operator++ - increment the specified argument;
//             change the value of the provided object
USDollar& USDollar::operator++()
{
    cents++;
    if (cents >= 100)
    {
       cents -= 100;
       dollars++;
    }
    return *this;
}


int main()
{
    USDollar d1(1, 60);
    USDollar d2(2, 50);
    USDollar d3(0, 0);
    d3 = d1 + d2;         //very straightforward in use
    ++d3;
    return 0;
}
```

The non-member function operator+(USDollar, USDollar) has been rewritten as the nonstatic member function USDollar::operator+(USDollar). At first glance, it appears that the member version has one less argument than the non-member version. If you think about it, however, you'll remember that this is the hidden first argument to all nonstatic member functions.

This difference is most obvious in USDollar::operator+() itself. In the following, I show the non-member and member versions for comparison:

```
//operator+ - the non-member version
USDollar operator+(USDollar& s1, USDollar& s2)
{
    unsigned int cents   = s1.cents   + s2.cents;
    unsigned int dollars = s1.dollars + s2.dollars;
    USDollar d(dollars, cents);
    return d;
}
//operator+ - the member version
USDollar USDollar::operator+(USDollar& s2)
{
    unsigned int c = cents   + s2.cents;
    unsigned int d = dollars + s2.dollars;
    USDollar t(d, c);
    return t;
}
```

You can see that the functions are nearly identical. Where the non-member version adds s1 and s2, however, the member version adds the "current object" — the one pointed at by this — to s2.

REMEMBER

The member version of an operator always has one less argument than the non-member version — the left-hand argument is implicit.

Yet Another Overloading Irritation

Just because you have overloaded operator*(double, USDollar&) doesn't mean you have operator*(USDollar&, double) covered. Because these two operators have different arguments, they have to be overloaded separately. This doesn't have to be a big drag, however.

First, nothing keeps one operator from referring to the other. In the case of operator*(), you would probably do something like the following:

```
USDollar operator*(double f, USDollar& s)
{
   //...implementation of function here...
}
inline USDollar operator*(USDollar& s, double f)
{
   //use the previous definition
   return f * s;
}
```

The second version merely calls the first version with the order of the operators reversed. Making it inline avoids any extra overhead.

A second approach is to provide a conversion path to an existing operator. Suppose, for example, that you provided a constructor to convert a double into a `USDollar`.

```
class USDollar
{
   friend USDollar operator+(USDollar& s1, USDollar& s2);
  public:
   USDollar(int d, int c);
   USDollar(double value)
   {
      dollars = (int)value;
      cents = (int)((value - dollars) * 100 + 0.5);
   }
   //...as before...
}

void fn(USDollar& s)
{
   //all of the following use
   //operator+(USDollar&, USDollar&)
   s = USDollar(1.5) + s;  //explicit conversion...
   s = 1.5 + s;      //...implicit conversion...
   s = s + 1.5;      //...in either order
   s = s + 1;        //even this works by converting the...
                     //...int into a double and then...
                     //...continuing as above
}
```

When to make operators members or non-members

When should the programmer implement an operator as a member and when as a non-member? The following operators must be implemented as member functions:

= Assignment

() Function call

[] Subscript

-> Class membership

Other than the operators listed, there isn't much difference between implementing an operator as a member or as a non-member, with the following exception. An operator like the following could not be implemented as a member function:

```
USDollar operator*(double factor,
   USDollar& s);
```

```
void fn(USDollar& principle)
{
   USDollar interestExpense = interest *
   principle
   //...
}
```

To be a member function, it would have to be a member of class `double`. Mere mortals cannot add operators to the intrinsic classes. Thus, operators such as the preceding must be non-member functions.

If you have access to the class internals, make the overloaded operator a member of the class. This is particularly true if the operator modifies the object upon which it operates.

Now you need to define neither `operator+(double, USDollar&)` nor `operator+(USDollar&, double)`. You can convert the `double` into a `USDollar` and use the `operator+(USDollar&, USDollar&)` already defined.

This conversion can be explicit, as shown in the first addition. It can also remain implicit, in which case C++ performs the conversion automatically.

Providing such conversion paths can save considerable effort by reducing the number of different operators the programmer must define.

WARNING!

Allowing C++ to make these conversions, however, can be dangerous. If multiple possible conversion paths exist, mysterious compiler errors can arise. Suppose, for example, that a constructor `USDollar(int)` existed. Then `s = s + 1` would no longer be allowed because the compiler would not know whether to convert 1 into a `double` and then into a `USDollar` using `USDollar(double)` or convert it directly into a `USDollar` using `USDollar(int)`.

Cast Operator

The cast operator can be overloaded as well. In practice, it looks like the following:

```
class USDollar
{
  public:
   USDollar(double value = 0.0);
   //the following function acts as a cast operator
   operator double()
   {
      return dollars + cents / 100.0;
   }
 protected:
   unsigned int dollars;
   unsigned int cents;
};
USDollar::USDollar(double value)
{
    dollars = (int)value;
    cents = (int)((value - dollars) * 100 + 0.5);
}
int main()
{
   USDollar d1(2.0), d2(1.5), d3;
   //invoke cast operator explicitly...
   d3 = USDollar((double)d1 + (double)d2);
   //...or implicitly
   d3 = d1 + d2;
   return 0;
}
```

A cast operator is the word operator followed by the desired type. The member function `USDollar::operator double()` provides a mechanism for converting an object of class `USDollar` into a double. For reasons that are beyond me, cast operators have no return type. (The argument is, "You don't need it because you can tell the return type from the name." I prefer a bit of consistency.)

As the preceding example shows, conversions using the cast operator can be invoked either explicitly or implicitly. Look at the implicit case carefully.

In trying to make sense of the expression `d3 = d1 + d2` in the earlier code snippet, C++ first looked for member function `USDollar::operator+ (USDollar)`. When that wasn't found, it looked for the non-member version of the same thing, `operator+(USDollar, USDollar)`. Lacking that as well, it started looking for an `operator+()` that it could use by converting one or the other arguments into a different type. Finally it found a match: If it converted both `d1` and `d2` to doubles, it could use the intrinsic `operator+(double, double)`. It then has to convert the resulting double back to `USDollar` using the constructor.

This demonstrates both the advantage and disadvantage of providing a cast operator. Providing a conversion path from `USDollar` to `double` relieves programmers of the need to provide their own set of operators. `USDollar` can just piggyback on the operators defined for double.

On the other hand, providing a conversion path removes the ability of programmers to control which operators are defined. By providing a conversion path to `double`, `USDollar` gets all of `double`'s operators whether they make sense or not. In addition, going through the extra conversions may not be the most efficient process in the world. For example, the simple addition just noted involves three type conversions with all of the attendant function calls, multiplications, divisions, and so on.

WARNING!

Be careful not to provide two conversion paths to the same type. For example, the following is asking for trouble:

```
class A
{
  public:
   A(B& b);
};
class B
{
  public:
   operator A();
};
```

If asked to convert an object of class `B` into an object of class `A`, the compiler will not know whether to use `B`'s cast operator `B:operatorA()` or `A`'s constructor `A::A(B&)`, both of which start out with a `B` and end up making an `A` out of it.

Perhaps the result of the two conversion paths would be the same, but the compiler doesn't know that. It must know which conversion path you really intended. If it can't determine this unambiguously, the compiler throws up its electronic hands and spits out an error.

Chapter 22

The Assignment Operator

In This Chapter

- Introduction to the assignment operator
- Why and when the assignment operator is necessary
- Similarities between the assignment operator and its first cousin, the copy constructor

Chapter 21 demonstrates how to go about overloading operators for classes that you define. Whether or not you start out overloading all operators, you need to learn to overload the assignment operator fairly early. The assignment operator can be overloaded for any user-defined class. By following the pattern provided in this chapter, you can avoid difficulty when overloading this operator.

Why Is Overloading the Assignment Operator So Critical?

C defines only one operator that can be applied to structure types: the assignment operator. In C, the following is legal and results in a bit-wise copy from source to destination:

```
void fn()
{
   struct MyStruct source, destination;
   destination = source;
}
```

To retain compatibility with C, C++ provides a default definition for `operator=()` for all user-defined classes. This default definition performs a member-by-member copy, like the default copy constructor (see Chapter 14 for a discussion of the default copy constructor). However, this default definition can be overloaded by an `operator=()` written specifically for the specified class.

The assignment operator is much like the copy constructor. In use the two look almost identical:

```
void fn(MyClass &mc)
{
    MyClass newMC = mc;    //this is the copy constructor
    newMC = mc;            //this is the assignment operator
}
```

The difference is that when the copy constructor was invoked on `newMC`, the object `newMC` did not already exist. When the assignment operator was invoked on `newMC`, it was already a `MyClass` object in good standing.

REMEMBER

The copy constructor is used when a new object is being created. The assignment operator is used if the left-hand object already exists. Like the copy constructor, an assignment operator should be provided whenever a shallow copy is not appropriate. (See the copy constructor in Chapter 14 for a further discussion of the fascinating topic of shallow copies versus deep copies.)

How Do I Overload the Assignment Operator?

Overloading the assignment operator is similar to overloading any other operator. For example, an assignment operator has been provided as an inline member function for the following class `Name`. (Remember, the assignment operator must be a member function of the class.)

```
#include <stdlib.h>
#include <string.h>
#include <ctype.h>
class Name
{
  public:
    Name()
    {
        pName = (char*)0;
    }
    Name(char *pN)
    {
        copyName(pN);
    }
    Name(Name& s)
    {
```

```
      copyName(s.pName);
    }
   ~Name()
    {
      deleteName();
    }
    //assignment operator
    Name& operator=(Name& s)
    {
      //delete existing stuff...
      deleteName();
      //...before replacing with new stuff
      copyName(s.pName);
      //return reference to existing object
      return *this;
    }
  protected:
    void copyName(char *pN);
    void deleteName();
    char *pName;
};
//copyName() - allocate heap memory to store name
void Name::copyName(char *pN)
{
    pName = (char*)malloc(strlen(pN) + 1);
    if (pName)
    {
      strcpy(pName, pN);
    }
}
//deleteName() - return heap memory
void Name::deleteName()
{
    if (pName)
    {
      delete pName;
      pName = 0;
    }
}

int main()
{
 Name s("Claudette");
    Name t("temporary");
    t = s;           //this invokes the assignment operator
    return 0;
}
```

The class Name retains a person's name in memory, which it allocates from the heap in the constructor. The constructors and destructor for class Name are similar to those described in Parts III and IV.

The assignment operator appears with the name operator=(). Notice how the assignment operator looks like a destructor followed by a copy constructor. This is typical. Consider the assignment in the example. The object t already has a name associated with it (temporary). In the assignment t = s, you must first call deleteName() to return to the heap the memory that the original name occupies. Only then can you call copyName() to allocate new memory into which to store the new name.

The copy constructor did not need to call deleteName() because the object didn't already exist. Therefore, memory had not already been assigned to the object when the constructor was invoked.

In general, an assignment operator has two parts. The first part resembles a destructor in that it deletes the assets that the object already owns. The second part resembles a copy constructor in that it allocates new assets.

Notice two details. First, the return type of operator=() is Name&. This matches the semantics of C. I could have made the return type void. If I did, however, the following would not work:

```
void otherFn(Name&);
void fn(Name& oldN)
{
   Name newN;
   otherFn(newN = oldN);
}
```

The results of the assignment newN = oldN would be void, the return type of operator=(), which does not match the prototype of otherFn(). Declaring operator=() to return a reference to the "current" object and returning *this retains the C semantics that you have all come to know and love.

The second detail to notice is that operator=() was written as a member function. Unlike other operators, the assignment operator cannot be overloaded with a non-member function.

The assignment operator must be a nonstatic member function. The special assignment operators, such as += and *=, have no special restrictions and can be non-member functions.

Protection

Providing your class with an assignment operator can add considerable flexibility to the application code. However, if this is too much for you or you can't make copies of your object, overloading the assignment operator with a protected or private function will keep anyone from accidentally making an unauthorized shallow copy. For example:

```
class Name
{
  //...just like before...
  protected:
   //assignment operator
   Name& operator=(Name& s)
   {
      return *this;
   }
};
```

With this definition, assignments such as the following are precluded:

```
void fn(Name &n)
{
    Name newN;
    newN = n;        //generates a compiler error -
                     //function has no access to op=()
}
```

This copy protection for classes may save you the trouble of overloading the assignment operator.

Chapter 23

Stream I/O

In This Chapter

- Rediscovering stream I/O as an overloaded operator
- Using stream file I/O
- Using stream buffer I/O
- Writing your own inserters and extractors
- Going behind the scenes with manipulators

Chapter 6 presents a quick look at stream I/O. What Chapter 6 didn't say was that stream I/O is not a new keyword or an exotic new syntax but just the right and left shift operators overloaded to perform input and output, respectively (you weren't ready for it back then). (If you skipped over it somehow, Chapter 21 explains overloading operators.)

In this chapter, I explain stream I/O in more detail. I must warn you that stream I/O is too large a topic to be covered completely in a single chapter — entire books are devoted to this one topic. I can get you started, though, so that you can perform the main operations.

How Does Stream I/O Work?

The operators that make up stream I/O are defined in the include file `iostream.h`. This file includes prototypes for several `operator>>()` and `operator<<()` functions. The code for these functions is included in the standard library, which your C++ program links with.

```
//for input we have:
istream& operator>>(istream& source, char *pDest);
istream& operator>>(istream& source, int  &dest);
istream& operator>>(istream& source, char &dest);
//...and so forth...
//for output we have:
```

(continued)

(continued)

```
ostream& operator<<(ostream& dest, char *pSource);
ostream& operator<<(ostream& dest, int   source);
ostream& operator<<(ostream& dest, char  source);
//...and so it goes...
```

Buzzword time: When overloaded to perform I/O, `operator>>()` is called the extractor and `operator<<()` is called the inserter.

Look in detail at what happens when I write the following:

```
#include <iostream.h>
void fn()
{
   cout << "My name is Randy\n";
}
```

First, C++ determines that the left-hand argument is of type `ostream` and the right-hand argument is of type `char*`. Armed with this knowledge, it finds the prototype `operator<<(ostream&, char*)` in `iostream.h`. C++ generates a call to the function for the `char*` inserter, passing the function the string `"My name is Randy\n"` and the object `cout` as the two arguments. That is, it makes the call `operator<<(cout, "My name is Randy\n")`. The `char*` inserter function, which is part of the standard C++ library, performs the requested output.

How did the compiler know that `cout` is of class `ostream`? This and a few other global objects are also declared in `iostream.h`. A list is shown in Table 23-1. These objects are constructed automatically at program start-up, before `main()` gets control.

This is analogous to the way `stdin` and `stdout` are opened by the C start-up code.

Table 23-1 Standard Stream I/O Objects

Object	*Class*	*Purpose*
cin	istream	Standard input
cout	ostream	Standard output
cerr	ostream	Standard error output
clog	ostream	Standard printer output

But why the shift operators?

In Chapter 6, I explain the desirability of stream I/O (mostly it's type safe and extensible). However, you might ask, "Why use the shift operators? Why not use another operator? Why not use another mechanism?"

It didn't have to be the shift operators. The developers of C++ could have agreed on some standard function name such as `output()` to perform output and simply overloaded that function name for all the intrinsic types. Compound output would have looked something like the following:

```
void displayName(char *pName, int age)
{
   output(cout, "The name passed was ");
   output(cout, pName);
   output(cout, "; his age is ");
   output(cout, age);
   output(cout, "\n");
}
```

The left shift operator was chosen instead for several reasons. First, it's a binary operator. This means that you can make the `ostream` object the left-hand argument and the output object the right-hand argument. Second, left shift is a very low priority operator. Thus, expressions such as the following work as expected:

```
#include <iostream.h>
void fn(int a, int b) {
   cout << "a + b" << a + b << "\n";
//operator+ has higher precedence than
   //operator<<
//so this expression is interpreted as
// cout << "a + b" << (a + b) << "\n";
//and not interpreted as
// (cout << "a + b" << a) + (b << "\n");
}
```

Third, the left shift operator binds from left to right. This is what allows you to string output statements together. For example, the previous function is interpreted as follows:

```
#include <iostream.h>
void fn(int a, int b) {
   ((cout << "a + b") << a + b) << "\n";
}
```

But having said all this, the real reason is probably just that it looks really neat. The double less than, <<, looks like something is moving out of the code, and the double greater than, >>, looks like something is coming in. And, hey, why not?

And just what is an `ostream` anyway? An `ostream` object contains the members necessary to keep track of output. In a similar vein, `istream` describes an input stream.

C STUFF

The C equivalent is struct `FILE`, which is defined in `stdio.h`. The function `fopen()` opens a file for input and output. `fopen()` returns a pointer to a `FILE` object into which it has stored the information necessary for subsequent I/O operations. This object is returned in calls to the `fx()` functions, such as `fprintf()`, `fscanf()`, and `fgets()`.

Also defined as part of the stream I/O library are a number of subclasses of `ostream` and `istream`. These subclasses are used for input and output to files and internal buffers.

The `fstream` Subclasses

The subclasses `ofstream`, `ifstream`, and `fstream` are defined in the include file `fstream.h` to perform stream input and output to a disk file in much the way the `fx()` functions (`fprintf()`, `fscanf()`, `fopen()`, `fclose()`, and others) perform file I/O in C. These three classes share a number of member functions that are used to control input and output, many of them inherited from `istream` and `ostream`. A complete list is provided with your compiler documentation, but let me get you started.

Class `ofstream`, which is used to perform file output, has several constructors, the most useful of which is

```
ofstream::ofstream(char *pFileName,
          int mode = ios::out,
          int prot = filebuff::openprot);
```

The first argument is a pointer to the name of the file to open. The second and third arguments specify how the file will be opened. The legal values for `mode` are listed in Table 23-2 and those for `prot` in Table 23-3. These values are bit fields that are ORed together. (The classes `ios` and `filebuff` are both parent classes of `ostream`.)

Table 23-2 Values for `mode` in the `ofstream` Constructor

Flag	*Meaning*
ios::ate	Append to the end of the file, if it exists
ios::in	Open file for input (implied for `istream`)
ios::out	Open file for output (implied for `ostream`)
ios::trunc	Truncate file if it exists (default)
ios::nocreate	If file doesn't already exist, return error
ios::noreplace	If file does exist, return error
ios::binary	Open file in binary mode (alternative is text mode)

Table 23-3 Values for `prot` in the `ofstream` Constructor

Flag	*Meaning*
filebuf::openprot	Compatibility sharing mode
filebuf::sh_none	Exclusive; no sharing
filebuf::sh_read	Read sharing allowed
filebuf::sh_write	Write sharing allowed

For example, the following program opens the file MYNAME and then writes some important and absolutely true information into that file:

```
#include <fstream.h>
void fn()
{
   //open the text file MYNAME for writing - truncate
   //whatever's there now
   ofstream myn("MYNAME");
   myn << "Randy Davis is suave and handsome\n"
       << "and definitely not balding prematurely\n";
}
```

The constructor `ofstream::ofstream(char*)` expects only a filename and provides defaults for the other file modes. If the file MYNAME already exists, it is truncated; otherwise, MYNAME is created. In addition, the file is opened in compatibility-sharing mode.

A second constructor `ofstream::ofstream(char*, int)` enables the programmer to specify other file I/O modes. For example, if I wanted to open the file in binary mode and append to the end of the file if the file already exists, I would create the `ostream` object as follows. (In binary mode, new-lines are not converted to carriage returns and line feeds on output nor converted back to new-lines on input.)

```
void fn()
{
   //open the binary file BINFILE for writing; if it
   //exists, append to end of whatever's already there
   ofstream bfile("BINFILE", ios::binary | ios::ate);
   //...continue on as before...
}
```

The member function `bad()` returns 1 if the file object has an error. To check whether the file was opened properly in the earlier example, I would have coded the following:

```
#include <fstream.h>
void fn()
{
   ofstream myn("MYNAME");
   if (myn.bad())         //if the open didn't work...
   {
      cerr << "Error opening file MYNAME\n";
      return;             //...output error and quit
   }
```

(continued)

(continued)

```
    myn << "Randy Davis is suave and handsome\n"
        << "and definitely not balding prematurely\n";
}
```

All attempts to output to an `ofstream` object that has an error have no effect until the error has been cleared by calling the member function `clear()`.

The destructor for class `ofstream` automatically closes the file. In the preceding example, the file was closed when the function exited.

Class `ifstream` works much the same way for input, as the following example demonstrates:

```
#include <fstream.h>
void fn()
{
   //open file for reading; don't create the file
   //if it isn't there

   ifstream bankStatement("STATEMNT", ios::nocreate);
   if (bankStatement.bad())
   {
      cerr << "Couldn't find bank statement\n";
      return;
   }
   while (!bankStatement.eof())
   {
      bankStatement >> accountNumber >> amount;
      //...process this withdrawal
   }
}
```

The function opens the file STATEMNT by constructing the object `bankStatement`. If the file does not exist, it is not created. (You assume that the file has information for you, so it wouldn't make much sense to create a new, empty file.) If the object is bad (for example, if the object was not created), the function outputs an error message and exits. Otherwise, the function loops, reading the `accountNumber` and `withdrawal` amount until the file is empty (end-of-file is true).

An attempt to read an `ifstream` object that has the error flag set, indicating a previous error, returns immediately without reading anything.

The class `fstream` is like an `ifstream` and an `ofstream` combined. (In fact, it inherits from both.) An object of class `fstream` can be created for input or output or both.

The strstream *Subclasses*

The classes `istrstream`, `ostrstream`, and `strstream` are defined in the include file `strstrea.h`. (The filename appears to be truncated because MS-DOS allows no more than eight characters for a filename.) These classes allow the operations defined for files by the `fstream` classes to be applied to character strings in memory. This is much like the `sx()` functions in C, `sprintf()` and `sscanf()`.

Although Windows 95 and NT relieve the eight plus three name restriction for the PC, `strstrea.h` remains truncated for historical reasons.

For example, the following code snippet parses the data in a character string using stream input:

```
#include <strstrea.h>
char* parseString(char *pString)
{
    //associate an istrstream object with the input
    //character string
    istrstream inp(pString, 0);

    //now input from that object
    int accountNumber;
    float balance;
    inp >> accountNumber >> balance;

    //allocate a buffer and associate an
    //ostrstream object with it
    char *pBuffer = new char[128];
    ostrstream out(pBuffer, 128);

    //output to that object
    out << "account number = " << accountNumber
        << ", balance = $" << balance;
        return pBuffer;
}
```

For example, `pString` might point to the following string:

```
"1234 100.0"
```

The object `inp` is associated with that string by the constructor for `istrstream`. The second argument to the constructor is the length of the string. In this example, the argument is 0, which means "read until you get to the terminating NULL."

On the output side, the object `out` is associated with the buffer pointed to by `pBuffer`. Here again, the second argument to the constructor is the length of the buffer. A third argument, which corresponds to the mode, defaults to `ios::out`. However, you can set this argument to `ios::ate`, if you want the output to append to the end of whatever is already in the buffer rather than overwrite it.

The buffer returned in the preceding code snippet given the example input would contain the string

```
"account number = 1234, balance = $100.00"
```

Manipulators

You can use stream I/O to output numbers and character strings using default formats. Usually the defaults are fine, but sometimes they don't cut it.

For example, I for one was less than tickled when the total from the example BUDGET program came back 249.600006 instead of 249.6 (or, better yet, 249.60). There must be a way to bend the defaults to my desires. True to form, C++ provides not one way but two ways to control the format of output.

Depending on the default settings of your compiler, you might get 249.6 as your output. Nevertheless, you really want 249.60.

First, the format can be controlled by invoking a series of member functions on the stream object. For example, the number of significant digits to display is set using the function `precision()` as follows:

```
#include <iostream.h>
void fn(float interest, float dollarAmount)
{
    cout << "Dollar amount = ";
    cout.precision(2);
    cout << dollarAmount;
    cout.precision(4);
    cout << interest
         << "\n";
}
```

In this example, the function `precision()` sets the precision to 2 immediately before outputting the value `dollarAmount`. This gives you a number such as 249.60, the nice type of result you want. It then sets the precision to 4 before outputting the interest.

A second approach is through what are called manipulators. (Sounds like someone behind the scenes of the New York Stock Exchange, doesn't it? Well, manipulators are every bit as sneaky.) Manipulators are objects defined in the include file `iomanip.h` to have the same effect as the member function calls. (You must include `iomanip.h` to have access to the manipulators.) The only advantage to manipulators is that the program can insert them directly into the stream rather than resort to a separate function call.

If you rewrite the preceding example to use manipulators, the program appears as follows:

```
#include <iostream.h>
#include <iomanip.h>
void fn(float interest, float dollarAmount)
{
   cout << "Dollar amount = "
        << setprecision(2) << dollarAmount
        << setprecision(4) << interest
        << "\n";
}
```

The most common manipulators and their corresponding meanings are given in Table 23-4.

Table 23-4 Common Manipulators and Stream Format Control Functions

Manipulator	*Member Function*	*Description*
dec	flags(10)	Set radix to 10
hex	flags(16)	Set radix to 16
oct	flags(8)	Set radix to 8
setfill(c)	fill(c)	Set the fill character to c
setprecision(c)	precision(c)	Set display precision to c
setw(n) characters *	width(n)	Set width of field to n

* This returns to its default value after the next field is output.

Watch out for the width parameter (`width()` function and `setw()` manipulator). Most parameters retain their value until they are specifically reset by a subsequent call, but the width parameter does not. The width parameter is reset to its default value as soon as the next output is performed. For example, you might expect the following to produce two eight-character integers:

```
#include <iostream.h>
#include <iomanip.h>
void fn()
{
   cout << setw(8)       //width is 8...
        << 10            //...for the 10, but...
        << 20            //...default for the 20
        << "\n";
}
```

What you get, however, is an eight-character integer followed by a two-character integer. To get two eight-character output fields, the following is necessary:

```
#include <iostream.h>
#include <iomanip.h>
void fn()
{
   cout << setw(8)       //set the width...
        << 10
        << setw(8)       //...now reset it
        << 20
        << "\n";
}
```

Thus, if you have several objects to output and the default width is not good enough, you must include a `setw()` call for each object.

Which way is better, manipulators or member function calls? Member functions provide a bit more control because there are more of them. In addition, the member functions always return the previous setting so you know how to restore it (if you want). Finally, a query version of each member function exists to enable you to just ask what the current setting is without changing it. This is shown in the following example:

```
#include <iostream.h>
void fn(float value)
{
   int previousPrecision;

   //...doing stuff here...

   //you can ask what the current precision is:
   previousPrecision = cout.precision();

   //or you can save the old value when you change it
   previousPrecision = cout.precision(2);
```

```
    cout << value;

    //now restore the precision to previous value
    cout.precision(previousPrecision);
    //...do more neat stuff...
}
```

Even with all these features, the manipulators are the more common, probably because they look neat. Use whatever you prefer, but be prepared to see both in other peoples' code.

Custom Inserters

The fact that C++ overloads the left shift operator to perform output is really exciting because you are free to overload the same operator to perform output on classes you define. (Okay, really exciting is a bit extreme. I suppose finding out that you just won the lottery would be really exciting. This falls more in the category of syntactically satisfying.)

This is the much-vaunted extensibility of stream I/O that I have alluded to but avoided explaining until now. Consider, for example, the `USDollar` class introduced in Chapter 21, extended with a `display()` member function:

```
#include <iostream.h>
#include <iomanip.h>
class USDollar
{
  public:
   USDollar(double v = 0.0)
   {
      dollars = v;
      cents = int((v - dollars) * 100.0 + 0.5);
   }
   operator double()
   {
      return dollars + cents / 100.0;
   }
   void display(ostream& out)
   {
      out << '$' << dollars << '.'
          //set fill to 0's for cents
          << setfill('0') << setw(2) << cents
          //now put it back to spaces
          << setfill(' ');
```

(continued)

(continued)

```
    }

  protected:
    unsigned int dollars;
    unsigned int cents;
};

//operator<< - overload the inserter for our class
ostream& operator<< (ostream& o, USDollar& d)
{
    d.display(o);
    return o;
}

int main()
{
    USDollar usd(1.50);
    cout << "Initially usd = " << usd << "\n";
    usd = 2.0 * usd;
    cout << "then usd = " << usd << "\n";
    return 0;
}
```

The `display()` function starts by displaying $, the dollar amount, and the obligatory decimal point. Notice that output is to whatever `ostream` object it is passed and not necessarily just to `cout`. This allows the same function to be used on `fstream` and `strstream` objects, both of which are subclasses of `ostream`.

When it comes time to display the cents amount, `display()` sets the width to two positions and the leading character to 0. This ensures that numbers smaller than 10 display properly.

Notice how class `USDollar`, instead of accessing the `display()` function directly, also defines an `operator<<(ostream&, USDollar&)`. The programmer can now output `USDollar` objects with the same ease and grace of the intrinsic types, as the example `main()` function demonstrates.

The output from this program is as follows:

```
Initially usd = $1.50
then usd = $3.00
```

You may wonder why the `operator<<()` returns the `ostream` object passed to it. This allows the operator to be chained with other inserters in a single expression. Because `operator<<()` binds from left to right, the following expression

```
void fn(USDollar& usd, float i)
{
   cout << "Amount " << usd << ", interest = " << i;
}
```

is interpreted as

```
void fn(USDollar& usd, float i)
{
   (((cout << "Amount ") << usd) << ", interest = ") << i;
}
```

The first insertion outputs the string `"Amount"` to cout. The result of this expression is the object `cout`, which is then passed to `operator<<(ostream&, USDollar&)`. It is important that this operator return its `ostream` object so that the object can be passed to the next inserter in turn.

Had you declared the return type of the insertion operator `void`, a perfectly valid usage, such as the preceding example, would generate a compiler error because you can't insert a string into a `void`. The following error is worse because it's more difficult to find:

```
ostream& operator<<(ostream& os, USDollar& usd)
{
   usd.display(os);
   return cout;
}
```

Notice that this function returns not the `ostream` object it was given but the ostream object `cout`. This is easy to do because `cout` is far and away the most commonly referenced `ostream` object. (`cout` has already been voted into the `ostream` Hall of Fame.)

This problem doesn't become visible until the following comes along:

```
void storeAccounts(int account,
                   USDollar balance,
                   char *pName)
{
   ofstream outFile("ACCOUNTS", ios::ate);
   outFile << account << balance << pName;
}
```

The `int` account outputs to `outFile` through the function `operator<<(ostream&, int&)`, which returns `outFile`. Then `USDollar` outputs to `outFile` through `operator<<(ostream&, USDollar&)`, which incorrectly returns `cout`, not `outFile`. Now `pName` outputs to `cout` instead of to the file as intended.

Smart Inserters

Many times, you would like to make the inserter smart. That is, you would like to say `cout << baseClassObject` and let C++ choose the proper subclass inserter in the same way that it chooses the proper virtual member function. Because the inserter is not a member function, you cannot declare it virtual directly. This is not a problem for the clever C++ programmer, as the following example demonstrates:

```
#include <iostream.h>
#include <iomanip.h>
class Currency
{
  public:
   Currency(double v = 0.0)
   {
      unit = v;
      cent = int((v - unit) * 100.0 + 0.5);
   }
   virtual void display(ostream& out) = 0;

  protected:
   unsigned int unit;
   unsigned int cent;
};

class USDollar : public Currency
{
  public:
   USDollar(double v = 0.0) : Currency(v)
   {
   }
   //display $123.00
   virtual void display(ostream& out)
   {
      out << '$' << unit << '.'
          << setfill('0') << setw(2) << cent
          << setfill(' ');
   }
```

```
};

class DMark : public Currency
{
 public:
   DMark(double v = 0.0) : Currency(v)
   {
   }
   //display 123.00DM
   virtual void display(ostream& out)
   {
      out << unit << '.'
          //set fill to 0's for cents
          << setfill('0') << setw(2) << cent
          //now put it back to spaces
          << setfill(' ')
          << " DM";
   }
};

ostream& operator<< (ostream& o, Currency& c)
{
   c.display(o);
   return o;
}

void fn(Currency& c)
{
   //the following output is polymorphic because
   //operator(ostream&, Currency&) is through a virtual
   //member function
   cout << "Deposit was " << c
        << "\n";
}
int main()
{
   //create a dollar and output it using the
   //proper format for a dollar
   USDollar usd(1.50);
   fn(usd);

   //now create a DMark and output it using its own format
   DMark d(3.00);
   fn(d);
   return 0;
}
```

The class `Currency` has two subclasses, `USDollar` and `DMark`. In `Currency`, the `display()` function is declared `pure virtual`. In each of the two subclasses, this function is overloaded with a `display()` function to output the object in the proper format for that type. The call to `display()` in `operator<<()` is now a virtual call. Thus, when `operator<<()` is passed `USDollar`, it outputs the object as a dollar. When passed `DMark`, it outputs the object as a deutsche mark.

Thus, although `operator<<()` is not virtual, because it invokes a virtual function the result is virtual perfection:

```
Deposit was $1.50
Deposit was 3.00 DM
```

This is another reason why I prefer to perform the work of output in a member function and let the non-member operator refer to that function.

Chapter 24

Object Validation and Signature Fields

In This Chapter

- Validating objects
- The results of invalid objects
- Turning validation off and on

Object validation is not actually a feature of C++, but I think it should be in every C++ programmer's toolbox. Therefore, I include it in this book.

Programmers, especially beginning programmers, complain a lot about pointers. One problem you may have is figuring out whether to use one asterisk or two asterisks and whether that ampersand is really necessary. Even after you get the compiler to accept your input, you're not out of the woods. Making sure that your pointers point to the right things is just as important.

Problems with pointers never correct themselves. For example, suppose that you have a linked list with a broken link. That is, one of the pointers in the linked list points not to the next member in the list but off into space. As your program comes puffing along through this linked list, it eventually encounters this diversion. With no way of knowing its mistake, the program vectors off into uncharted memory like a train that has jumped the track. The chances that the program will find the way back home are just about as good as the chances of a derailed train hopping back onto the track.

In addition, pointer problems often don't become apparent until the program has progressed some distance from the source of the problem. The broken link in the example may exist for some time before the program encounters it and crashes. This makes finding pointer problems extremely difficult.

Of course, the best approach is to not make any pointer mistakes. Write only perfect programs and you don't have to worry about pointer problems. Barring that, the next best approach is to identify pointer problems as close to the source as possible so that the problem can be identified and corrected.

What strong typing is and what it is not

Many programmers misunderstand when I say, "Invoke a member function with an invalid object address." I get responses like, "But that's what strong typing is for! If I call function `fn(MyClass*)` with something other than a pointer to `MyClass`, the compiler is supposed to generate a compiler error!" Not so. Strong typing catches problems like the following:

```
void fn2(MyClass*);
void fn()
{
    ScmeOtherClass soc;
    fn2(&soc);         //the argument type is
                       //wrong
}
```

Here the object is valid. That is, it's a valid `SomeOtherClass` object, but it's not the type of object `fn2()` is expecting.

The type of problem I'm looking for is shown in the following:

```
void fn2(MyClass*);
void fn()
{
  MyClass *pMC;
  fn2(pMC);
//the argument type is correct
}
```

Here `pMC` is declared to be a pointer to a `MyClass` object, which is what `fn2()` expects. But `pMC` doesn't, in fact, point to a `MyClass` object because it hasn't been initialized yet. Like all uninitialized auto variables, it contains garbage, white noise, nada. This is the type of problem to which I refer here. (This example is obvious, but pointer problems can arise in myriad and subtle ways.)

Accessing Data Members with Invalid Pointers

In order to recognize the problems caused by invalid pointers, seeing the results of using an invalid pointer is helpful. Consider something like the following class definition:

```
class SomeClass
{
   int member1;
   int member2;
};
```

The data members `member1` and `member2` represent offsets within some object (in the case of `fn2()`, the object pointed at by `pObj`). You may assume that the offset of `member1` is 0 and that of `member2` is 4 (or some other small multiple of 2). Even though the standard doesn't say that this is, in fact, the case, for the purposes of this discussion I say that it is.

Now consider the following simple code snippet:

```
void fn2(SomeClass* pObj)
{
   pObj->member2 = 0;  // initialize 'member2'
}
void fn()
{
    SomeClass obj;
    SomeClass *pObj = &obj;

    fn2(pObj);          // pass the first object to fn2()

    pObj++;             // increment the pointer; now
                        // it points "nowhere"

    fn2(pObj)           // pass the now invalid pointer
                        // to fn2()
}
```

The function `fn2()` initializes the member `member2` to 0. It does this by accepting the pointer passed it, `pObj`, adding 4 to it (the offset of `member2`), and then storing a 0 at that address.

The function `fn()` first allocates an object of class `SomeClass` off of the stack. It then stores the address of this object in the pointer `pObj`. Next, it passes this address to the function `fn2()`. `fn2()` goes through the steps outlined in the previous paragraph to set `obj.member2` to 0.

Next `fn()` increments the pointer `pObj`, which moves it to the next `SomeClass` object. The only problem is, there isn't another `SomeClass` object. The result is that `pObj` now points to some random data on the stack. Unfortunately, not knowing this error, `fn2()` goes through the same steps of adding 4 and storing a 0 at the resulting address, blissfully ignorant of the damage it may be causing.

The main problem with errors involving invalid pointers is that they tend to have erratic results. If the resulting address in the preceding example is somewhere in unused memory, pointing to invalid memory doesn't matter, and the program will continue to work until some seemingly unimportant change is made that renders the target address critical to the workings of the program.

Invoking Member Functions with Invalid Pointers

Consider the consequences of invoking a member function with an invalid object address.

Three different possibilities exist, as shown in the following example function:

```
class MyClass
{
  public:
   static  void staticFn();    //case 1
           void normalFn();    //case 2
   virtual void virtualFn();   //case 3
};


void fn(MyClass *pMC)
{
   pMC->staticFn();
   pMC->normalFn();
   pMC->virtualFn();
}
```

If `pMC` doesn't contain a valid address upon entry into the function `fn()`, what is the effect of each of the three function calls?

Case 1: Static functions don't use the address of the object; only the type of the object is used to determine the class. Therefore, invoking a static member function with an invalid object address has no deleterious effect.

Case 2: Normal functions receive the address of the current object as the hidden first argument, the `this` pointer. When invoked with a bad object address, the `this` pointer is invalid. If the function tries to save anything into the current object, it writes into uncharted memory. Whatever the function tries to read from the object is garbage. Therefore, invoking a normal function with an invalid object address causes erratic results and may result in memory being overwritten.

Case 3: Virtual functions use information hidden in the object to find the function to call. If the object is invalid, the call is immediately fatal.

Table 24-1 summarizes these results.

Table 24-1 Results of Calling a Member Function with a Bad Object

Function Type	*Result*
Static	No problem
Normal	Unpredictable and maybe fatal results
Virtual	Immediately fatal

TECHNICAL STUFF

You can recognize the results of invoking a virtual member function with an invalid address in the debugger. An attempt to single step into the call hangs the computer or terminates the computer immediately, without ever arriving at the function.

You may think that Case 3 is the worst case, but actually it's probably the best for the developer. The fact that the program immediately bombs forces the programmer to find and fix the problem. The worst case is undoubtedly Case 2 because it tends to be erratic, sometimes crashing, sometimes not.

So What Do You Do about Invalid Pointers?

Given what havoc an invalid pointer can wreak, careful C++ programmers outfit their classes with extra bulwarking to detect when the object is invalid, as would be the case when using an invalid pointer. For example, the programmer can define a nonstatic data member to contain a signature field unique to the class. This field is initialized in the constructors and cleared in the destructor. By checking this field, the programmer can determine at other times whether the object is valid.

The following shows the class `USDollar` outfitted with a signature field:

```
#include <iostream.h>
#include <iomanip.h>
class USDollar
{
  public:
   USDollar(double v = 0.0)
   {
      dollars = v;
      cents = int((v - dollars) * 100.0 + 0.5);
      signature = 0x1234;    //it's a valid object now
```

(continued)

(continued)

```
   }
  ~USDollar()
   {
      if (isLegal("destructor"))
      {
         signature = 0;       //it's no longer a valid object
      }
   }
   operator double()
   {
      if (isLegal("double"))
      {
         return dollars + cents / 100.0;
      }
      else
      {
         return 0.0;
      }
   }
   void display(ostream& out)
   {
      if (isLegal("display"))
      {
         out << '$' << dollars << '.'
             << setfill('0') << setw(2) << cents
             << setfill(' ');
      }
   }
   int isLegal(char *pFunc);
  protected:
   unsigned int signature;
   unsigned int dollars;
   unsigned int cents;
};
//isLegal - check the signature field. If it doesn't
//          check out, generate error and return indicator
int USDollar::isLegal(char *pFunc)
{
   if (signature != 0x1234)
   {
      cerr << "\nInvalid USDollar object address passed to "
           << pFunc
           << "\n";
      return 0;
   }
```

```
    return 1;
}
ostream& operator<< (ostream& o, USDollar& d)
{
    d.display(o);
    return o;
}

void printSalesTax(USDollar &amount)
{
    cout << "Tax on "
         << amount
         << " = "
         << USDollar(0.0825 * amount)
         << "\n";
}
int main()
{
     cout << "First case\n";
    USDollar usd(1.50);
    printSalesTax(usd);
    cout << "\n";
    cout << "Second case\n";
    USDollar *pUSD;
    printSalesTax(*pUSD);
    return 0;
}
```

The signature field is set in the constructor and cleared in the destructor. Each class presumably gets a unique signature value. Instead of checking the signature field directly, a member function `isLegal()` is used to compare the signature with the expected 0x1234. If there is not a match, `isLegal()` outputs a warning message and returns an indication to the caller.

I added a call to `isLegal()` to the beginning of each member function. If the signature does not check out, each function returns without storing anything in the faulty object and thereby doing unknown harm. (The warning message from `isLegal()` alerts the programmer to the problem.)

The little program provided shows how `isLegal()` works. The first dollar amount, `usd`, is declared properly. The addition of `isLegal()` has no visible effect on the output.

The pointer `pUSD`, however, has not been declared properly. The programmer has forgotten to initialize it. Thus, `pUSD` doesn't point to anything in particular.

When printSalesTax() attempts to use this invalid object, the error messages start to fly, making the problem immediately obvious:

```
First case
Tax on $1.50 = $0.12
Second case
Invalid USDollar object address passed to double
Tax on
Invalid USDollar object address passed to display
 = $0.00
```

When these error messages begin to appear, the programmer knows to set a breakpoint on the output statement in isLegal() and rerun the program. As soon as the breakpoint is encountered, the programmer can then backtrack to determine how things managed to get so screwed up.

What Else Can isLegal() Do?

Although the test function isLegal() is not limited to checking the signature field, this is the single most important check it can make. You can add any other checks you like as well.

For a class Student, you may want to check that the social security number is nine digits, that the name is present and legal, that the age is not less than 0 or more than 150, and on and on and on. The more checks you can add, the more likely you are to catch bugs during debugging before they slip unnoticed into the field.

You may be worried about the overhead introduced by isLegal(), especially because it is called at the beginning of every member function. "I can't afford that," you say. "My programs have to be lean and efficient."

This is a classic case of having your cake and eating it, too. After you have completed debugging the program, replace the definition of isLegal() with an inline "do nothing" version as follows:

```
class USDollar
{
   //...everything the same as before...
   int isLegal(char *pF)
   {
      return 1;
   }
   //...carry on...
};
```

Calling this function generates no overhead (especially if the function is inlined). You should keep a copy of the original definition of `isLegal()`, however, so that you can reinstall it if an unexpected bug pops up.

A really shrewd optimizer (which is what you want to be using if you're generating the final version anyway) may even notice that the error paths of the calling functions have been rendered unreachable by an `isLegal()` that always returns 1, and consequently remove the "dead code."

Borland C++ and Microsoft Visual C++ are really shrewd optimizers.

Saving Time with Object Validation

Object validation is a voluntary technique. To many, it may seem like too much work. But I assure you that object validation saves much more time than it costs. Pointer problems are often difficult and time-consuming to track down. Avoiding such problems or catching them early is worth the few extra checks.

Chapter 25

Handling Errors — Exceptions

In This Chapter

- Introducing exceptions
- Finding what's wrong with good ol' error returns
- Examining throwing and catching exceptions more closely
- Packing more heat into that throw

C++ introduces a new mechanism for capturing and handling errors. Called *exceptions,* this mechanism is based on the keywords `try`, `catch`, and `throw` (that's right, more variable names that you can't use). In outline, it works like this: A function `try`s to get through a piece of code. If the code detects a problem, it `throw`s an error indication that the calling function must `catch`.

The following code snippet demonstrates how that works in 1s and 0s:

```
#include <iostream.h>

// factorial - compute factorial
int factorial(int n)
{
    // you can't handle negative values of n
    if (n < 0)
    {
        throw "Argument for factorial negative";
    }

    // go ahead and calculate factorial
    int accum = 1;
    while(n > 0)
    {
        accum *= n;
        n--;
    }
```

(continued)

(continued)

```
return accum;
}

// any old function will do
void someFunc()
{
    try
    {
        // this will generate an exception
        cout << "Factorial of -1 is " << factorial(-1) << endl;

        // control will never get here
        cout << "Factorial of 10 is " << factorial(10) << endl;
    }
    // control passes here
    catch(char* pError)
    {
        cout << "Error occured: " << pError << endl;
    }
}
```

`someFunc()` starts out by creating a block outfitted with the `try` keyword. Within this block, it can do whatever it wants. In this case, `someFunc()` attempts to calculate the factorial of a negative number. Not to be hoodwinked, the clever `factorial()` function detects the bogus request and throws an error indication using the `throw` keyword. Control passes to the `catch` phrase, which immediately follows the closing brace of the `try` block. The second call to `factorial()` is not performed.

Why Do I Need a New Error Mechanism?

What's wrong with error returns like FORTRAN used to make? Factorials cannot be negative, so I could have said something like "Okay, if `factorial()` detects an error, it will return a negative number. The actual value will indicate the source of the problem." What's wrong with that? That's how it's been accomplished for ages.

Unfortunately, several problems arise. First, although it's true that the result of a factorial cannot be negative, other functions are not so lucky. For example, you can't take the log of a negative number either, but the negative return value trick won't work here — logarithms can be either negative or positive.

Second, there's just so much information that you can store in an integer. Maybe you can have -1 for "argument is negative" and -2 for "argument is too large." But if the argument is too large, I'd like to know what the argument was because it may help me to debug the problem. There's no place to store that type of information.

Third, the processing of error returns is optional. Suppose someone writes `factorial()` so that it dutifully checks the argument and returns a negative number if the argument is out of range. If the code that calls that function doesn't check the error return, it doesn't do any good. Sure, I make all kinds of menacing threats like "You will check your error returns or else," but you all know that the language can't force anyone.

Even if I do check the error return from `factorial()` or any other function, what can my function do with the error? It can probably do nothing more than output an error message of my own and return another error indication to my caller, which probably does the same. Pretty soon all code begins to have the following appearance:

```
// call some function, check the error return, handle it,
// and return
errRtn = someFunc();
if (errRtn)
{
    errorOut("Error on call to someFunc()");
    return MY_ERROR_1;
}

errRtn = someOtherFunc();
if (errRtn)
{
    errorOut("Error on call to someOtherFunc()");
    return MY_ERROR_1;
}
```

This mechanism has several problems:

- It's highly repetitive.
- It forces the user to invent and keep track of numerous error return indications.
- It mixes the error handling code into the normal code flow, thereby obscuring the normal, non-error path.

These problems don't seem so bad in this simple example, but they become increasingly worse as the calling code becomes more complex. The result is that error handling code doesn't get written to handle all the conditions that it should.

The exception mechanism addresses these problems by removing the error path from the normal code path. Further, exceptions make error handling obligatory. If your function doesn't handle the thrown exception, control passes up the chain of called functions until C++ finds a function to handle the error. This also gives you the flexibility to ignore errors that you can't do anything about anyway. Only the functions that can actually correct the problem need to catch the exception.

How Do Exceptions Work?

Take a closer look at the steps that the code goes through to handle an exception. When the `throw` occurs, C++ first copies the thrown object to some neutral place. It then begins looking for the end of the current `try` block.

If a `try` block is not found in the current function, control passes to the calling function. A search is then made of that function. If no `try` block is found there, control passes to the function that called it, and so on up the stack of calling functions. This process is called *unwinding the stack*.

An important feature of stack unwinding is that as each stack is unwound, any objects that go out of scope are destructed just as if the function had executed a return statement. This keeps the program from losing assets or leaving objects dangling.

When the encasing `try` block is found, the code searches the first `catch` phrase immediately following the closing brace of the `catch` block. If the object thrown matches the type of argument specified in the `catch` statement, control passes to that `catch` phrase. If not, a check is made of the next `catch` phrase. If no matching `catch` phrases are found, the code searches for the next higher level `try` block in an ever outward spiral until an appropriate `catch` can be found. If no `catch` phrase is found, the program is terminated.

Consider the following example:

```
#include <iostream.h>
class Obj
{
  public:
    Obj(char c)
    {
        label = c;
        cout << "Constructing object " << label << endl;
    }
    ~Obj()
```

```
    {
        cout << "Destructing object "  << label << endl;
    }

  protected:
    char label;
};

void f1();
void f2();

int main(int, char*[])
{
    Obj a('a');
    try
    {
        Obj b('b');
        f1();
    }
    catch(float f)
    {
        cout << "Float catch" << endl;
    }
    catch(int i)
    {
        cout << "Int catch" << endl;
    }
    catch(...)
    {
        cout << "Generic catch" << endl;
    }
    return 0;
}

void f1()
{
    try
    {
        Obj c('c');
        f2();
    }
    catch(char* pMsg)
    {
        cout << "String catch" << endl;
    }
}
```

(continued)

(continued)

```
void f2()
{
    Obj d('d');
    throw 10;
}
```

The output from executing this program appears as follows:

```
Constructing object a
Constructing object b
Constructing object c
Constructing object d
Destructing object d
Destructing object c
Destructing object b
Int catch
Destructing object a
```

First you see the four objects `a`, `b`, `c`, and `d` being constructed as control passes through each declaration before `f2()` throws the `int` 10. Because no `try` block is defined in `f2()`, C++ unwinds `f2()`'s stack, causing object `d` to be destructed. `f1()` defines a `try` block, but its only `catch` phrase is designed to handle `char*`, which does not match the `int` thrown. Therefore, C++ continues looking. This unwinds `f1()`'s stack, resulting in object `c` being destructed.

Back in `main()`, C++ finds another `try` block. Exiting that block causes object `b` to go out of scope. The first `catch` phrase is designed to catch `float`s that don't match our `int`, so it's skipped. The next `catch` phrase matches the `int` exactly, so control stops there. The final `catch` phrase, which would catch any object thrown, is skipped because a matching `catch` phrase was already found.

What Kinds of Things Can I Throw?

The thing following the `throw` keyword is actually an expression that creates an object of some kind. In the examples so far, I've always thrown integers, but `throw` can handle any type of object. This means that you can throw almost as much information as you want. Consider the following class definition:

```
#include <iostream.h>
#include <iostream.h>
#include <string.h>
```

```
// Exception - generic exception handling class
class Exception
{
  public:
    Exception(char* pMsg, char* pFile, int nLine)
    {
        strncpy(msg, pMsg, sizeof msg);
        msg[sizeof msg - 1] = '\0'; // make sure it's
                                    // terminated
        strncpy(file, pFile, sizeof file);
        file[sizeof file - 1] = '\0';
        lineNum = nLine;
    }

    virtual void display(ostream& out)
    {
        out << "Error <" << msg << ">\n";
        out << "Occurred on line #" << lineNum
            << ", file " << file << endl;
    }

  protected:
    // error message
    char msg[80];

    // file name and line number where error occurred
    char file[80];
    int lineNum;
};
```

The `throw` looks like the following:

```
throw Exception("Negative argument to factorial", __FILE__,__LINE__);
```

`__FILE__` and `__LINE__` are intrinsic `#define`s that are set to the name of the source file and the current line number in that file, respectively.

The corresponding `catch` is straightforward:

```
void myFunc()
{
    try
    {
```

(continued)

(continued)

```
        //. . .whatever calls
    }
    // catch an Exception object
    catch(Exception x)
    {
        // use the built-in display member function
        x.display(cerr);
    }
}
```

The `catch` snags the `Exception` object and then uses the built-in `display()` member function to display the error message.

The `Exception` class represents a generic error reporting class. However, this class can be extended by subclassing from it. For example, I can define an `InvalidArgumentException` class that stores the value of the invalid argument in addition to the message and location of the error:

```
class InvalidArgumentException : public Exception
{
  public:
    InvalidArgumentException(int arg, char* pFile, int nLine)
      : Exception("Invalid argument", pFile, nLine)
    {
        invArg = arg;
    }

    virtual void display(ostream& out)
    {
        Exception::display(out);
        out << "Argument was " << invArg << endl;
    }

  protected:
    int invArg;
};
```

Notice that the calling function automatically handles the new `InvalidArgumentException` because an `InvalidArgumentException` is an `Exception` and the `display()` member function is polymorphic.

Chapter 26
Templates

In This Chapter

- Investigating template functions
- Comparing templates to macros
- Expanding templates into classes
- Building and using template libraries

When I was at school learning my craft ("Teach him any craft," my parents begged, just so he doesn't come back home), much was made of functional and procedural programming and the role that functions played in making code more modular. All types of benefits issued forth from modularity: Function programs were easier to write, easier to debug, and easier to maintain. With all this propaganda, forgetting that functions were invented simply as a labor-saving device is easy.

Back in the early days of programming, people noticed that they were writing certain blocks of code over and over. For example, the following code snippet for finding the larger of two numbers got high Nielsen ratings:

```
// save the larger of two numbers nX1 and nX2
int nX = nX1;
if (nX < nX2)
{
    nX = nX2;
}
```

By moving commonly repeated blocks of code into a function, such duplication could be avoided with a resulting savings in both computer memory (which was expensive) and programmer effort (which was even more expensive):

```
// max - return the larger of two numbers
int max(int nX1, int nX2)
{
    // retain X1
```

(continued)

(continued)

```
int nX = nX1;

// if X1 is smaller than X2...
if (nX < nX2)
{
    // ...then retain X2 instead
    nX = nX2;
}
    return nX;
}

// some silly function somewhere
void otherFunc(int nX)
{
    // process the larger of x and 0
    int nArg = max(nX, 0);

    // use max to implement absolute value function
    int nAbsX = max(nX, -nX);

    // ...and so it goes...
}
```

(Of course, programmers in those days didn't have C++, but you get the idea.)

Unfortunately, as useful as strong typing was in ferreting out pesky programming errors, it meant that the nifty function `max(int, int)` worked great for arrays of `int`s but couldn't be used to find the maximum of two `float`s or `double`s or anything else. What was needed was a way to get the same reuse capabilities of the old days in today's strongly typed world.

It is possible to rewrite the function for each different type:

```
// max - return the larger of two numbers
int max(int nX1, int nX2)
{
    // retain X1
int nX = nX1;
// if X1 is smaller than X2...
if (nX < nX2)
{
    // ...then retain X2 instead
    nX = nX2;
}
    return nX;
```

```
}
float max(float fX1, float fX2)
{
float fX = fX1;
if (fX < fX2)
{
    fX = fX2;
}
    return fX;
}
double max(double dX1, double dX2)
{
double dX = dX1;
if (dX < dX2)
{
    dX = dX2;
}
    return dX;
}
```

This solution works, but it involves a lot of seemingly needless typing. With lazy programmers being what they are (lazy), it wasn't long before they had devised the *template* mechanism for writing generic functions and classes that can be used for more than one type of object. In this chapter, I start by demonstrating the template function. I then expand the concept to template classes and show you how libraries of template classes are built and used in modern, professional programs to save both time and space.

Why Do I Need Templates?

The recalcitrant C programmer is no doubt thinking, "Aha. Now here's a feature that C has had for years in the form of macros." Because the macro preprocessor is not part of the C++ compiler, building typeless routines is often possible. A macro version of the preceding might look something like this:

```
#define MAX(x, y) ((x) > (y) ? (x) : (y))
```

I have several responses to this argument (besides a good ol' Bronx cheer).

One response to this argument is that the problems of macros are well known and are documented in this book (for example, check out Chapter 5). Macros are fraught with errors due to the precedence rules conflicting with operations in the macro definition. In addition, invoking macros on arguments with side effects is generally disastrous.

Another response is that macros don't have the desired effect. Typeless macros do not provide the protection offered by the C++ compiler. The goal was not to generate typeless functions, which is what a macro is, but to generate generic functions where the type can be provided after the fact.

Third, macros are limited in what they can legitimately do. This means that it is often necessary to force the limits of the language (and the programmer) to write the function in the form of a macro. The result is more difficult to write and to read. (Compare the `MAX()` macro with the `max()` functions that it pretends to replace.)

Templates, by working as part of the C++ language and not part of some preprocessor, avoid these problems while remaining generic.

Template Functions

Go back to the definition of the three `max()` functions and compare them. Except for the extra comments in `max(int, int)`, the only difference in the three functions is that the first function has `int`, the second has `float`, and the third has `double`. What if you could replace all three functions with one single function template in which the types `int`, `float`, and `double` are replaced by some placeholder, such as `T`. To turn this pattern into a "real" function, you would only need to provide a class (such as `int`) in place of `T`. This is the way C++ *template functions* work.

The following is a version of the template function `max<T>(T, T)`:

```
// max - return the maximum of two numbers of type T
template <class T>
T max(T tX1, T tX2)
{
    T tX = tX1;
    if (tX < tX2)
    {
        tX = tX2;
    }
    return tX;
}
```

`max<T>(T, T)` is not a function but a template function.

The keyword `template` is followed by angle brackets containing one or more type names, each preceded by the keyword `class`, or a constant, or both. Following the angle brackets is what looks like a normal function definition. Each of the names appearing in the template list must be used somewhere in the template function definition. In this case, the template function `T max<T>(T t1, T t2)` returns the larger of two objects `t1` and `t2`, each of which is of type `T`, where `T` is some class to be defined later.

Template functions are useless until they have been converted into real functions by providing a class in place of `T`. The following code snippet demonstrates how you could do this:

```
void someFunc()
{
    // the following prototype causes C++ to create a
    // function max(int, int) from the template function
    // max<T>(T, T) int max(int, int);

    // the following creates a new, separate function
    // max(double, double)
    double max(double, double);

    // ...
}
```

By comparing the prototype declaration to the function template, C++ can tell that the programmer wants to create a function `int max(int, int)` by replacing `T` with `int`. C++ goes through the template doing exactly that: Everywhere it sees a `T`, C++ replaces it with `int`. The compiler then goes back and compiles the resulting function.

C++ can't compile the function until the template is expanded into a real function. If your template function has compile errors, you probably won't know it until you instance the template function.

Simply referring to the template function is enough to tell C++ what you want. Consider the following example:

```
// abs - return the absolute value of the argument
int abs(short nArg)
{
    // simply referencing the function expands the template
    // to be expanded into a function
    return max(nArg, -nArg);
}
```

Here C++ can tell that the programmer wants the template function `max<class T>(T, T)` expanded into `max(short, short)`. This can lead to a bit of confusion, as demonstrated by the following example:

```
// first define a generic template function...
template <class T>
T max(T tX1, T tX2)
{
    T tX = tX1;
    if (tX < tX2)
    {
        tX = tX2;
    }
    return tX;
}

// ...followed by a separate explicit function
int max(int nX1, char nC1)
{
    int nX2 = nC1;
    int nX = nX1;
    if (nX < nX2)
    {
        nX = nX2;
    }
    return nX;
}

int abs(int nArg)
{
    // now, which one of the above is called?
    return max(nArg, 0);
}
```

Which function is called now? The compiler has two options here. It could convert the second argument into a `char` and then call `max(int, char)`, or it could instance the template function into `max(int, int)` and call it. To avoid confusion, C++ uses the following rules when trying to determine which function to invoke:

1. First, the compiler looks for an explicit function whose arguments match exactly.
2. Next, the compiler looks for a function template that could be expanded into a function whose arguments match exactly.
3. Finally, the compiler looks for an explicit function that could be called by converting one or more arguments.

Notice that the compiler does not look for a template that could be invoked by converting one or more arguments. Thus, the following would not work:

```
// same old template function
template <class T>
T max(T tX1, T tX2)
{
    T tX = tX1;
    if (tX < tX2)
    {
        tX = tX2;
    }
    return tX;
}

// convertSpecial - convert special characters below a
//                  space to a space
char convertSpecial(char c)
{
    // this doesn't work
    return (char)max(c, 0x20);
}
```

The template function `max<T>(T, T)` is not expanded because the two arguments, `c` and `0x20`, are not of the same type. C++ does not notice that it could expand `max<T>(T, T)` into `max(int, int)` and then convert `c` into an `int`.

Perhaps one reason is that this answer is not unique: It could also convert `max<T>(T, T)` into `max(char, char)` and then convert `0x20` into a `char`.

Instancing Template Functions with Classes

So far I have considered only the case where `T` is replaced with an intrinsic class in the expansion of the `max<T>(T, T)` template function. `T` can also be a user-defined class, as the following example demonstrates:

```
#include <math.h>

template <class T>
T max(T& tX1, T& tX2)
{
```

(continued)

(continued)

```
    T tX = tX1;
    if (tX < tX2)
    {
        tX = tX2;
    }
    return tX;
}

// Complex - this is a minimal complex class
class Complex
{
  protected:
    double dReal, dImagine;

  public:
    Complex(double dR = 0, double dI = 0)
    {
        dReal = dR;
        dImagine = dI;
    }

    double abs()
    {
        return sqrt(dReal * dReal +
                    dImagine * dImagine);
    }
};

int operator < (Complex& c1, Complex& c2)
{
    return c1.abs() < c2.abs();
}

int main()
{
    Complex c1(2.0);
    Complex c2(1.0);
    Complex c3 = max(c1, c2);
    return 0;
}
```

Notice, however, that the definition of `max<T>(T, T)` makes use of `operator<(T, T)`. This is why I had to define `operator<(Complex&, Complex&)`. (Making the arguments referential just saved the cost of passing the entire object on the call stack.) If this operator did not exist, a compiler error would be generated at the call to `max(c1, c2)` because this statement caused the template function to be expanded with class `Complex`.

Template Classes

C++ also allows the programmer to define template classes. A *template class* follows the same principle of using a conventional class definition with a placeholder for some unknown support classes:

```
template <class T>
class Array
{
  protected:
    int nSize;
    T*  ptArray;

  public:
    Array(int nArraySize)
    {
        nSize = nArraySize;
        ptArray = new T[nSize];
    }

    int size()
    {
        return nSize;
    }

    T& operator[](int nIndex)
    {
        if (nIndex < 0 || nIndex >= nSize)
        {
            throw "Range of Array object exceeded";
        }
        return ptArray[nIndex];
    }
};
```

Notice that `Array<T>::operator[](int)` returns a reference to a `T`. What's a `T`? I don't know and neither does C++. Therefore, C++ can't do anything with this definition until `T` is provided. As soon as you provide a definition for `T`, C++ can compile the function with alacrity.

I can create a real class from the template class `Array<T>` by providing a type for `T` in the same way that I did for template functions:

```
int main()
{
    // create an array of ints
    Array<int> arrayOfInts(10);

    int i;
    for (i = 0; i < arrayOfInts.size(); i++)
    {
        arrayOfInts[i] = i;
    }
    return 0;
}
```

This snippet declares the object `arrayOfInts` to be of type `Array<int>`. If I had a class `Student`, I could create an array of `Student` objects just as easily:

```
#include "Student.h"

int main()
{
    // first create an array of ints
    Array<int> arrayOfInts(10);

    // now create an array of Students
    Array<Student> arrayOfStudents(100);

    // ...whatever the program needs to do...
}
```

In this example, C++ creates two separate classes, `Array<int>` and `Array<Student>`. C++ sees no similarity between the two classes. In particular, they are not assignment compatible.

Do I really need template classes?

"But," you say, "can't I just create a simple Array class? Why mess with templates?"

Sure you can, if you know a priori what types of things you need arrays of. For example, if all I ever need is arrays of integers, I have no reason to create a template `Array<T>`. I could just create the class `IntArray` and be finished.

The only other alternative I have is to create an `ArrayOfVoid` class designed to handle an array of `void*`, such as the following example:

```
#include <stdlib.h>
#include <iostream.h>

typedef void* VoidPtr;

class ArrayOfVoid
{
  protected:
    int nSize;
    VoidPtr*  pArray;

  public:
    ArrayOfVoid(int nArraySize)
    {
        // store off the number of elements
        nSize = nArraySize;

        // allocate enough room to hold nSize pointers
        pArray = (VoidPtr*)malloc(nArraySize * sizeof↩ (void*));
    }

    int size()
    {
        return nSize;
    }

    VoidPtr& operator[](int nIndex)
    {
        if (nIndex < 0 || nIndex >= nSize)
        {
            throw "Range of Array object exceeded";
        }
        return pArray[nIndex];
    }
};
```

In the preceding example, I use a pointer to `void` because `void*` can point to any type of object. That way, I can add any type of object to this array using `addElement()`. I must then recast the pointer returned by `getElement()` into a pointer to the proper type of object before I can use it:

```
// calculate the average grade in the class
void averageGrade(ArrayOfVoidPtr& array)
{
    double dAcc = 0.0;

    int nIndex;
    for (nIndex = 0; nIndex < array.size(); nIndex++)
    {
        // fetch the grade of that student - assume that
        // some class Student exists and that it contains a
        // member function grade() which returns the grade
        // of the Student
        dAcc += ((Student*)array[nIndex])->grade();
    }
}
```

The problem with such an approach is that it circumvents the typing system. I must recast the pointer returned by `operator[]` into a `Student*`. But what if the pointer didn't point to a `Student`? The call to `grade()` would at best return garbage and at worst be fatal. With strong typing thwarted, C++ can do little to detect the problem.

By comparison, the template class is instantiated with a given class:

```
// calculate the average grade in the class
double averageGrade(Array<Student>& array)
{
    double dAcc = 0.0;

    int nIndex;
    for (nIndex = 0; nIndex < array.size(); nIndex++)
    {
        // fetch the grade of that student
        dAcc += array[nIndex].grade();
    }
    return dAcc / array.size();
}
```

Not only is this solution easier to read, but I have some assurance that `array` actually contains `Student` objects.

Template member functions

The member functions of a template class are automatically template functions. Template member functions defined in the class don't appear much different from their more concrete member function brethren.

Template member functions may also be defined outside the class, although the syntax is a bit tortured until you get used to it.

The first thing to remember is that template functions must be declared with the `template` keyword. In addition, you must remember that the name of the template function must appear with the name of the template class attached.

Thus, if I had defined `size()` as an external function, it would look like the following:

```
// size - return the size of the Array<T> object
template <class T>
int Array<T>::size()
{
    return nSize;
}
```

The full name of the `size()` member template function is `Array<T>::size()`.

Similarly, when written outside of the class, the index operator appears as follows:

```
template <class T>
T& Array<T>::operator[](int nIndex)
{
    if (nIndex < 0 || nIndex >= nSize)
    {
        throw "Range of Array object exceeded";
    }
    return ptArray[nIndex];
}
```

Tips for using templates

You need to remember a few things when using templates. First, no code is generated for a template. (Code is generated after the template is converted into a concrete class or function.) This implies that a .cpp source file is almost never associated with a template class. The entire template class definition, including all the member functions, is contained in the `.h` include file so that it can be available for the compiler to expand.

Second, a template class does not consume any memory. Therefore, there is no penalty for creating template classes if they are never instanced. On the other hand, a template class uses memory every time it is instanced. Thus, the code for `Array<Student>` consumes memory even if `Array<int>` already exists.

Finally, a template class cannot be compiled and checked for errors until it has been converted into a real class. Thus, a template class `Array` might compile even though it contains obvious syntax errors. The errors won't appear until a class such as `Array<int>` or `Array<Student>` is created.

If an error does appear when instancing a template class, it does not necessarily mean that the template class has a problem. For example, suppose the template class `Array<T>` contains a method `sort()` that uses the template function `operator<(T&, T&)`. Such a template class cannot be instanced with the class `Student` unless `operator<(Student&, Student&)` exists. (You can't sort students until you define the sequencing function.) This is not an error in `Array<T>`, per se; it's merely an incompatibility between `Array<T>` and `Student`.

Example Application

One of the most common uses of templates is in the area of class containers. A *container* is a class designed to contain objects. For example, a linked list is a container, as is an array, a matrix, a file, and a stack. Upon reflection, the reasons are clear. Almost every programmer needs, for example, a linked list from time to time. Rather than write a linked list for a given class, say `Account`, why not write a linked list template class that can be used to contain different types of objects?

Hey, that gives me an idea. Maybe I can create a template linked list class and then use it to contain `Account` objects in the BUDGET application.

Template class SLL

The following code shows the template class `SLL`:

```
                                                 //Note 1
//SLL.H - SLL represents a singly linked list container
//        template class.

// SLLNode - represents a node in the linked list chain.
//           Each node contains a pointer to the next node
//           in the list plus a pointer to the data.
template <class T>                               // Note 2
class SLLNode
```

```
{
public:
    SLLNode<T>(T* pD)
    {
        pNext = 0;
        pData = pD;
    }

    SLLNode<T>* pNext; // pointer to next node   // Note 3
    T*          pData; // pointer to data
};

// SLL - this class represents a               // Note 2
//       single list class.
//       A singly linked list consists of a list of nodes
//       each of which points to the data.
template <class T>
class SLL
{
  protected:
    SLLNode<T>*  pFirst; // pointer to first node // Note 4
    SLLNode<T>*  pLast;      // pointer to last node
    SLLNode<T>*  pCurrent;   // pointer to "current" node
    int nMembers;            // number of members in list

  public:
    SLL();

    // add - add member to end of list
    void add(T* pData)
    {
        // create a node which points to our data
                                              // Note 5
        SLLNode<T>* pNode = new SLLNode<T>(pData);

        // add it to the end of the list
        if (pLast)
        {
            pLast->pNext = pNode;
        }
        pLast = pNode;

        // if this is the only member in the list...
        if (pFirst == 0)
        {
```

(continued)

(continued)

```
            // ...make it first member also
            pFirst = pNode;
        }

        // now count it
        nMembers++;
    }

    // count - return the number of accounts
    int count()
    {
        return nMembers;
    }


    // provide navigation functions
    // current - return the data pointer of current node
    T*  current();
    // over - move over to the next node
    void over()
    {
        pCurrent = pCurrent->pNext;
    }
    // reset - reset to beginning of list
    void reset()
    {
        pCurrent = pFirst;
    }
};

// constructor - build an empty list
template <class T>
SLL<T>::SLL()
{
    pFirst = pLast = (SLLNode<T>*)0;
    pCurrent = (SLLNode<T>*)0;
    nMembers = 0;
}
// current - return the data pointer of current node
template <class T>
T* SLL<T>::current()
{
    // assume data pointer is zero...
    T* pData = (T*)0;
```

```
    // if we aren't off the end of list...
    if (pCurrent)
    {
        // ...then replace with actual data ptr
        pData = pCurrent->pData;
    }
    return pData;
}
```

The first thing to notice (`Note 1`) is that `SLL` is contained in an `.h` file. None of the code of a template class, even the non-inline functions, are defined in a .cpp file. The singly linked list actually consists of two template classes (`Note 2`). The template class `SLL` maintains a singly linked list of nodes. `SLL` contains a pointer to the first and last node in the list (`Note 4`); each node contains a pointer to the data as well as to the next node in the list (`Note 3`). These nodes are of type `SLLNode`. The data pointer in `SLLNode` is of type `T*`, making this singly linked list a template class pair.

Take a closer look at one of the member functions, in this case `add()` (`Note 5`). `add()` takes a pointer of type `T*`. (In the application, `T` will eventually be `Account`, but for now act like you don't know that.) `add()` allocates a node to hold the data pointer. The address of this node is kept in the pointer `pNode`. Notice that the type of `pNode` is `SLLNode<T>*` and not `SLLNode*`. From that point on, `add()` simply adds the node to the end of the list.

`SLLNode` is a template class and not a class, so `SLLNode*` doesn't make sense. You can't define a pointer to a template class because you can't create an object with a template class.

Having said all this about container template classes, I should point out the Standard Template Library includes numerous template classes, including some really neat containers. However, this library is more than a little complex and certainly beyond the scope of this humble treatise.

Using SLL, the BUDGET6 program

The following shows the BUDGET program converted to use the SLL template class:

```
//BUDGET6.CPP - Budget program using a template container
//              class to hold the account objects rather
//              than embed that information into the class.

#include <iostream.h>
#include <stdlib.h>
```

(continued)

(continued)

```
#include <ctype.h>

// use the template class SLL
#include "sll.h"

//Account - this abstract class incorporates properties
//          common to both account types Checking and
//          Savings; however, it's missing the concept
//          withdrawal(), which is different between the two
class Account
{
  protected:
    Account(Account &c)
    {
        throw "No creating funds\n";
    }

  public:
    Account(unsigned accNo, float initialBalance = 0.0);

    //access functions
    int accountNo()
    {
        return accountNumber;
    }
    float acntBalance()
    {
        return balance;
    }

    //transaction functions
    void deposit(float amount)
    {
        balance += amount;
    }
    virtual void withdrawal(float amount) = 0;

    //display function for displaying self on 'cout'
    void display()
    {
        cout << "Account " << accountNumber
             << " = "      << balance
             << "\n";
    }

  protected:
```

```
    unsigned   accountNumber;
    float      balance;
};

Account::Account(unsigned accNo, float initialBalance)
{
    accountNumber = accNo;
    balance = initialBalance;
}

//Checking - this class contains properties unique to
//           checking accounts. Not much left, is there?
class Checking : public Account
{
  public:
    //here the constructor defined inline
    Checking(unsigned accNo, float initialBalance = 0.0) :
             Account(accNo, initialBalance)
    {
    }

    //overload pure virtual functions
    virtual void withdrawal(float amount);
};

void Checking::withdrawal(float amount)
{
    if (balance < amount )
    {
        cout << "Insufficient funds: balance " << balance
             << ", check "                     << amount
             << "\n";
    }
    else
    {
        balance -= amount;

        //if balance falls too low, charge service fee
        if (balance < 500.00)
        {
            balance -= 0.20F;
        }
    }
}
```

(continued)

(continued)

```
//Savings - same story as Checking except it also has
//          a unique data member
class Savings : public Account
{
  public:
    //here constructor is defined as separate function
    //just to show you the difference
    Savings(unsigned accNo, float initialBalance = 0.0);

    //transaction functions
    virtual void withdrawal(float amount);


  protected:
    int noWithdrawals;
};

Savings::Savings(unsigned accNo, float initialBalance) :
   Account(accNo, initialBalance)
{
    noWithdrawals = 0;
}
void Savings::withdrawal(float amount)
{
    if (balance < amount)
    {
        cout << "Insufficient funds: balance " << balance
             << ", withdrawal "                << amount
             << "\n";
    }
    else
    {
        if (++noWithdrawals > 1)
        {
            balance -= 5.00F;
        }
        balance -= amount;
    }
}

//prototype declarations
unsigned getAccntNo();
void process(Account &account);

//main - accumulate the initial input and output totals
```

```
int main()
{
    // loop until someone enters an 'X' or 'x'
    Account *pA;
    char     accountType;     //S or C

    try
    {
        // keep the accounts in an account container
        SLL<Account> books;                         // Note 1

        unsigned keepLooping = 1;
        while (keepLooping)
        {
            cout << "Enter S for Savings, "
                    "C for Checking, X for exit\n";
            cin  >> accountType;

            switch (accountType)
            {
              case 'c':
              case 'C':
                pA = new Checking(getAccntNo());
                if (pA == 0)
                {
                    throw "Out of memory";
                }
                process(*pA);
                books.add(pA);                      // Note 2
                break;

              case 's':
              case 'S':
                pA = new Savings(getAccntNo());
                if (pA == 0)
                {
                     throw "Out of memory";
                }
                process(*pA);                       // Note 2
                books.add(pA);
                break;

              case 'x':
              case 'X':
                keepLooping = 0;
                break;
```

(continued)

(continued)

```
            default:
               cout << "I didn't get that.\n";
            }
         }

         //now present totals
         float total = 0.0;
         cout << "Account totals:\n";
                                                     // Note 3
         for (books.reset(); pA = books.current(); books.over())
         {
             pA->display();
             total += pA->acntBalance();
         }
         cout << "Total worth   = " << total << "\n";
     }

     // char* exception is a general, internal error
     catch(char* pReason)                            // Note 4
     {
         cout << "Exception: " << pReason << endl;
     }
     catch(...)
     {
         cout << "Unknown exception\n" << endl;
     }
     return 0;
}

//getAccntNo - return the account number entered
unsigned getAccntNo()
{
     unsigned accntNo;
     cout << "Enter account number:";
     cin  >> accntNo;
     return accntNo;
}

//process(Account) - input the data for an account*/
void process(Account &account)
{
     cout << "Enter positive number for deposit,\n"
             "negative for withdrawal, 0 to terminate";
```

```
    float transaction;
    do
    {
        cout << ":";
        cin  >> transaction;

        //deposit
        if (transaction > 0)
        {
            account.deposit(transaction);
        }

        //withdrawal
        if (transaction < 0)
        {
            account.withdrawal(-transaction);
        }
    } while (transaction != 0);
}
```

Compare BUDGET6 to BUDGET5, and you notice that this version is considerably simpler. For example, the concept of a singly linked list has been removed from that of a bank account. This leaves behind only 100 percent account stuff in the class.

The main changes are in `main()` (pun intended). First, `main()` declares a `try` block to catch any exceptions that might get thrown during the program. Then `main()` declares a book's object of type `SLL<Account>` to contain the accounts (`Note 1`). This means that each time an account is created, it must be added to the books (`Note 2`).

After all the accounts have been created, the program goes back through the books calculating the total worth (`Note 3`). Notice in particular the `for` loop. `reset()` resets the pointer to the beginning of the list, `over()` moves the pointer to the next member, and `current()` returns the address of the current account or zero if the list has been exhausted. The member functions of SLL were defined to facilitate `for` loop traversal of the list.

The only type of exception thrown in this program is an ASCIIZ string containing the reason for the exception. The corresponding `catch` block at the bottom of `main()` (`Note 4`) simply catches the exception and prints the reason before exiting normally.

Forget Those Macros

By being type-safe, template functions provide one more reason not to resort to macros. Template classes allow the programmer to define a single solution to a problem, such as containing objects, and then reuse that solution for any number of different object types.

Chapter 27
Multiple Inheritance

In This Chapter

- Introduction to multiple inheritance
- Avoiding ambiguities with multiple inheritance
- Avoiding ambiguities with virtual inheritance
- The ordering rules for multiple constructors
- Problems with multiple inheritance

In the class hierarchies discussed so far, each class has inherited from a single parent. This is the way things usually are in the real world. Some classes, however, represent the blending of two classes into one.

An example of such a class is the sleeper sofa. As the name implies, it is a sofa and also a bed (although not a very comfortable bed). Thus, the sleeper sofa should be allowed to inherit bed-like properties. To address this situation, C++ allows a derived class to inherit from more than one base class. This is called *multiple inheritance.*

How Does Multiple Inheritance Work?

To see how multiple inheritance works, I can expand on the sleeper sofa example. Figure 27-1 shows the inheritance graph for class SleeperSofa. Notice how this class inherits from class Sofa and from class Bed. In this way, it inherits the properties of both.

The code to implement class SleeperSofa looks like the following:

```
class Bed
{
  public:
   Bed();
   void sleep();
```

(continued)

(continued)

```
    int weight;
};
class Sofa
{
  public:
    Sofa();
    void watchTV();
    int weight;
};

//SleeperSofa - is both a Bed and a Sofa
class SleeperSofa : public Bed, public Sofa
{
  public:
    SleeperSofa();
    void foldOut();
};

int main()
{
    SleeperSofa ss;
    //you can watch TV on a sleeper sofa...
    ss.watchTV();          //Sofa::watchTV()
    //...and then you can fold it out...
    ss.foldOut();          //SleeperSofa::foldOut()
    //...and sleep on it (sort of)
    ss.sleep();            //Bed::sleep()
    return 0;
}
```

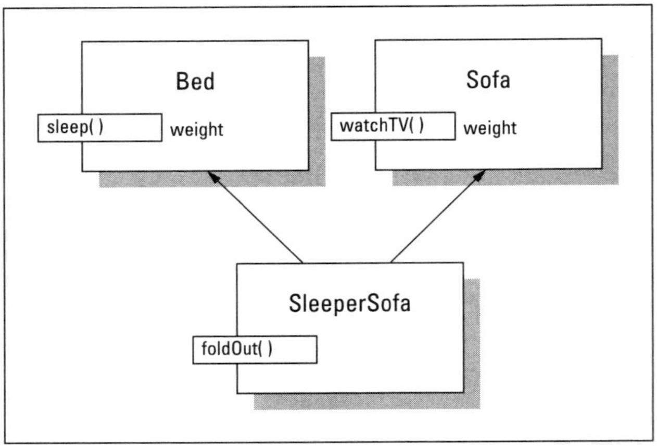

Figure 27-1: Class hierarchy of a sleeper sofa.

Here the class SleeperSofa inherits from both Bed and Sofa. This is apparent from the appearance of both classes in the class declaration. SleeperSofa inherits all the members of both base classes. Thus, both of the calls ss.sleep() and ss.watchTV() are legal. You can use a SleeperSofa as a Bed or a Sofa. Plus the class SleeperSofa can have members of its own, such as foldOut(). Is this a great country or what?

Inheritance Ambiguities

Although multiple inheritance is a powerful feature, it introduces several possible problems. One is apparent in the preceding example. Notice that both Bed and Sofa contain a member weight. This is logical because both have a measurable weight. The question is, "Which weight does SleeperSofa inherit?"

The answer is "both." SleeperSofa inherits a member Bed::weight and a separate member Sofa::weight. Because they have the same name, unqualified references to weight are now ambiguous. This is demonstrated in the following snippet:

```
#include <iostream.h>
void fn()
{
   SleeperSofa ss;
   cout << "weight = "
        << ss.weight     //illegal - which weight?
        << "\n";
}
```

The program must now indicate one of the two weights by specifying the desired base class. The following code snippet is correct:

```
#include <iostream.h>
void fn()
{
   SleeperSofa ss;
   cout << "sofa weight = "
        << ss.Sofa::weight    //specify which weight
        << "\n";
}
```

Although this solution corrects the problem, specifying the base class in the application function isn't desirable because it forces class information to leak outside the class into application code. In this case, fn() has to know that SleeperSofa inherits from Sofa. These types of so-called name collisions were not possible with single inheritance but are a constant danger with multiple inheritance.

Virtual Inheritance

In the case of SleeperSofa, the name collision on weight was more than a mere accident. A SleeperSofa doesn't have a bed weight separate from its sofa weight. The collision occurred because this class hierarchy does not completely describe the real world. Specifically, the classes have not been completely factored.

Thinking about it a little more, it becomes clear that both beds and sofas are special cases of a more fundamental concept: furniture. (I suppose I could get even more fundamental and use something like object_with_mass, but furniture is fundamental enough.) Weight is a property of all furniture. This relationship is shown in Figure 27-2.

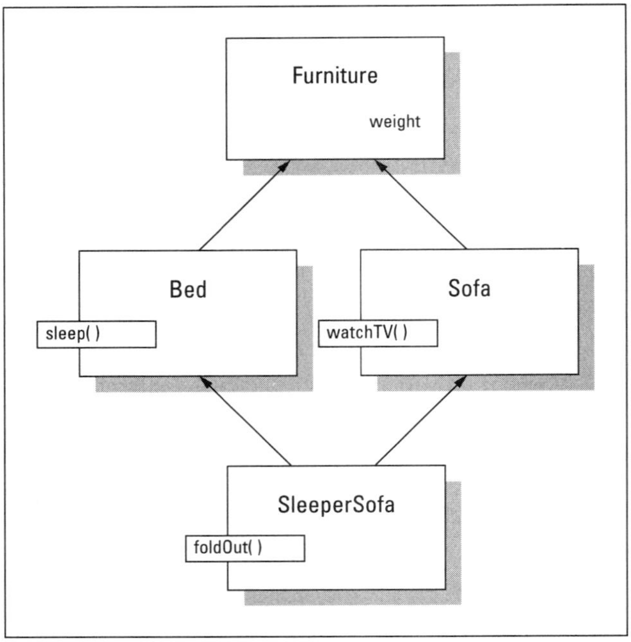

Figure 27-2: Further factoring of beds and sofas (by weight).

Factoring out the class Furniture should relieve the name collision. With much relief and great anticipation of success, I generated the following C++ class hierarchy:

```
#include <iostream.h>

//Furniture - more fundamental concept; this class
//            has "weight" as a property
class Furniture
{
  public:
   Furniture();
   int weight;
};

class Bed : public Furniture
{
  public:
   Bed();
   sleep();
};
class Sofa : public Furniture
{
  public:
   Sofa();
   void watchTV();
};
class SleeperSofa : public Bed, public Sofa
{
  public:
   SleeperSofa();
   void foldOut;
};

void fn()
{
   SleeperSofa ss;
   cout << "weight = "
        << ss.weight     //problem solved; right?
        << "\n";
}
```

Imagine my dismay when I find that this doesn't help at all — weight is still ambiguous. (I wish my weight were as ambiguous!) "Okay," I say (not really understanding why weight is still ambiguous), "I'll try casting ss to a Furniture."

```
#include <iostream.h>
void fn()
{
   SleeperSofa ss;
   Furniture *pF;
   pF = (Furniture*)&ss; //use a Furniture pointer...
   cout << "weight = "   //...to get at the weight
        << pF->weight
        << "\n";
};
```

Casting `ss` to a `furniture` doesn't work either. Now I get some strange message that the cast of `SleeperSofa*` to `Furniture*` is ambiguous. What's going on?

The explanation is straightforward. `SleeperSofa` doesn't inherit from `Furniture` directly. Both `Bed` and `Sofa` inherit from `Furniture` and then `SleeperSofa` inherits from them. In memory, a `SleeperSofa` looks like Figure 27-3.

You can see that a `SleeperSofa` consists of a complete `Bed` followed by a complete `Sofa` followed by some `SleeperSofa` unique stuff. Each of these subobjects in `SleeperSofa` has its own `Furniture` part, because each inherits from `Furniture`. Thus, a `SleeperSofa` contains two `Furniture` objects!

I haven't created the hierarchy shown in Figure 27-2 after all. The inheritance hierarchy I have actually created is the one shown in Figure 27-4.

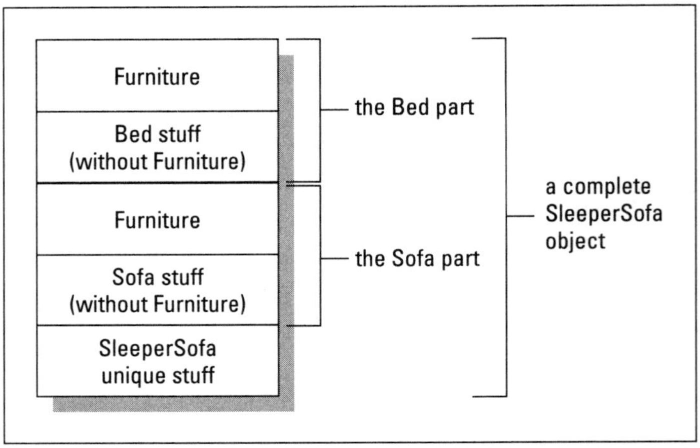

Figure 27-3: Memory layout of a `SleeperSofa`.

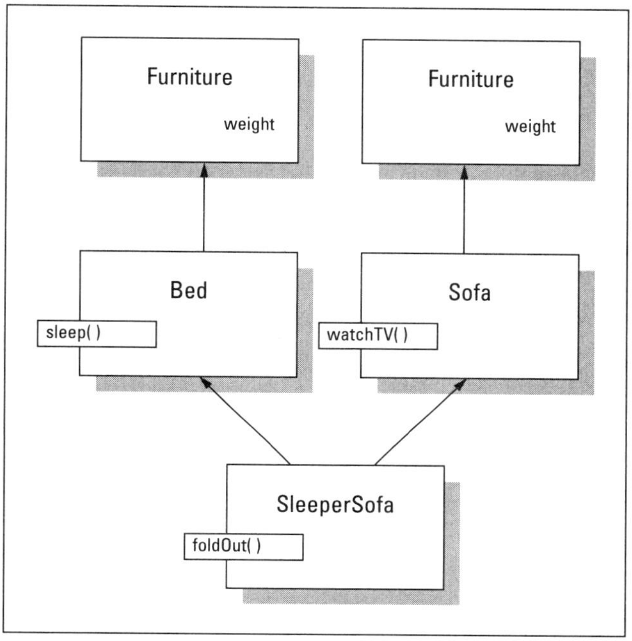

Figure 27-4: Actual result of my first attempt.

But `Sleepersofa` containing two `Furniture` objects is nonsense. `SleeperSofa` needs only one copy of `Furniture`. I want `SleeperSofa` to inherit only one copy of `Furniture`, and I want `Bed` and `Sofa` to share that one copy. C++ calls this *virtual inheritance* because it uses the virtual keyword.

I hate this overloading of the term *virtual* because virtual inheritance has nothing to do with virtual functions.

Armed with this new knowledge, I return to class `SleeperSofa` and implement it as follows:

```
#include <iostream.h>
class Furniture
{
  public:
   Furniture() {}
   int weight;
};
class Bed : virtual public Furniture
{
```

(continued)

(continued)

```
  public:
    Bed() {}
    void sleep();
};
class Sofa : virtual public Furniture
{
  public:
    Sofa() {}
    void watchTV();
};
class SleeperSofa : public Bed, public Sofa
{
  public:
    SleeperSofa() : Sofa(), Bed() {}
    void foldOut();
};

void fn()
{
    SleeperSofa ss;
    cout << "weight = "
         << ss.weight
         << "\n";
}
```

Notice the addition of the keyword virtual in the inheritance of `Furniture` in `Bed` and `Sofa`. This says, "Give me a copy of `Furniture` unless you already have one somehow, in which case I'll just use that one." A `SleeperSofa` ends up looking like Figure 27-5 in memory.

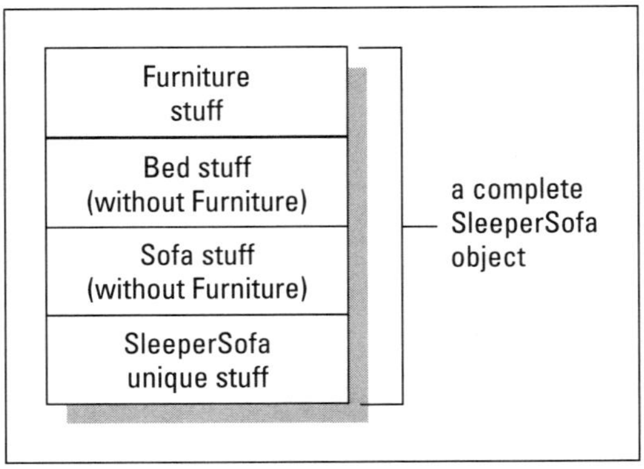

Figure 27-5: Memory layout of `SleeperSofa` with virtual inheritance.

Here you can see that a `SleeperSofa` inherits `Furniture`, and then `Bed` minus the `Furniture` part, followed by `Sofa` minus the `Furniture` part. Bringing up the rear are the members unique to `SleeperSofa`. (Note that this may not be the order of the elements in memory, but that's not important for the purpose of this discussion.)

Now the reference in `fn()` to `weight` is not ambiguous because a `SleeperSofa` contains only one copy of `Furniture`. By inheriting `Furniture` virtually, you get the desired inheritance relationship as expressed in Figure 27-2.

If virtual inheritance solves this problem so nicely, why isn't it the norm? The first is because virtually inherited base classes are handled internally much differently than normally inherited base classes, and these differences involve extra overhead. The second reason is because sometimes you want two copies of the base class (although this is unusual).

As an example of the latter, consider a `TeacherAssistant` who is both a `Student` and a `Teacher`, both of which are subclasses of `Academician`. If the university gives its teaching assistants two IDs — a student ID and a separate teacher ID — class `TeacherAssistant` will need to contain two copies of class `Academician`.

Constructing the Objects of Multiple Inheritance

The rules for constructing objects need to be expanded to handle multiple inheritance. The constructors are invoked in the following order:

- First, the constructor for any virtual base classes is called in the order in which the classes are inherited.
- Then the constructor for any nonvirtual base classes is called in the order in which the classes are inherited.
- Next, the constructor for any member objects is called in the order in which the member objects appear in the class.
- Finally, the constructor for the class itself is called.

Notice that base classes are constructed in the order in which they are inherited and not in the order in which they appear on the constructor line.

A Contrary Opinion

I should point out that not all object-oriented practitioners think that multiple inheritance is a good idea. In addition, many object-oriented languages don't support multiple inheritance.

Multiple inheritance is not an easy thing for the language to implement. This is mostly the compiler's problem (or the compiler writer's problem). But multiple inheritance adds overhead to the code when compared to single inheritance, and this overhead can become the programmer's problem.

More importantly, multiple inheritance opens the door to additional errors. First, ambiguities such as those mentioned in the section "Inheritance Ambiguities" pop up. Second, in the presence of multiple inheritance, casting a pointer from a subclass to a base class often involves changing the value of the pointer in sophisticated and mysterious ways. Let me leave the details to the language lawyers and compiler writers. I want to point out, however, that this can result in unexpected results. For example:

```
#include <iostream.h>
class Base1 {int mem;};
class Base2 {int mem;};
class SubClass : public Base1, public Base2 {};

void fn(SubClass *pSC)
{
   Base1 *pB1 = (Base1*)pSC;
   Base2 *pB2 = (Base2*)pSC;
   if ((void*)pB1 == (void*)pB2)
   {
      cout << "Members numerically equal\n";
   }
}
int main()
{
   SubClass sc;
   fn(&sc);
   return 0;
}
```

`pB1` and `pB2` are not numerically equal even though they came from the same original value, `pSC`, and the message "Members numerically equal" doesn't appear. (Actually, if `fn()` is passed a zero because C++ doesn't perform these transmigrations on `null`, the message does appear; for any nonzero address, the message doesn't appear. See how strange it gets?)

I suggest that you avoid using multiple inheritance until you are comfortable with C++. Single inheritance provides enough expressive power to get used to. Later, you can study the manuals until you're sure that you understand exactly what's going on when you multiply inherit. One exception is the use of commercial libraries such as Microsoft's Foundation Classes and Borland's Object-Window Library, which use multiple inheritance quite a bit. These classes have been checked out and are safe.

Don't get me wrong. I'm not out and out against multiple inheritance. The fact that Borland, Microsoft, and others use multiple inheritance effectively in their class libraries proves that it can be done. If multiple inheritance weren't worth the trouble, they wouldn't use it. However, multiple inheritance is a feature that you might want to hold off on using until you're ready.

Part VII
The Part of Tens

In this part . . .

What *...For Dummies* book would be complete without a "Part of Tens"? In Chapter 28, I cover ten ways to avoid adding bugs to your C++ program. (Most of these suggestions work for C programs too at no extra charge.) Chapter 29 lists the ten most important compiler options (plus a few more) from the ocean of possibilities.

Chapter 28

Ten Ways to Avoid Adding Bugs to Your Program

In This Chapter

- Enabling all warnings and error messages
- Insisting on clean compiles
- Using a clear and consistent coding style
- Limiting the visibility
- Adopting a signature field
- Adding comments to your code while you write it
- Single stepping every path at least once
- Avoiding overloaded operators
- Using exceptions to handle errors
- Avoiding multiple inheritance

Enabling All Warnings and Error Messages

The syntax of C++ allows for a lot of error checking. When the compiler encounters a construct that it cannot decipher, it has no choice but to generate an error message. Although the compiler attempts to synch back up with the next statement, it does not attempt to generate an executable program.

Disabling warning and error messages is a bit like unplugging the red lights on your car dashboard because they bother you. Ignoring the problem will not make it go away. If your compiler has a Syntax Check from Hell mode, enable it. Both Microsoft and Borland have an Enable All Messages option — set it. You save time in the end.

During all its digging around in your source code, a good C++ compiler also looks for suspicious-looking syntactical constructs, such as the following code snippet:

```
#include "student.h"
#include "class.h"
Student* addNewStudent(Class class, char *pName, SSNumber ss)
{
   Student pS;
  if (pName != 0)
   {
      pS = new Student(pName, ss);
      class.addStudent(pS);
   }
   return pS;
}
```

Here you see that the function first creates a new `Student` object that it then adds to the `Class` object provided. (Presumably `addStudent()` is a member function of `Class`.)

If a name is provided (that is, `pName` is not 0), a new `Student` object is created and added to the `class`. With that done, the function returns the `Student` created to the caller. The problem is that if `pName` is 0, `pS` is never initialized to anything. A good C++ compiler, such as the Visual C++ compiler, can detect this path and generate a warning that there is a possibility that `pS` is never initialized when it is returned to the caller and maybe you should look into the problem, or words to that effect.

Insisting on Clean Compiles

Don't start debugging your code until you remove or at least understand all the warnings generated during compilation. Enabling all the warning messages if you then ignore them does you no good. If you don't understand the warning, look it up. What you don't know *will* hurt you.

Adopting a Clear and Consistent Coding Style

Coding in a clear and consistent style not only enhances the readability of the program but also results in fewer coding mistakes. Remember, the less brain power you have to spend deciphering C++ syntax, the more you have left over for thinking about the logic of the program at hand. A good coding style should enable you to do the following with ease:

- Differentiate class names, object names, and function names
- Know something about the object based on its name
- Differentiate preprocessor symbols from C++ symbols (that is, `#defined` objects should stand out)
- Identify blocks of C++ code at the same level (this is the result of consistent indentation)

In addition, you need to establish a standard module header that provides information about the functions or classes in the module, the author (presumably, that's you), the date, the version of the compiler that you are using, and a modification history.

Finally, all programmers involved in a single project should use the same style. Trying to decipher a program with a patchwork of different coding styles is confusing.

Limiting the Visibility

Limiting the visibility of class internals to the outside world is a cornerstone of object-oriented programming. The class is responsible for its own internals; the application is responsible for using the class to solve the problem at hand.

Specifically, limited visibility means that data members should not be accessible outside the class — that is, they should be marked as private or protected. In addition, member functions that the application software does not need to know about should also be protected.

A related rule is that public member functions should trust application code as little as possible. Any argument passed to a public member function should be treated as though it may cause bugs until it has been proven safe. A function such as the following is an accident waiting to happen:

```
class Array
{
  public:
   Array(int s)
   {
       size = 0;
       pData = new int[s];
```

(continued)

(continued)

```
        if (pData)
        {
            size = s;
        }
    }

    ~Array()
    {
        delete pData;
        size = 0;
        pData = 0;
    }

    //either return or set the array data

    int data(int index)
    {
        return pData[index];
    }

    int data(int index, int newValue)
    {
        int oldValue = pData[index];
        pData[index] = newValue;
        return oldValue;
    }

  protected:
    int size;
    int *pData;
};
```

The function `data(int)` allows the application software to read data out of `Array`. This function is too trusting; it assumes that the `index` provided is within the data range. What if the `index` is not? The function `data(int, int)` is even worse because it overwrites an unknown location.

What's needed is a check to make sure that the `index` is in range. In the following, only the `data(int)` function is shown for brevity:

```
int data(unsigned int index)
{
    if (index >= size)
    {
```

```
        cout << "Array index out of range (" << index << ")\n";
        return 0;
    }
    return pData[index];
}
```

Now an out-of-range index will be caught by the check. (Making index unsigned precludes the necessity of adding a check for negative index values.)

Using a Signature Field

In the preceding example, you were able to add a check to the function to make sure that the index was within the legal range for the given Array object. But what if the Array object itself were invalid? One of the few ways that you can determine whether the object itself is valid is to add a type of ID field, which I refer to as a signature field in this book.

The addition of a signature field allows the member function one further level of testing. A signature field can be coupled with an isLegal() type function to confirm that the object being passed into the public member function is, in fact, in good health. (I would love to cover this topic again, but it is covered so well in Chapter 24.)

Commenting Your Code While You Write It

I think you can avoid errors if you comment your code while you write it rather than wait until everything works and then go back and add comments. I can understand not taking the time to write voluminous headers and function descriptions until later, but you always have time to add short comments while writing the code.

Short comments should be enlightening. If they're not, they aren't worth much and you should be doing something else instead. You need all the enlightenment you can get while you're trying to make your program work. When you look at a piece of code you wrote a few days ago, comments that are short, descriptive, and to the point can make a dramatic contribution to helping you figure out exactly what it was you were trying to do.

In addition, consistent code indentation and naming conventions make the code easier to understand. It's all very nice when the code is easy to read after you're finished with it, but it's just as important that the code be easy to read while you're writing it. That's when you need the help.

Single Stepping Every Path at Least Once

As a programmer, it's important for you to understand what your program is doing. Nothing gives you a better feel for what's going on under the hood than single stepping the program with a good debugger. (The debuggers included in the IDE of interactive compilers work just fine.)

Beyond that, as you write a program, you sometimes need raw material to figure out some bizarre behavior. Nothing gives you that material better than single stepping new functions as they come into service.

Finally, when a function is finished and ready to be added to the program, every logical path needs to be traveled at least once. Bugs are much easier to find when the function is examined by itself rather than after it's been thrown into the pot with the rest of the functions — and your attention has gone on to new programming challenges.

Avoid Overloading Operators

Other than using the two stream I/O operators `operator<<()` and `operator>>()` and the assignment operator `operator=()`, you should probably hold off overloading operators until you feel comfortable with C++. Although a good set of overloaded operators can increase the utility and readability of a new class, overloading operators other than the three just listed is almost never necessary and can significantly add to your debugging woes as a new programmer. You can get the same effect by defining and using the proper public member functions instead.

After you've been C-plus-plusing for a few months, feel free to return and start overloading operators to your heart's content.

Using Exceptions to Handle Errors

The exception mechanism in C++ is designed to handle errors conveniently and efficiently. Now that this feature has been standardized, you should use it. The resulting code is easier to write, easier to read, and easier to maintain. Besides, other programmers have come to expect it — you wouldn't want to disappoint them, would you?

Avoiding Multiple Inheritance

Multiple inheritance, like operator overloading, adds another level of complexity that you don't need to deal with when you're just starting out. Fortunately, most real-world relationships can be described with single inheritance. (Some people claim that multiple inheritance is not necessary at all — I'm not one of them.)

Feel free to use multiple-inherited classes from commercial libraries, such as the Microsoft MFC classes. Microsoft has spent a considerable amount of time setting up its classes, and it knows what it's doing.

After you feel comfortable with your level of understanding of C++, experiment with setting up some multiple inheritance hierarchies. That way, you'll be ready when the unusual situation that requires multiple inheritance to describe it accurately does arise.

Chapter 29

The Ten Most Important Microsoft Visual C++ Compiler Switches

In This Chapter

- Producing a command line program
- Changing your project settings
- Using the General Settings tab: MFC and directories
- Choosing debug factors
- Getting to the good stuff from the General tab
- Changing C++ language settings
- Controlling code generation
- Customizing your C++ language extensions
- Regulating compile optimizations
- Enabling precompiled headers

The compiler that is most often used on the PC to generate applications is the Visual C++ compiler from Microsoft. This chapter explains the ten most important settings of the Microsoft Visual C++ compiler when used to generate command line programs.

Because this is not a Windows programming book, I am not covering settings used in the generation of Windows programs.

Generating a Command Line Program

Because the Microsoft name is so tightly coupled with that of Windows and because the Visual C++ compiler has some neat tools for generating Microsoft Windows applications, people often assume that Visual C++ will not generate a *DOS-like* command line type application. This simply isn't the case. In fact, all the programs in this book were tested with the Visual C++ compiler.

Small (or was it compact?) Windows

The command line programs we have been producing using Visual C++ are called console applications. Console applications are still Windows applications. In fact, they are still Windows-32 applications, meaning that they execute under Windows using 32-bit registers. To execute a console application, select it as you would any other program. The output from a Windows console application looks a lot more like the output from a UNIX or MS-DOS program.

The fact that these Windows applications are 32-bit applications relieves the programmer from worrying about 16-bit memory models. Such memory models are given names like Small, Medium, Compact, or Large. Another memory model is called the Huge memory model.

Because no one uses these earlier models for 16-bit processors anymore, Visual C++ stopped supporting several releases ago (Version 1.52 was the last version that included support for 16-bit applications). Since then, 16-bit considerations have faded away like a bad dream.

To create a command line program (what Microsoft calls a *console application*), first select File, New, and then Projects. From the list of program types to create, select Win32 Console Application. Before you can select OK, you must select a Project name. Each program that you create must have a project associated with it and each project goes into its own directory. The project describes the details of how the program was created (the flags are described in this chapter). You can change the base directory for the project by editing the path specified in Location. Select OK to have Visual C++ create a project. At this point, you should be looking at an empty work space (it's empty in the sense that there are no C++ source files associated with the project).

To create a new C++ source file, select File, New, and then Files. From this, you should see a list of possible types of files that you can create. Select C++ Source File, and type in the new file name. Selecting OK opens a new window into which you can type your program. In addition, Visual C++ automatically adds the new file to the currently open project.

You also can add previously created C++ source files to your project. Select Project, Add To Project, and then Files to open the File dialog box. Select the source files that you would like to add to the project.

Changing Project Settings

To view the project settings, select Project and then Settings to reveal a screen like Figure 29-1. Notice that Visual C++ allows you to maintain multiple, different project setting configurations. In fact, it creates two settings for you from the very beginning: Debug and Release. The difference between these two settings is that the Debug setting tends to have all the project settings to the value that is most convenient for the debugger. Because these settings are also the slowest possible settings, the Production setting is provided to produce the fastest, smallest executable for the final build prior to release of the software.

To change a setting, select the configuration for which you want the settings changed by selecting the drop-down menu next to the Settings For label. Selecting All Configurations changes the setting in all possible configurations.

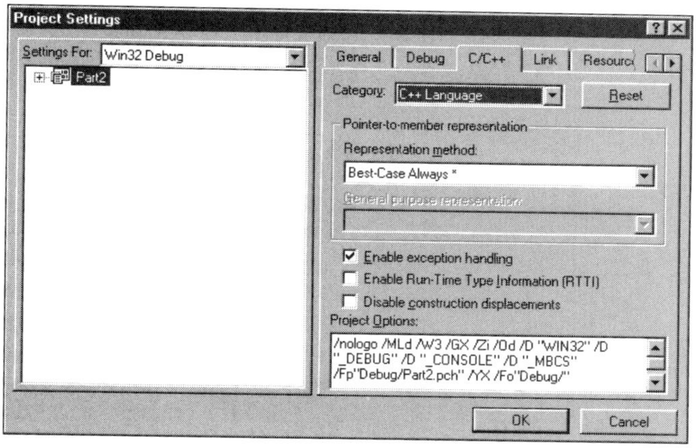

Figure 29-1: The Project Settings window.

Choosing General Settings

The General Settings tab window, which is shown in Figure 29-2, contains two settings of interest. First, are you or are you not using MFC? MFC stands for Microsoft Foundation Classes and applies to Windows development, so the answer here is basically No.

The second question concerns directories. Visual C++ generates several intermediate files while both editing and compiling. Normally, these files go into the current directory. However, Visual C++ allows you to place these temporaries in a different directory if you like. About the only reason for this would be if the current directory were full (unlikely) or if you had a really fast disk (like a RAM disk) off to the side that you could use for temporary files. In this same section, Visual C++ allows you to place the file executable in any directory you like.

TIP

The directory name provided is relative, so if you want the output directory to be completely independent of the current directory, provide a full path as is shown in Figure 29-2 for the Output directory.

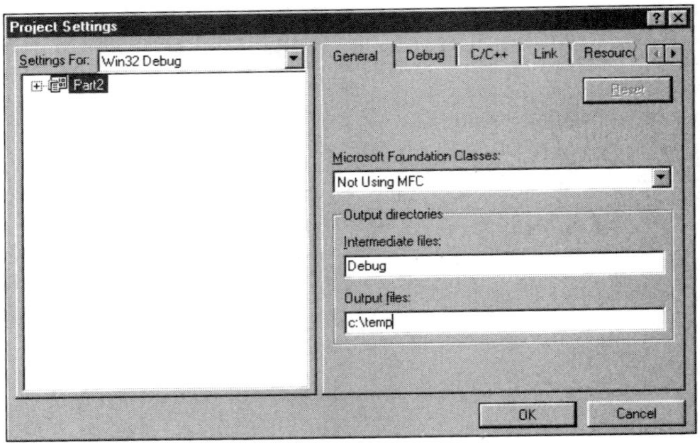

Figure 29-2: The General tab window.

Selecting Settings for Debug

The Debug Settings tab, shown in Figure 29-3, has four catch-all questions. Only the second and third text fields affect much.

The second text field specifies the Working Directory. This directory is much the same as the Intermediate File directory specified under the General tab, which allows the user to direct intermediate debug files to a separate location.

The third text field allows the programmer to enter any arguments to the program during debug. These arguments would normally follow the program name when executing it from the command line prompt.

A second category under the Debug Settings tab is Additional DLL. Here DLL stands for Dynamic Link Library. Most readers of this book will have little use for this setting.

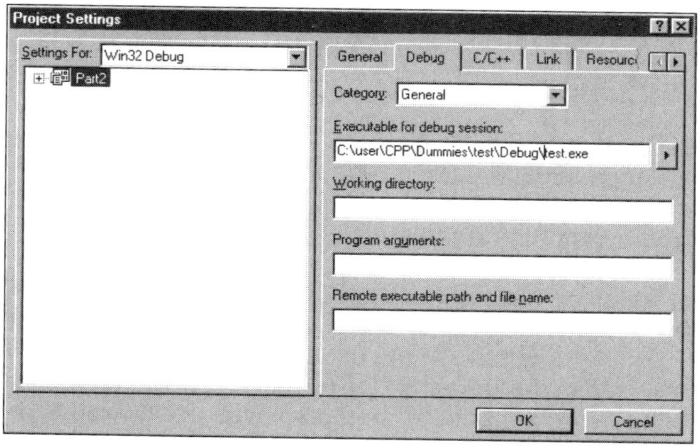

Figure 29-3: The Debug tab window.

Choosing General Options for C/C++

The C/C++ tab hides most of the "good stuff" starting right from the General category, as shown in Figure 29-4.

The Warning Level tells the compiler how hard to look for errors. A level of 0 says overlook all but the most heinous infractions. Level 4 says don't let much of anything get by. The default is 3, although I prefer the higher level of 4.

Normally, the compiler continues with the link step after all the source files have compiled, even if warnings were generated. If the Warnings as Errors check box is selected, the link step is not performed if any warnings are generated.

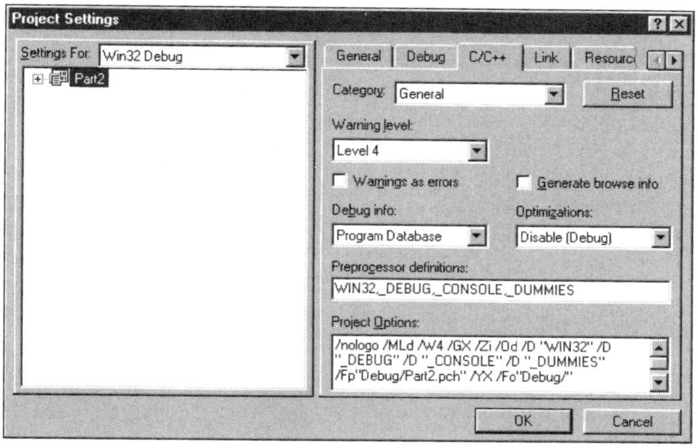

Figure 29-4: The General category of the C/C++ tab window.

The Debug Info select box allows the user to select the form that the debug information takes. You probably don't have a reason to mess with this setting.

Browsing of variables during debug requires browser information to be generated during compilation; however, this is not the default because it increases the size of the object files while slowing down compilation a lot. To enable this, select the Generate Browse Info check box.

The Optimizations setting controls the amount of optimization that the compiler performs. During debug, you really don't want any optimizations performed because it can cause the debugger to do some confusing things. When you are ready to generate a "for release" version, enable either the Maximum Speed or Minimum Size options. If you prefer, you can select Customize and select the particular optimizations from the list provided that you would like to perform.

Finally, the Preprocessor Definitions window allows you to define any preprocessor `#define`s you would like. For example, notice that I have added the `#define _DUMMIES`. This allows me to control how my code is compiled via preprocessor directives within the code. You can add whatever you want, but be careful not to remove or modify any directives that are already there.

Controlling C++ Language Settings

The C++ language category allows the programmer to control those settings that are unique to C++. Some of these settings are rather confusing, so you may want to skip this category. This window is shown in Figure 29-5.

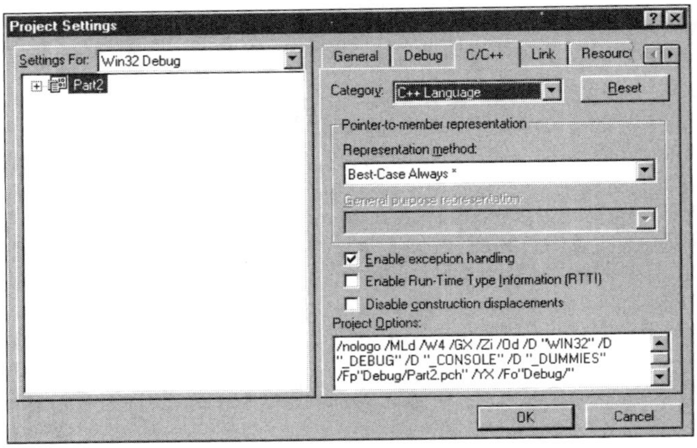

Figure 29-5: The C++ category of the C/C++ tab window.

Visual C++ supports different formats for the way that pointers to virtual member functions are handled. The default is Best-Case Always, which allows the compiler to select the format. However, if you want to control the case, select General Purpose under Representation method and you will be afforded three options: Point to Any Class, Point to Single- and Multiple-Inheritance Classes, and Point to Single-Inheritance Classes. The first two options generate more complicated code than the single-inheritance option; however, select it and the compiler will no longer support multiple inheritance.

The next three check boxes also allow you to simplify the code generated by the compiler. If you are not using exception handling (you should be), deselect Enable Exception Handling for a small decrease in the time to call a function. Leave the next two deselected — they represent features that I don't discuss.

Choosing Code Generation Settings

The Code Generation window shown in Figure 29-6 controls the final step in the compilation process.

The Processor allows the user to select the type of CPU for which the compiled code is designed. The default Blend produces a blend of code that is optimized for most 80386 and later processors. You can select other specific variations of the Intel 80 x 86 processor; however, the resulting code may not execute on earlier processors.

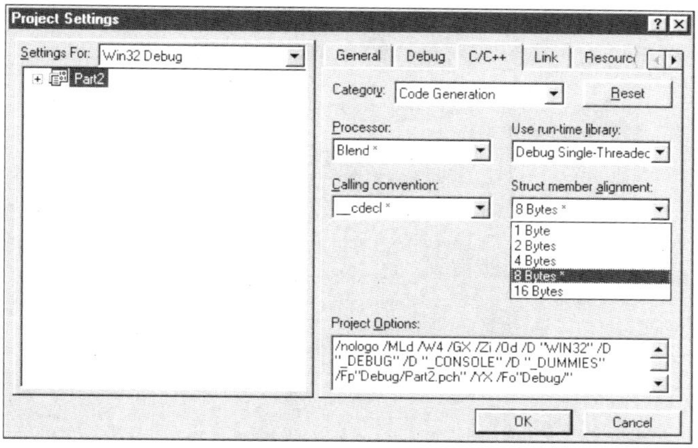

Figure 29-6: The Code Generation category of the C/C++ tab window.

The Calling Convention drop-down menu refers to the default way in which arguments are passed to functions. The default `cdecl` refers to the way in which most compilers pass arguments to C functions, by pushing arguments from left to right. The selection `stdcall` passes functions in the opposite direction. The third selection fastcall passes the first two arguments by caching them in a register. This can significantly speed up the performance of very small functions.

The third drop-down menu, Use Run-time Library, refers to the set of .lib functions you want to link with. Normally, you will want to link with the Single-threaded or Debug Single-threaded. If you are creating multiple threads in your program (I didn't in this book), you will need to select the Multi-threaded versions.

The final drop-down menu allows the user to select the alignment of structures. Making this number too large will waste a small amount of space but have no other affect. Making this number too small can significantly slow down the execution speed of the program. When generating code for modern Intel processors, this number should not be less than 4 and perhaps not smaller than 8.

Customizing with the Code Generation Window

The Code Generation window of the C/C++ tab window, shown in Figure 29-7, contains a series of individual check boxes.

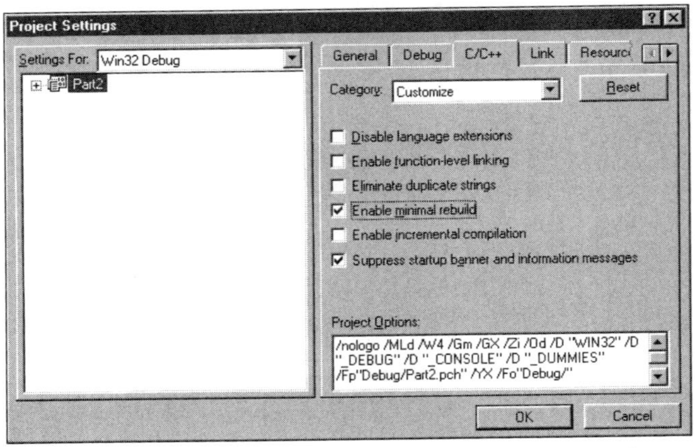

Figure 29-7: The Customize category of the C/C++ tab window.

Visual C++ enables a few language extensions to make Windows programming easier. It is often a good idea to disable these language extensions if you are trying to write code that will be ported to a different environment.

Enabling Minimal Rebuild can save programmer time by only relinking those parts of the program that have changed since the last time the program was linked. Because this results in a larger executable file, you'll eventually want to perform a full relink, but it's worthwhile when you're in the constant compile/relink cycle common during development.

Enabling Incremental Compilation can also save time in that it recompiles only those functions that have changed since the last time the module has been compiled.

Controlling Compile Optimizations

The Optimizations category allows the programmer to control the types of compile optimizations that are performed (see Figure 29-8).

The three most common selections are Debug (meaning perform no optimizations), Optimize for Speed, or Optimize for Size. A fourth option, Customize, allows the user to select the specific customizations that she would like to perform. I don't recommend this setting, however, because some of the optimizations are not safe. Without knowing what you're doing, you can generate code that does not work from perfectly correct source code.

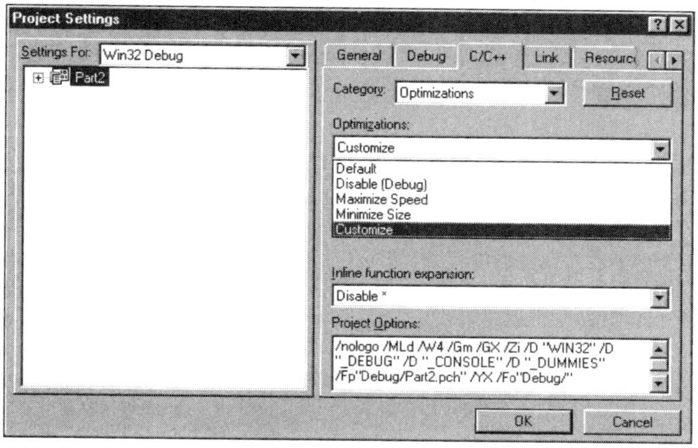

Figure 29-8: The Optimizations category of the C/C++ tab window.

The Inline function expansion setting has three positions. In debug mode, the default is Disable, meaning that all functions are outlined whether they are declared inline or not. A second setting inlines functions that are specifically declared with the inline keyword, but none else. The final setting, Any Suitable, enables inlining for any function, which fulfills the requirements for inlining. See Chapter 5 for details on function inlining.

Selecting Precompiled Headers

The Standard C++ include files almost never change. Compiling these include files over and over again can result in a significant waste of time, because they seldom, if ever, change. To address this, the window shown in Figure 29-9 shows the support in Visual C++ for precompiled headers.

When precompiled headers are enabled, the first time you compile your source file, the compiler writes the results of compiling the .H include files to a separate file, with the file extension .PCH. The next time you compile that module, or any other module that includes the same .H files, the compiler reads this saved information instead of recompiling the same files. Often, the Standard C++ include files are considerably larger than the application code, so enabling precompiled headers can increase compilation speed considerably.

To get the maximum benefit from precompiled headers, try to include the same .H files in the same order in each module. Enabling precompiled headers should have no effect on the executable file produced. When precompiled headers are turned on, they should automatically sense a change to a header file and cause the precompiled headers to rebuild. If you suspect otherwise, you can turn precompiled headers off.

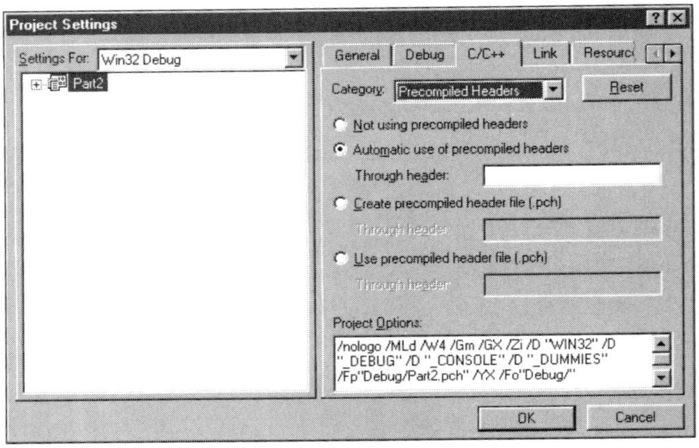

Figure 29-9: The Precompiled Headers category of the C/C++ tab window.

Appendix A: Glossary

abstract class: A class that contains one or more pure virtual functions. Such a class cannot be instanced with an object.

abstraction: The concept of simplifying a real-world concept into its essential elements. Abstraction allows software classes to represent what would otherwise be hopelessly complicated real-world concepts.

analysis phase: The phase of development during which the problem is analyzed to determine its essential elements.

base class: A class from which another class inherits.

callback function: A function invoked by the operating system when a specific event occurs.

class member: Another term for static member.

classification: The grouping of similar objects. For example, warm-blooded, live-bearing, suckling animals are grouped into the classification *mammals.*

code segment: The part of a program containing executable instructions.

coding phase: The phase during which the results of the design phase are turned into code.

constructor: A special member function invoked automatically when an object is created.

copy constructor: A constructor whose argument is a reference to an object of the same class. For example, the copy constructor for class `Z` is declared `Z::Z(Z&)`.

data segment: The block of memory where C and C++ keep global and static variables. See *code segment* and *stack segment.*

deep copy: A copy made by replicating the object plus any assets owned by the object, including objects pointed at by data members of the object being copied.

default constructor: The constructor that has a *void* argument list.

derived class: A class that inherits from another class.

design phase: The phase of development during which the solution to the problem is formulated. The input to this phase is the result of the analysis phase.

disambiguation: The process of deciding which overloaded function a call refers to by comparing the use to the prototypes of the overloaded functions.

early binding: The normal, non-polymorphic calling method. All calls in C are bound early.

expression: A sequence of subexpressions and operators. A C or C++ expression always has a type and a value.

extensibility: The capability to add new features to a class without modifying existing code that uses that class.

friend: A function or class that is not a member of the class but is granted access to the private and protected members of the class.

function declaration: The description of a function giving its name, the name of the class with which the function is associated (if any), the number and type of any arguments, and the type of any value returned by the function.

function prototype declaration: A function declaration that contains no code.

function signature: Another name for the full function name (including argument types and return type).

global variable: A variable declared outside a function and therefore accessible to all functions.

heap: Memory allocated to the program through calls to `malloc()`. Such memory must be returned to the heap through calls to `free()`.

inheritance: The capability of a class in C++ to assume the properties of an existing class.

inline function: A function expanded at the point it is called, much like a macro definition.

instance member: Another term for a normal, nonstatic member.

instance of a class: A declared object of the specified type. For example, in the `int i` declaration, `i` is an instance of class `int`.

IS_A: The relationship between a subclass and its base class. For example, a `Mallard` IS_A `Duck`, meaning that an object of class `Mallard` is also a `Duck`.

late binding: The process by which polymorphism is accomplished in C++.

local variable: A variable declared in a function and therefore accessible to only that function.

member function: A function defined as part of a class in the same way that a data member is defined.

method: Another term for member function.

object-oriented programming: Programming that is based on the principles of data hiding, abstraction, inheritance, and polymorphism.

operator overloading: Defining a meaning for intrinsic operators when applied to a user-defined class.

outline function: A conventional function that is expanded at the point it is declared. Any subsequent references to the function generate a call to the point in memory where the function is expanded. See *inline function.*

overloading: Giving two different functions the same name. Such functions must be differentiable by the number or types of their arguments.

overriding: Providing a function in a subclass with the same name and arguments as a function in the base class. See *polymorphism* and *virtual member function.*

paradigm: A way of thinking; an approach to programming. Used in the context of the object-oriented paradigm or the functional programming paradigm. (Pronounced "pair-a-dime," as in 20 cents.)

pointer variable: A variable that contains an address.

polymorphism: The capability to decide which overloaded member function to invoke on the basis of the real-time type of the object, not the declared type of the object.

private: A class member accessible only to other members of the same class.

protected: A class member accessible to other members of the same class and members of any subclass. Protected members are not accessible publicly.

public: A class member accessible outside the class.

pure virtual function: A virtual member function that has no implementation.

reference variable: A variable that serves as an alias to another variable.

shallow copy: A binary, bit-for-bit copy.

short-circuit evaluation: A technique by which the right-hand subexpression of a binary expression is not evaluated if its value would not affect the value of the overall expression. This occurs with two operators, `&&` and `||`. For example, in the expression `a && b`, if the left-hand argument evaluates to 0 (false), there is no need to evaluate the right-hand argument because the result will still be 0.

signature field: A nonstatic data member that is given a particular value. This value can be checked in the member functions to determine whether `this` points to a valid object. This is a highly effective debugging technique.

stack segment: The part of a program in memory that contains the nonstatic, local variables.

static data member: A data member not associated with the individual instances of the class. For each class, one instance of each static data member exists, irrespective of how many objects of that class are created.

static member function: A member function that has no `this` pointer.

stream I/O: C++ input/output based on overloading `operator<<` and `operator>>`. The prototypes for these functions are in the include file `iostream.h`.

subclass: A class that inherits publicly from a base class. If `Undergraduate` is a subclass of `Student`, then `Undergraduate` IS_A `Student`.

`this`: The pointer to the current object. `this` is an implicit, hidden, first argument to all nonstatic member functions. `this` is always of type "pointer to the current class."

variable type: Specifies the size and internal structure of the variable. The built-in, or intrinsic, variable types are `int`, `char`, `float`, and `double`.

virtual member function: A member function that is called polymorphically. See *polymorphism*.

v_table: A table that contains the addresses of the virtual functions of a class. Each class that has one or more virtual member functions must have a v_table.

Appendix B

About the CD

On the CD-ROM:

- Getting your CD up and running
- Installing the code for this book

System Requirements

Make sure that your computer meets the following minimum system requirements listed. If your computer doesn't match up to most of these requirements, you may have problems using the contents of the CD.

- A PC with a 486 or faster processor.
- Microsoft Windows 3.1 or later.
- At least 8MB of total RAM installed on your computer. For best performance, I recommend that Windows 95–equipped PCs that have at least 16MB of RAM installed.
- At least 200KB of hard drive space available to install all the code from this CD. (You need less space if you don't install every program.)
- A CD-ROM drive — double-speed (2x) or faster.
- A monitor capable of displaying at least 256 colors or grayscale.

If you need more information on the basics, check out *PCs For Dummies,* 4th Edition, by Dan Gookin; *Macs For Dummies,*4th Edition, by David Pogue; *Windows 95 For Dummies* by Andy Rathbone; or *Windows 3.11 For Dummies,* 3rd Edition, by Andy Rathbone (all published by IDG Books Worldwide, Inc.).

Using the CD with Microsoft Windows

To install the items from the CD to your hard drive, follow these steps.

1. **Insert the CD into your computer's CD-ROM drive.**

   Give your computer a moment to take a look at the CD.

2. **When the light on your CD-ROM drive goes out, double-click on the My Computer icon. (It's probably in the top-left corner of your desktop.)**

   This action opens the My Computer window, which shows you all the drives attached to your computer, the Control Panel, and a couple other handy things.

3. **Double-click on the icon for your CD-ROM drive.**

   Another window opens, showing you all the folders and files on the CD.

4. **Double-click the file called License.txt.**

   This file contains the end-user license that you agree to by using the CD. When you are finished reading the license, close the program, most likely NotePad, that displayed the file.

5. **Double-click the file called Readme.txt.**

   This file contains the most up-to-date information about the code.

6. **You can copy individual folders from the CD to an appropriately named folder on your hard drive, or you can run the self-extractor, CODE.EXE.**

The self-extractor will place all the files on your hard drive and maintain the folder structure of the CD. The default location for the files to be installed is C:\C++ FD CODE, but you can change the name of this folder in the self-extractor dialog box.

What You'll Find

The CD includes all the programs you'll need to use with this book. Each folder on the CD represents a chapter in the book. The programs are numbered sequentially within each folder. The CD also includes a 25-Minute Workout (see the Introduction for more information about the Workout). The questions for each part are in the QUESTION.TXT file. The answers are in the corresponding part file.

If You've Got Problems (Of the CD Kind)

I tried my best to compile programs that work on most computers with the minimum system requirements. Alas, your computer may differ, and some programs may not work properly for some reason.

The two likeliest problems are that you don't have enough memory (RAM) for the programs you want to use, or you have other programs running that are affecting installation or running of a program. If you get error messages like `Not enough memory` or `Setup cannot continue`, try one or more of these methods and then try using the software again:

- **Turn off any anti-virus software that you have on your computer.** Installers sometimes mimic virus activity and may make your computer incorrectly believe that it is being infected by a virus.
- **Close all running programs.** The more programs you're running, the less memory is available to other programs. Installers also typically update files and programs; if you keep other programs running, installation may not work properly.
- **In Windows, close the CD interface and run demos or installations directly from Windows Explorer.** The interface itself can tie up system memory, or even conflict with certain kinds of interactive demos. Use Windows Explorer to browse the files on the CD and launch installers or demos.
- **Have your local computer store add more RAM to your computer.** This is, admittedly, a drastic and somewhat expensive step. However, if you have a Windows 95 PC, adding more memory can really help the speed of your computer and enable more programs to run at the same time.

If you still have trouble installing the items from the CD, please call the IDG Books Worldwide Customer Service phone number: 800-762-2974 (outside the U.S.: 317-596-5430).

Index

• Symbols •

• A •

• C •

• D •

(continued)

• G •

• H •

• I •

• *p* •

• R •

• T •

• V •

• W •

Notes

IDG Books Worldwide, Inc., End-User License Agreement

READ THIS. You should carefully read these terms and conditions before opening the software packet(s) included with this book ("Book"). This is a license agreement ("Agreement") between you and IDG Books Worldwide, Inc. ("IDGB"). By opening the accompanying software packet(s), you acknowledge that you have read and accept the following terms and conditions. If you do not agree and do not want to be bound by such terms and conditions, promptly return the Book and the unopened software packet(s) to the place you obtained them for a full refund.

1. **License Grant.** IDGB grants to you (either an individual or entity) a nonexclusive license to use one copy of the enclosed software program(s) (collectively, the "Software") solely for your own personal or business purposes on a single computer (whether a standard computer or a workstation component of a multiuser network). The Software is in use on a computer when it is loaded into temporary memory (RAM) or installed into permanent memory (hard disk, CD-ROM, or other storage device). IDGB reserves all rights not expressly granted herein.

2. **Ownership.** IDGB is the owner of all right, title, and interest, including copyright, in and to the compilation of the Software recorded on the disk(s) or CD-ROM ("Software Media"). Copyright to the individual programs recorded on the Software Media is owned by the author or other authorized copyright owner of each program. Ownership of the Software and all proprietary rights relating thereto remain with IDGB and its licensers.

3. **Restrictions on Use and Transfer.**

   (a) You may only (i) make one copy of the Software for backup or archival purposes, or (ii) transfer the Software to a single hard disk, provided that you keep the original for backup or archival purposes. You may not (i) rent or lease the Software, (ii) copy or reproduce the Software through a LAN or other network system or through any computer subscriber system or bulletin-board system, or (iii) modify, adapt, or create derivative works based on the Software.

   (b) You may not reverse engineer, decompile, or disassemble the Software. You may transfer the Software and user documentation on a permanent basis, provided that the transferee agrees to accept the terms and conditions of this Agreement and you retain no copies. If the Software is an update or has been updated, any transfer must include the most recent update and all prior versions.

4. **Restrictions on Use of Individual Programs.** You must follow the individual requirements and restrictions detailed for each individual program in the "About the CD" section of this Book. These limitations are also contained in the individual license agreements recorded on the Software Media. These limitations may include a requirement that after using the program for a specified period of time, the user must pay a registration fee or discontinue use. By opening the Software packet(s), you will be agreeing to abide by the licenses and restrictions for these individual programs that are detailed in the "About the CD" section and on the Software Media. None of the material on this Software Media or listed in this Book may ever be redistributed, in original or modified form, for commercial purposes.

5. **Limited Warranty.**

   (a) IDGB warrants that the Software and Software Media are free from defects in materials and workmanship under normal use for a period of sixty (60) days from the date of purchase of this Book. If IDGB receives notification within the warranty period of defects in materials or workmanship, IDGB will replace the defective Software Media.

   (b) **IDGB AND THE AUTHOR OF THE BOOK DISCLAIM ALL OTHER WARRANTIES, EXPRESS OR IMPLIED, INCLUDING WITHOUT LIMITATION IMPLIED WARRANTIES OF MERCHANTABILITY AND FITNESS FOR A PARTICULAR PURPOSE, WITH RESPECT TO THE SOFTWARE, THE PROGRAMS, THE SOURCE CODE CONTAINED THEREIN, AND/OR THE TECHNIQUES DESCRIBED IN THIS BOOK. IDGB DOES NOT WARRANT THAT THE FUNCTIONS CONTAINED IN THE SOFTWARE WILL MEET YOUR REQUIREMENTS OR THAT THE OPERATION OF THE SOFTWARE WILL BE ERROR FREE.**

   (c) This limited warranty gives you specific legal rights, and you may have other rights that vary from jurisdiction to jurisdiction.

6. **Remedies.**

   (a) IDGB's entire liability and your exclusive remedy for defects in materials and workmanship shall be limited to replacement of the Software Media, which may be returned to IDGB with a copy of your receipt at the following address: Software Media Fulfillment Department, Attn.: *C++ For Dummies,* 3rd Edition, IDG Books Worldwide, Inc., 7260 Shadeland Station, Ste. 100, Indianapolis, IN 46256, or call 800-762-2974. Please allow three to four weeks for delivery. This Limited Warranty is void if failure of the Software Media has resulted from accident, abuse, or misapplication. Any replacement Software Media will be warranted for the remainder of the original warranty period or thirty (30) days, whichever is longer.

   (b) In no event shall IDGB or the author be liable for any damages whatsoever (including without limitation damages for loss of business profits, business interruption, loss of business information, or any other pecuniary loss) arising from the use of or inability to use the Book or the Software, even if IDGB has been advised of the possibility of such damages.

   (c) Because some jurisdictions do not allow the exclusion or limitation of liability for consequential or incidental damages, the above limitation or exclusion may not apply to you.

7. **U.S. Government Restricted Rights.** Use, duplication, or disclosure of the Software by the U.S. Government is subject to restrictions stated in paragraph (c)(1)(ii) of the Rights in Technical Data and Computer Software clause of DFARS 252.227-7013, and in subparagraphs (a) through (d) of the Commercial Computer–Restricted Rights clause at FAR 52.227-19, and in similar clauses in the NASA FAR supplement, when applicable.

8. **General.** This Agreement constitutes the entire understanding of the parties and revokes and supersedes all prior agreements, oral or written, between them and may not be modified or amended except in a writing signed by both parties hereto that specifically refers to this Agreement. This Agreement shall take precedence over any other documents that may be in conflict herewith. If any one or more provisions contained in this Agreement are held by any court or tribunal to be invalid, illegal, or otherwise unenforceable, each and every other provision shall remain in full force and effect.

C++ FOR DUMMIES®

DELUXE COMPILER KIT

by Stephen R. Davis

IDG BOOKS WORLDWIDE

IDG Books Worldwide, Inc.
An International Data Group Company

Foster City, CA ✦ Chicago, IL ✦ Indianapolis, IN ✦ New York, NY

C++ For Dummies® Deluxe Compiler Kit

Published by
IDG Books Worldwide, Inc.
An International Data Group Company
919 E. Hillsdale Blvd.
Suite 400
Foster City, CA 94404
www.idgbooks.com (IDG Books Worldwide Web site)
www.dummies.com (Dummies Press Web site)

Part #: MM007

Printed in the United States of America

10 9 8 7 6 5 4 3 2 1

IP/TQ/QW/ZZ/IN

Distributed in the United States by IDG Books Worldwide, Inc.

Distributed by CDG Books Canada Inc. for Canada; by Transworld Publishers Limited in the United Kingdom; by IDG Norge Books for Norway; by IDG Sweden Books for Sweden; by Woodslane Pty. Ltd. for Australia; by Woodslane (NZ) Ltd. for New Zealand; by TransQuest Publishers Pte Ltd. for Singapore, Malaysia, Thailand, Indonesia, and Hong Kong; by ICG Muse, Inc. for Japan; by Norma Comunicaciones S.A. for Colombia; by Intersoft for South Africa; by Eyrolles for France; by International Thomson Publishing for Germany, Austria and Switzerland; by Distribuidora Cuspide for Argentina; by Livraria Cultura for Brazil; by Ediciones ZETA S.C.R. Ltda. for Peru; by WS Computer Publishing Corporation, Inc., for the Philippines; by Contemporanea de Ediciones for Venezuela; by Express Computer Distributors for the Caribbean and West Indies; by Micronesia Media Distributor, Inc. for Micronesia; by Grupo Editorial Norma S.A. for Guatemala; by Chips Computadoras S.A. de C.V. for Mexico; by Editorial Norma de Panama S.A. for Panama; by American Bookshops for Finland. Authorized Sales Agent: Anthony Rudkin Associates for the Middle East and North Africa.

For general information on IDG Books Worldwide's books in the U.S., please call our Consumer Customer Service department at 800-762-2974. For reseller information, including discounts and premium sales, please call our Reseller Customer Service department at 800-434-3422.

For information on where to purchase IDG Books Worldwide's books outside the U.S., please contact our International Sales department at 317-596-5530 or fax 317-596-5692.

For consumer information on foreign language translations, please contact our Customer Service department at 1-800-434-3422, fax 317-596-5692, or e-mail rights@idgbooks.com.

For information on licensing foreign or domestic rights, please phone +1-650-655-3109.

For sales inquiries and special prices for bulk quantities, please contact our Sales department at 650-655-3200 or write to the address above.

For information on using IDG Books Worldwide's books in the classroom or for ordering examination copies, please contact our Educational Sales department at 800-434-2086 or fax 317-596-5499.

For press review copies, author interviews, or other publicity information, please contact our Public Relations department at 650-655-3000 or fax 650-655-3299.

For authorization to photocopy items for corporate, personal, or educational use, please contact Copyright Clearance Center, 222 Rosewood Drive, Danvers, MA 01923, or fax 978-750-4470.

Publisher's Acknowledgments

We're proud of this book; please register your comments through our IDG Books Worldwide Online Registration Form located at `http://my2cents.dummies.com`.

Some of the people who helped bring this book to market include the following:

Acquisitions, Editorial, and Media Development

Project Editor: Jade Leah Williams

Acquisitions Editor: Greg Croy

Copy Editor: Barry Childs-Helton

Technical Editor: Oran Sands

Associate Permissions Editor: Carmen Krikorian

Editorial Manager: Leah Cameron, Rev Mengle

Media Development Manager: Heather Heath Dismore

Editorial Assistant: Beth Parlon

Production

Project Coordinator: Melissa Stauffer

Layout and Graphics: Angela F. Hunckler, Brent Savage, M. Anne Sipahimalani

Proofreader: Brian Massey

General and Administrative

IDG Books Worldwide, Inc.: John Kilcullen, CEO; Steven Berkowitz, President and Publisher

IDG Books Technology Publishing Group: Richard Swadley, Senior Vice President and Publisher; Walter Bruce III, Vice President and Associate Publisher; Steven Sayre, Associate Publisher; Joseph Wikert, Associate Publisher; Mary Bednarek, Branded Product Development Director; Mary Corder, Editorial Director

IDG Books Consumer Publishing Group: Roland Elgey, Senior Vice President and Publisher; Kathleen A. Welton, Vice President and Publisher; Kevin Thornton, Acquisitions Manager; Kristin A. Cocks, Editorial Director

IDG Books Internet Publishing Group: Brenda McLaughlin, Senior Vice President and Group Publisher; Diane Graves Steele, Vice President and Associate Publisher; Sofia Marchant, Online Marketing Manager

IDG Books Production for Dummies Press: Michael R. Britton, Vice President of Production; Debbie Stailey, Associate Director of Production; Cindy L. Phipps, Manager of Project Coordination, Production Proofreading, and Indexing; Shelley Lea, Supervisor of Graphics and Design; Debbie J. Gates, Production Systems Specialist; Robert Springer, Supervisor of Proofreading; Laura Carpenter, Production Control Manager; Tony Augsburger, Supervisor of Reprints and Bluelines

◆

The publisher would like to give special thanks to Patrick J. McGovern, without whom this book would not have been possible.

◆

The program included on this kit's CD-ROM was reproduced by IDG Books Worldwide, Inc. under a special arrangement with Microsoft Corporation. For this reason, IDG Books Worldwide, Inc. is responsible for the product warranty and for support. If your CD is defective, please return it to IDG Books Worldwide, Inc., which will arrange for its replacement. PLEASE DO NOT RETURN IT TO MICROSOFT CORPORATION. Any product support will be provided, if at all, by IDG Books Worldwide, Inc. PLEASE DO NOT CONTACT MICROSOFT CORPORATION FOR PRODUCT SUPPORT. End users of this Microsoft program shall not be considered "registered owners" of a Microsoft product and therefore shall not be eligible for upgrades, promotions or other benefits available to "registered owners" of Microsoft products.

Installing and Configuring Microsoft Visual C++ 6.0 Introductory Edition

In This Booklet

- Removing old versions of C++ programs
- Installing Microsoft Visual C++ 6.0
- Customizing and changing your installation options
- Customizing the Visual C++ 6.0 user interface
- Creating, building, and executing a program
- Staying bug-free

Congratulations! You are the proud owner of the C++ For Dummies Deluxe Compiler Kit. (Program packages always start with praise, trying to convince you that you didn't make a big mistake and that you shouldn't go cancel the check before it clears.) Since you've already ripped open the box, you know that this kit consists of three parts: *C++ For Dummies* book, a CD-ROM containing Microsoft Visual C++ 6.0 Introductory Edition, and this installation guide. (Actually, there's a fourth part: a CD-ROM lurking in the back jacket of the big book, containing the programs from the book. The deal keeps getting better all the time.)

The CD-ROM tucked in the back cover contains the programs from *C++ For Dummies*. This CD-ROM is meant to save you the work of typing in the programs by hand. This also eliminates the frustration of knowing that you typed in something wrong, but you just can't seem to find it. If you still can't find your problem, don't take it up with IDG Books Worldwide — you know how busy publishers are. You can contact me directly at `www.stephendavis.com`.

Sorting through C++ programs

What's the difference between the Introductory Edition of Visual C++ and the Standard Edition (or the departing edition, for that matter)? Not much, it turns out — except for one thing: you are not allowed to distribute programs that you create with the Introductory Edition. In other words, you can only play that great card game that you generated with Introductory Visual C++ at home. Your friend can't take a copy home to play — she can only play the game at your house (hey, that doesn't sound too bad after all).

If using the Introductory Edition convinces you that Visual C++ is the killer programming tool of your dreams, you may decide to register and shell out for the Enterprise Edition of Visual C++ — the Big Kahuna unlimited edition. (That *is* the idea behind introversions of software. But you knew that.) In addition to having access to all the cool C++ capabilities, you'll be street-legal when you share the programs you make with the Enterprise Edition.

You may be familiar with Visual Studio 6 — an industrial-strength set of programming tools from Microsoft that includes a here's-the-kitchen-sink version of Visual C++. Visual Studio 6 is really for nerds who write programs for a living and wear the pocket protector with pride. Visual Studio 6 includes a raft of language tools such as Visual Basic, Visual J++, and Visual SourceSafe. While these tools are useful, some of the tools in the package have nothing to do with programming in C++ at home. Let's stick closer to home and concentrate on Visual C++ itself in this kit.

If you're wondering what the practical difference is between Visual C++ and other C++ programs, the answer is — not much (whoa, déjà vu all over again) — except for the vigorous popularity of Visual C++. In all fairness, Visual C++ is true to the C++ standard. That is, there is no noticeable difference in capability between Visual C++ and the C++ Standard programming language.

If you're ready to start compiling and executing all those fine programs in the C++ book, as well as those you may later write yourself, then you have one minor chore to do first: install Visual C++ 6.0. (Details, details . . .) In their proper order, the three phases of this useful and exciting procedure are as follows:

1. **Removing any previous version of Visual C++.**
2. **Installing the most current product, including whatever options you prefer.**
3. **Installing the C++ documentation included on the disc.**

A closer look at each phase is right, fitting, and next.

Removing Earlier Versions of Visual C++

If you are completely, utterly, reliably sure that you do *not* have another version of Visual C++ installed on your computer, skip this section and go straight to the "Installing Microsoft Visual C++ 6.0 Introductory Edition" section of this booklet. If an old version of C++ *is* lurking on your system, you're where you need to be — push on.

Version 6 is capable of installing itself over earlier versions of Visual C++. My personal preference is to remove the older versions before starting the installation process. It's generally safer; when it comes to giving an automated process *carte blanche,* I am a software coward. Besides, should anything go wrong during that automated installation, removing any earlier version of C++ becomes an absolute necessity anyway. Might as well get it over with now.

You may want to reconsider your options before you start removing that earlier version of Visual C++ from your system. If the programs covered in *C++ For Dummies* execute just fine under Visual C++ 5.0 — for example, if you happen to have a full-blown Version 5 installed on your computer — you may not want to install the Introductory Edition of Version 6. Installing the Introductory Edition of Version 6 will take away your right to freely distribute the programs you write. To regain that right after installing Version 6, you must either reinstall your old version of Visual C++ prior to uninstalling the introductory issue or forge ahead and buy the Enterprise Edition of Version 6.0.

To uninstall an earlier version of Visual C++:

1. **Close all programs that are currently executing on your PC, but keep Windows 95 or 98 running.**
2. **Open the Control Panel by double-clicking the small computer (My Computer) icon on your desktop (isn't it cute?) and then double-clicking the Control Panel icon.**
3. **Double-click the Add/Remove Programs icon in the Control Panel window.**

   A window appears, showing a list of all the programs installed on your computer.
4. **Select Microsoft Visual C++ *X* from the list of programs installed on your PC where *X* is the version you already have installed.**

   If no such label is present, then your computer doesn't have an earlier version and you can merrily skip to the "Installing Microsoft Visual C++ 6.0 Introductory Edition" section later in this booklet. You should not be overly concerned with any other version of C++ that might be present on your machine. Non-Microsoft versions of C++ do not interfere with Visual C++.
5. **Select Add/Remove.**

   A special installation window appears. If you get some error such as "Can't execute Installation program" (details may vary in your location), then someone (couldn't have been you, could it?) has deleted some part of the Visual C++ directory without uninstalling it first. Your best option is to reinstall the old version and then uninstall it. (It's crazy, but it works. Apparently reinstalling the old package restores it to pristine condition so that the uninstall program can find what it expects to see during removal.)
6. **Select Remove All.**

   A pop-up window appears to confirm that yes, indeed, you are crazy enough to want to remove their fine product over which they sweated bullets just for your entertainment.
7. **Select Yes and sit back.**

   The install/remove program removes an impressive list of files.

8. **Reboot your computer if the installation program doesn't automatically reboot for you or if your computer appears to hang.**

You are now ready to proceed with the preliminary steps required to install Microsoft Visual C++ 6.0.

Navigating Through the Opening Screens prior to Installing Visual C++

Gone are the days when copying the files onto your hard disk was sufficient to install a program. Now days, you go through a sometimes confusing set of installation instructions before you can begin playing with your new toy.

You need to install Visual C++ 6.0 Introductory Edition from the CD-ROM provided onto your hard disk with this booklet. You cannot execute Visual C++ 6.0 directly from the CD-ROM.

Follow these steps prior to installing Microsoft Visual C++ 6.0.

1. **Remove the Visual C++ 6.0 CD-ROM from your compiler kit box and insert it into your computer.**

   The setup program executes automatically. If it doesn't, open and read the contents of the CD-ROM in the Windows Explorer. Double-click `Setup.exe` to open the Installation Wizard.

   The window opens, displaying a button that allows you to easily scan the Readme file.

2. **Click the View Readme file button to view special installation instructions.**

The Visual C++ Readme file contains more warnings than a TV ad for a prescription drug. I've studied the list and you need only concern yourself with one. Visual C++ 6.0 requires a Protected Mode CD-ROM driver (as opposed to a Real Mode driver). Unless you have a really old CD-ROM (say, pre-Windows 95), you're probably okay and can skip ahead to Step 7.

3. **Open the Control Panel again and double-click the System icon located near the bottom of the window.**

4. **When the list of System Properties appears select the Device Manager tab.**

5. **Select the CD-ROM icon from the list of devices.**

   A small exclamation point appears next to the name of the CD-ROM if it's a Real Mode driver or if there is something amiss with your CD-ROM driver. (A Real Mode driver is an "old style" driver written during the MS-DOS days. Windows 95 and later grudgingly support these older drivers but you really need to get them replaced.)

   If the System's window shows that your CD-ROM driver is working without complaint, proceed on to the next installation step.

   If your CD-ROM has a Real Mode driver, you need to contact the manufacturer of your CD-ROM for an update. You can probably download a new one over the Web. To find your manufacturer's Web address, try combining the name with www and .com. For example, `www.sony.com`. If that doesn't work, do a web search for your manufacturer's name.

6. **Back out gracefully by closing the System and Control Panel windows before proceeding. (You don't *have* to close the System and Control Panel windows, but if you don't, the screen becomes amazingly messy.)**

7. **Closing the Control Panel window reveals the installation window sitting patiently in the background. Click Next to move to the End User License Agreement window.**

   Actually, the End User License Agreement lists the limitations that you will need to accept as part of using Visual C++ 6.0 Introductory Edition.

8. **Click I Accept the Agreement.**

   If you are not prepared to accept the agreement, you can always use the CD-ROM as a coaster.

9. **Click Next to move to the Product Number and User ID window.**

10. **Enter your name and, optionally, your company's name.**

    If you are paranoid, enter someone else's name. The Visual C++ package will associate you by this name. Your name may appear if you have installed certain other Microsoft products previously. Because this is the Introductory version, no keyword is required.

At this point, the installer will check to see if you have Microsoft's Internet Explorer version 4.01 or newer installed on your computer. If you do, the IE takes over and you may skip to Step 11.

If IE 4.01 is not on your computer, follow the subset of instructions in the sidebar, "Installing Internet Explorer 4.01" for installation. The installation of IE 4.01 is necessary to run Visual C++6.0.

Installing Internet Explorer 4.01

If you were in the preliminary process of installing Microsoft Visual C++ 6.0 and discovered that you didn't have the Internet Explorer installed on your computer, then this section is for you.

Follow these steps to install IE 4.01 on your computer:

1. **The Install Internet Explorer dialog box appears and asks if you wish to install the new version of I.E. Click Next to proceed.**
2. **The Active Setup dialog box appears. Click Next to continue.**
3. **The End-User License Agreement dialog box appears. Click I accept and then click the Next button.**
4. **The next dialog box allows you to select between the standard or full installation. Select your preference and then click Next.**
5. **If you wish to install the Windows Desktop Update, click Yes. If you fear change (or at least prefer to keep your desktop the way that it currently is), click No.**
6. **Select your country of residence and then click Next.**
7. **Select the folder or drive where you want to install I.E. 4 and click Next.**

   The installer now begins to install the various components of IE 4. If this procedure is interrupted, a message appears saying, "Setup was unable to install all the components. Please close all applications and try running Setup again." Do as the message requests and start over with Step 1. The installer automatically restarts the IE 4 installer again. Click Back as requested.
8. **A message appears telling you to reboot your computer. Click No.**

   This choice returns you to the IE 4 install screen.

(continued)

(continued)

9. **Click Exit and then reboot your computer in the normal manner.**
10. **After Windows restarts, return to the preceding Step 1 and start the pre-installation steps again. (See the "Navigating Through the Opening Screens prior to Installing Visual C++" section.)**
11. **The active Setup box appears again asking you to finish the installation. Click OK.**
12. **The installer will configure your system properly and then ask to reboot your machine again. Click OK.**
13. **After rebooting, the IE4 installer dialog box reappears. Click Next to proceed with the pre-installation of Visual C++ 6.0.**
14. **The Install DCOM98 (sounds like a trade show doesn't it?) dialog box appears. This is one more item that Visual C++ 6.0 requires to operate. Click Next.**
15. **Upon completion, the Install Wizard box appears and offers to reboot your machine again. Click OK.**

11. **Click Next to continue to the Choose Common Install Folder window.**

    This window allows you to select the lucky folder in which to install Visual C++. (A word to the wise and the impatient: Changing the installation folder from the default given is just asking for trouble.) As noted, you need 50 megabytes of available disk space to successfully install Visual C++ 6.0 Introductory Edition (the Enterprise Edition takes much more disk space than that). There was a time when 50 megabytes would have been considered outrageous, even on a NASA mainframe, but that's small in today's world of bloated software.

12. **Click Next and proceed to the Introductory Setup program.**

    The opening window of the Introductory Setup program asks you to read the End User License Agreement again. (Is there an echo here somewhere?)

13. **Click Continue to proceed.**

    This window displays your product ID. You will need your ID should you ever call Microsoft for help (in which case, good luck — you'll need it, along with a comfortable chair).

If you miss your ID, don't worry — you can always retrieve this number by clicking About from the Help menu once you are executing Visual C++.

14. **Select OK.**

    The installation program searches your hard disk to make sure you have the necessary disk space, and to see what other Microsoft-language products you may have installed. To customize your installation, see the section on "Installing Microsoft Visual C++ 6.0."

Installing Microsoft Visual C++ 6.0

The Introductory Setup program does not install every option present on the CD-ROM. To do so would waste valuable disk space with options that you may not need or don't care to use. (You don't want to blow that skimpy 50-meg allotment, now, do you? For example, do you really *need* a database driver to interface with dBase III?)

The Setup program gives you two options: Custom installation and Typical installation. The Custom installation allows you to select exactly the options that you want to install — the problem is that you must select the options that you want to install. The Typical installation saves you the trouble by installing the options that most programmers need without asking.

To install the program:

1. **Select the Typical or Custom button from the Introductory Setup window, shown in Figure 1, according to the type of setup you desire.**

   Choose Typical to install the default settings. If you choose Typical and later want to change your options, see "Changing Visual C++ Installation" section later in this booklet.

   Choose Custom to customize your setting and then go on to Step 2. This setting enables you to reduce the amount of disk space required through installing only those components that you need.

Don't agonize too much about this decision. You can always add or remove components later.

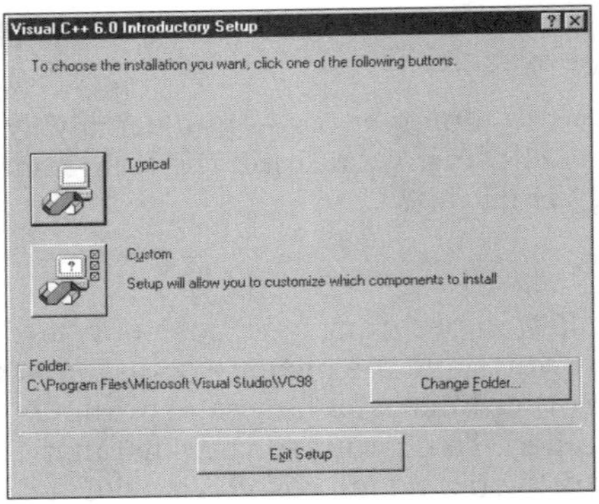

Figure 1: The Introductory Setup window allows the user to select the default settings by choosing Typical, or to customize by choosing Custom.

2. **To add or remove components, choose from the Options list box on the left, as shown in Figure 2.**

   The number to the right of the component refers to the available hard disk space. The number in the lower-left corner (next to "Space Required on C:") shows the total space required and the total space available for installing the selected components.

   Some options are all-or-nothing affairs. Click them off and you get nothing — click them on and you get the full Monty. Some options have sub-selections. A checkbox appears gray if some part but not all of an option is selected. The initial settings reflect what would have been installed had you selected the Typical default setting.

   For example, suppose you want to add the capability to access a FoxPro database. You could do it by following these steps:

   2a. Select the Data Access option (it contains all the database-access functions - there's no way to know that FoxPro access is hidden under Data Access except to search around).

   2b. Click the Change Option button.

   2c. Select ODBC drivers from the next window. (FoxPro accesses through an ODBC driver, whatever that is.)

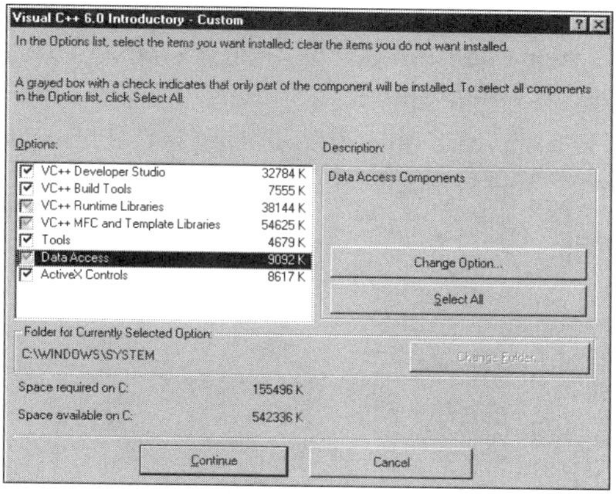

Figure 2: The Custom window displays the types of installation components that the operator can modify.

2d. **Again, click the Change Option button to make the Microsoft ODBC Drivers window appear.**

2e. **Select the FoxPro button. A check mark appears in the box.**

2f. **Select OK to exit the ODBC drivers window.**

2g. **Click OK to return to the top-level window.**

2h. **Click Continue when you've finished messing around selecting the options you want.**

3. **Click the Continue button after completing your installation setup.**

   The Setup program copies the Visual C++ files from the CD-ROM to your hard disk, as shown in Figure 3. In addition, the Visual C++ Setup program stores the data you entered (such as name, rank, favorite pet, and serial number) into the Windows Registry. (Big Bill's got in his registry now.)

4. **Click OK to complete installation of Visual C++.**

   The final menu window of the Introductory Setup program displays the Environment Variable message. You can ignore this message unless you plan to execute Visual C++ by using an MS-DOS command. (Visual C++ isn't very "Visual" from the command line.) To install documentation to support development, see the following section on "Installing Visual C++ 6.0 Introductory Documentation."

This is actually the only step during installation that makes any real changes. Up until now, you could click Cancel at any point without having made any permanent change to your hard disk.

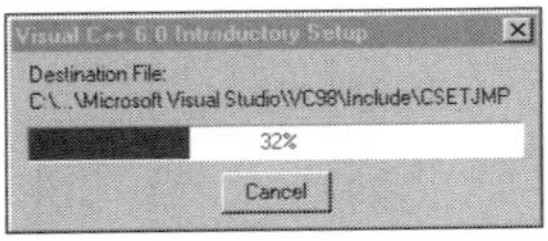

Figure 3: The actual installation of files to the hard disk occurs in the final installation step.

Installing Visual C++ 6.0 Introductory Documentation

A little knowledge is a dangerous thing; a little documentation is a pretty good life preserver. The Visual C++ 6.0 Introductory Documentation, included with the Introductory Edition, provides information that you can use with the C++ For Dummies book. The documentation also includes information on the Visual C++ 6.0 package, the Standard C++ library, the C++ language, and Windows programming.

Once Visual C++ 6.0 has been safely installed, the setup program gives you the option of installing the Visual C++ 6.0 Introductory Documentation from the window. This program installs a full set of documentation to support development.

To install the documentation package, click through the series of Nexts and provide the requested information. If you don't want to install the package, click the checkmark to deselect the documentation installation. Install this package unless you've decided to live "on the edge" without it (or you're a computer genius and don't need the documentation except as a little light reading).

If the window shown in Figure 4 appears, you have successfully completed the installation process. If you see anything else on-screen instead of that window, it's a sign of complete and ignominious failure.

If the installation is not successful, uninstall Visual C++ (by using the Add/Remove icon from the Control Panel or by executing `Setup.exe` from the CD-ROM as described at the beginning of this section) and start over again. If that doesn't work, examine the Readme file for further aid. If you still can't get anywhere, you might try the FAQ (frequently asked questions) sheet on `www.stephendavis.com`. When you determine what went wrong, please send along the fix to `CPPFIX@www.stephendavis.com` so that I can pass it along to others.

Though not absolutely required when you have finished installing Visual C++, you should reboot your PC anyway. It's one way to make sure everything is cleaned up properly. (Hmmm. Would it help if I rebooted my son to get his room cleaned up?)

Please don't reboot with the "three finger salute" (Ctrl + Alt + Delete) unless Windows has crashed. It's far better to reboot by clicking Start⇨Shut Down from the Start menu.

You can now remove the Visual C++ CD-ROM and put it away (in a safe place, not in a home for repeat-offender CDs).

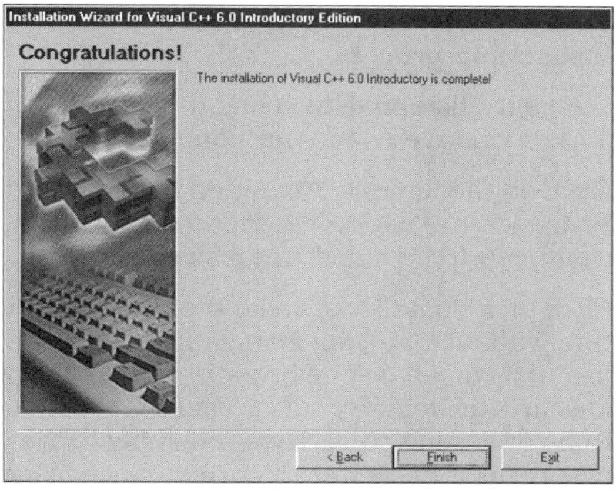

Figure 4: The Congratulations message signals a successful completion of the installation procedure.

Changing Visual C++ Installation

The Custom installation option allowed you to choose the options you want from the menu of your choice. If you selected the Typical option, you got the Daily Special. Unlike the faire at my local greasy spoon, you can change your options even after you finish dinner (if you get indigestion from your choices).

Adding and removing configuration options

The Setup program allows you to add or remove options to your Visual C++ configuration at any time, including the documentation.

1. **Put the installation CD-ROM into the drive. Inserting the CD-ROM executes the Setup program automatically. If it does not, don't worry. Open the CD-ROM in the Windows Explorer. Double-click `Setup.exe` to start the setup process.**

   The Setup program detects that Visual C++ 6.0 is on your computer. Setup then dutifully opens the window so you can update the current installation.

2. **Select the Workstation Tools and Components options to update the Visual C++ 6.0 installation.**

3. **Click on the Next button to take you back through the installation process.**

4. **Click on Customize to select the options you'd like to add or remove from your configuration.**

   Click on the Remove All option to remove the entire Visual C++ 6.0 package from the disk. This returns the vast majority of your hard disk space.

   Click on Reinstall to refresh the Visual C++ 6.0 installation without changing installation options. This is useful if somehow one or more of your Visual C++ 6.0 files are deleted. Try this if Visual C++ 6.0 doesn't seem to be operating correctly — crashing in the wrong places (as if there were a correct place to crash).

   Click on Add/Remove to change the installation options.

5. **Click on and off the installation options from the customization window that appears. This window is identical to the window that appears when you click the Custom button during the original installation.**
6. **Click on Continue when you have finished selecting the Visual C++ 6.0 installation options.**
7. **Click OK from the Installation Successful window that appears.**

   Pat yourself on the back for a job well done.

Updating your options

Since your first installation of Visual C++ 6.0, new and better documentation may be available. The following steps show you how to update the documentation that you already have. Execute the following steps to update the Visual C++ documentation.

1. **Put the installation CD-ROM into the drive. Inserting the CD-ROM executes the Setup program automatically. If it does not, don't worry. Open the CD-ROM in the Windows Explorer. Double-click** `Setup.exe` **to start the setup process.**

   The Setup program detects that Visual C++ 6.0 is on your computer. Setup then dutifully opens the window so you can update your current installation.
2. **Select the MSDN option to update the Visual C++ 6.0 documentation. (MSDN stands for Microsoft Developer Network).**
3. **Click the Next button. Make sure the Install Visual C++ 6.0 Introductory Documentation check box is checked.**
4. **Click Next to continue to the Visual C++ 6.0 Docs Setup window. This window allows you to either Install, Reinstall, or Remove the Visual C++ 6.0 documentation.**
5. **Click Reinstall to update the Visual C++ 6.0 Introductory Documentation.**
6. **Click Remove All to remove the Introductory documentation.**

Adding C++ Introductory Documentation later

If you chose not to install the Visual C++ 6.0 Introductory Documentation during your initial installation setup, you can install it now. Follow these steps to install the Visual C++ 6.0 Introductory Documentation:

1. **Insert the installation CD-ROM into your computer.**

   Inserting the CD-ROM automatically executes the Setup program. If it does not, don't worry. Open the CD-ROM in the Windows Explorer. Double-click `Setup.exe` to start the setup process.

   The Setup program detects that Visual C++ 6.0 is on your computer. Setup then dutifully opens the window so you can update your current installation.

2. **Select the MSDN option to update the Visual C++ 6.0 documentation. (MSDN stands for Microsoft Developer Network).**
3. **Click the Next button. Make sure the Install Visual C++ 6.0 Introductory Documentation check box is checked.**
4. **Click Continue to display the Product ID window.**
5. **Click OK to proceed to the License Agreement window. Read the License Agreement window.**
6. **Click I Agree, to install the Visual C++ 6.0 Introductory Documentation.**
7. **Click Typical installation from the Docs Setup window. (It's the only option available.) Setup installs the full set of Visual C++ 6.0 Introductory Documentation.**
8. **Click OK to acknowledge installation.**

Using Visual C++ 6.0

Let's get started using Visual C++ by loading, compiling, and running the C++ source files from the C++ For Dummies CD-ROM.

Building and executing a program

Your first project is to create something you can actually execute from the lifeless mass of confusion that we call a C++ program. As an example, we'll start with `Budget1.cpp`, a snappy little number from the first exercise in C++ For Dummies.

To load `Budget1.cpp`:

1. **Insert the C++ For Dummies CD-ROM into your drive (not the Visual C++ 6.0 Introductory CD-ROM — it's the yellow-and-black CD-ROM with the Dummies figure on the front).**
2. **Examine the contents of the CD-ROM in Windows Explorer.**
3. **Double-click on** `the C__dD.exe` **file. (Could they have thought of a stranger name for a program than that?)**
4. `C__fD.exe` **is a self-extracting ZIP file. Running the program opens the WinZip window, as shown in Figure 5.**

   This self-extracting WinZIP file should pop up the window, as shown in Figure 5.
5. **Click on Unzip to extract the 78 program files into the directory** `C:\C++ FD` **When the extraction is complete, return to the Start menu.**

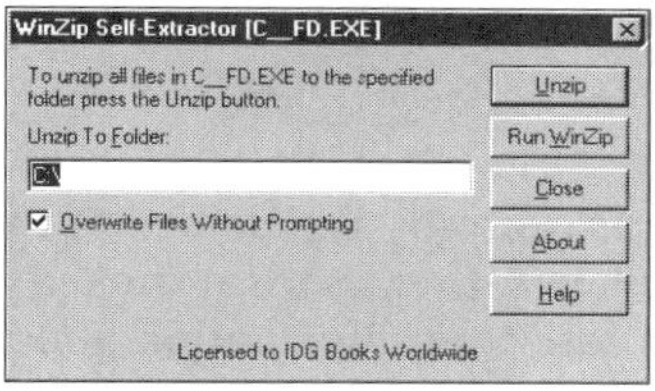

Figure 5: The self-extracting `C__fD` program on the C++ For Dummies CD-ROM provides a convenient mechanism for loading the C++ programs to your hard disk.

You have now installed the entire suite of programs from C++ For Dummies into a newly created directory with the unlikely name of C++ FD on your hard disk.

Creating your first program

1. **From the Start menu, start the Microsoft Visual C++ 6.0 program by clicking Start⇨Programs⇨Microsoft Visual C++ 6.0. (Look for the icon under the list of programs.)**

TIP: To save time, you can open the Taskbar Settings window and select the Start Menu's Programs tab. Under the Advanced window, behold the list of the Start Programs icons. Grab a copy of the Microsoft Visual C++ 6.0 icon for your desktop by holding down the Ctrl key while you drag the icon to your desktop area. This shortcut enables you to execute Visual C++ by double-clicking the desktop icon, instead of laboriously slogging through menu items to find your program.

   The first thing you should see is a screen containing a set of windows with a Did You Know tip window on top. (Hey, Microsoft, *did you know* that Did You Know windows are a pain in the neck?) Close the Tip window. The remaining windows are empty because you haven't loaded a program yet.

2. **From the menu toolbar, click File⇨Open.**

   Navigate to the `C:\C++FD\Budgets` directory. You should see the files `Budget1.cpp` through `Budget5.cpp`, classics all. Figure 6 shows `Budget1.cpp` opened in Visual C++.

3. **Click `Budget1.cpp` ⇨Open. This opens a window displaying the program source file.**

4. **Select Build from the Build menu item. Visual C++ 6.0 opens a dialog box asking permission to create a Project file.**

TIP: The Project file contains not only the names of the C++ files that are destined to link together to form the executable file, but also an assortment of other information about the program. Visual C++ requires this information to proceed. Fortunately, Visual C++ is capable of building a default project file without help.

5. **Click on the OK to allow Visual C++ 6.0 to create a project.**

   Visual C++ compiles `Budget1.cpp` and links it with the C++ library files to create the awesome executable file, `Build1.exe`.

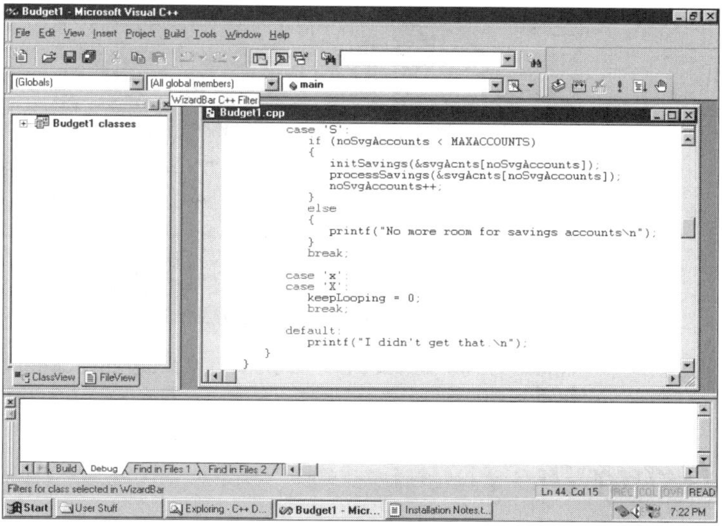

Fig 6: Visual C++ deploys a number of useful windows to facilitate development.

It's now time to execute this "wonder of modern man" program.

6. **Click** `Execute Budget1.exe` **from within the Build menu (or press Ctl+F5) to tell Visual C++ to execute the program.**

   Before it executes the Budget1 program, Visual C++ Introductory Edition puts a warning that this version doesn't permit redistribution for executables created with this program. That is, you alone can use what you create, but no one else.

7. **Click the OK button to calm its fears; Visual C++ opens an MS-DOS window in which the program executes.**

   See the Budget1 exercise in *C++ For Dummies* for details on what the program is expecting in the way of input. For a glimpse of the output from such a trial execution, take a look at Figure 7.

8. **Type X and then Return to go back to the development environment.**

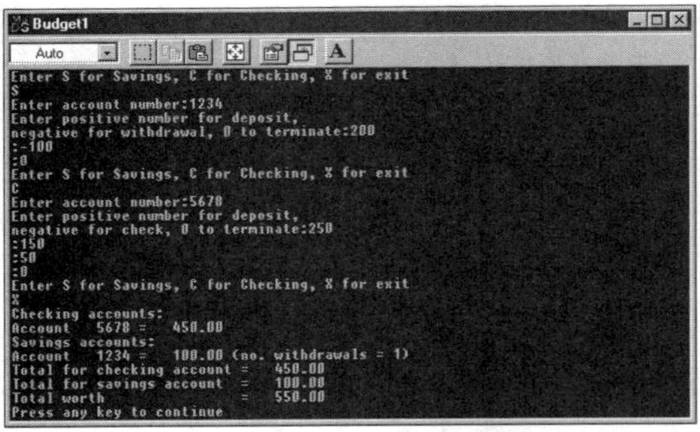

Figure 7: The output from a non-Win32 program appears in an MS-DOS window.

Using the Debugger

It's all very nice to build and execute programs that have no bugs (well, we can hope). But that usually doesn't happen on this planet. It's likely that the program you first execute has at least one big, healthy bug. Though flyswatters don't work on this type of bug and Raid only gunks up the keyboard, you do have some available ways to debug a program. The time-honored (and time-intensive) try-try-again approach involves adding print statements to the program, perhaps making some random changes that might nail the problem, and then rerunning the program. (And you thought TV reruns were bad.) This was the way I debugged my FORTRAN programs in the Pre-PC Period. Today we use modern tools like the Debugger that's built into the Visual C++ environment.

To demonstrate the use of the Debugger, I will introduce a bug into `Build1` and then find it. Nothing up my sleeve. . . .

Introducing an error into the source file

(Source file, allow me to introduce this nice error. Error, meet source file. . . .) While still in the `Budget1` project, place a `//` comment in front of the statements that initialize the two variables `noChkAccounts` and `noSvgAccounts` within `Budget1.cpp`. Forgetting to initialize variables is a common problem, especially in non-object-oriented programs such as `Budget1` (that's the reason for constructors, as seen in the *C++ For Dummies* book).

The modified `Budget1.cpp` code appears as follows:

```
/*main - accumulate the initial input and output
totals*/
int main()
{
   char     accountType;        /*S or C*/
   unsigned keepLooping;        /*0 -> get out of
loop*/
   float    chkTotal;           /*total in checking
accounts*/
   float    svgTotal;           /*total in savings
accounts*/
   float    total;              /*total of all
accounts*/
   int      i;
   int      noChkAccounts;      /*no. of checking
accounts*/
   int      noSvgAccounts;      /*no. of savings
accounts*/

   /*loop until someone enters X or x*/
   //noChkAccounts = 0;// commented out incor-
rectly
   //noSvgAccounts = 0;
   keepLooping = 1;
   while (keepLooping)
   {
```

Note the comment marks in front of the two assignments.

To ascertain that you are introducing a program, rebuild and execute the program by pressing F7 followed by F5. (You can choose to update a Savings account by pressing S.) Next, enter the account number — it doesn't really matter what the value is, for example 1234. After you enter a value and press Return, the program halts and displays a message. Aha — success!

When prompted to enter the path for INPUT.C, ignore this message for now and click Cancel. The failed execution of `Budgt1.exe` automatically puts you into the Debug mode.

Using the Debugger

Before using the Debugger, consider what a Debugger is and how it works. The Debugger is a utility that controls your program by inserting stopping points into the program. The program stops executing when it encounters one of these stop instructions. That gives the Debugger a chance to look at the code and hunt for glitches. Then the Debugger restarts the program by jumping to the stop point and continuing execution until the program reaches another stop instruction. During those times when the program stops, the Debugger can examine the values of different properties of the program, including any variables as shown in Figure 8.

To demonstrate the use of the Debugger, rebuild `Budget1` just to make sure. Now press the F10 key. This starts the Debugger at the first line of the program.

The Debugger begins execution with the ubiquitous "The terms of this agreement do not permit redistribution" warning message. This time clicking the OK button does not cause the program to continue execution. Instead, control immediately passes back to the Debugger.

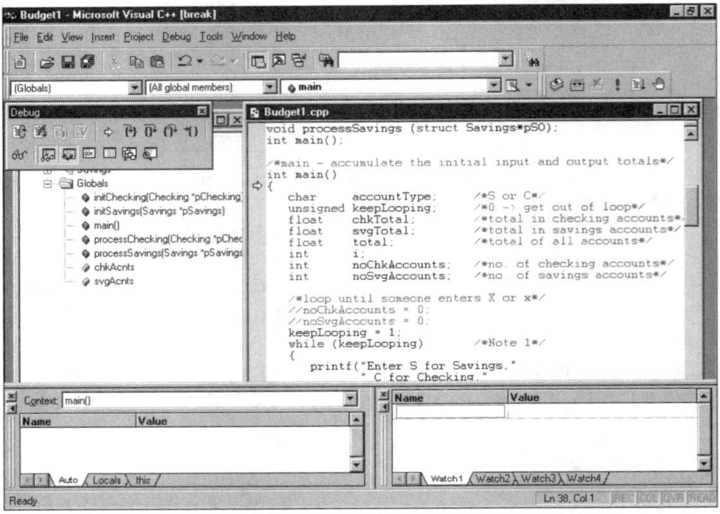

Figure 8: The Debugger display includes the source code, a table of the local variables, and a table of "watch" variables.

Examine the Visual C++ interface in debug mode. Visual C++ displays the source code with an indicator of the current location (the small yellow arrow), a display of the current variables in the lower left window, and a window of *watch* variables on the right. Both of these latter two windows are empty - I'll demonstrate them later.

In addition, Visual C++ opens a new menu, the Debug menu. This menu offers an assortment of Debugger commands. Don't worry if these new buttons are not familiar to you. You can use screen tips to determine the meanings of the various menu items. If you're not sure what a button does, hold the cursor over the button a second or two until a small, yellow bubble opens, containing a short explanation of the button. These bubbles are known as *screen tips*.

Let's continue the program to the first command in the program, the `keepLooking1` assignment. Set the cursor on the assignment and then set a breakpoint by clicking on the hand icon or entering F9. A small stop sign appears on the index next to the assignment. Now tell the Debugger to continue execution by clicking the little page-down icon (next to the hand icon) or by entering F5. The MS-DOS window flashes open as the program begins executing and then immediately disappears as control encounters the break point. The resulting display is shown in Figure 9.

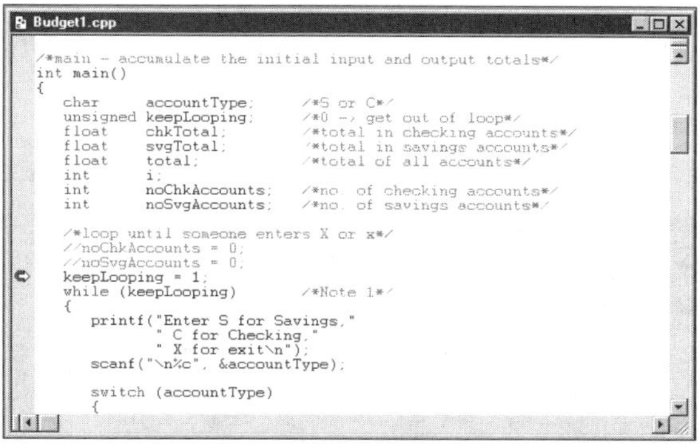

Figure 9: A small stop sign marks the location of a breakpoint — a small yellow arrow indicates where the program stopped.

Set a breakpoint on the statement and press F5 again to continue execution to the next statement.

Now examine the Variables window. Now you see the variables that are defined in the function. Most of these variables contain "ridiculous" numbers, such as `-85899764` in many of the integer values. The local variables contain garbage since we have yet to store anything there.

Unlike its neighbors, `keepLooking` is set to a variable reasonable `1`. This is because we have just executed the assignment.

We could continue stepping through the program by alternately setting breakpoints and then continuing, however, this can get tedious. Fortunately, the Visual C++ Debugger offers an alternative: the single-step command.

The single-step command executes a single source line and then returns control to the Debugger. To execute the next statement and stop, enter F10 (there is a Debugger icon that does the same thing, but it's difficult to describe it). The yellow arrow moves to the semicolon of the multiline `printf()` statement — the pointer always stops at the end of a statement.

Enter F10 one more time to pass control to the `scanf()` statement. Executing the `printf()` should have updated the program display. To check this, click the `Budget1` button on the Windows task bar to display the program window. The resulting display is shown in Figure 10.

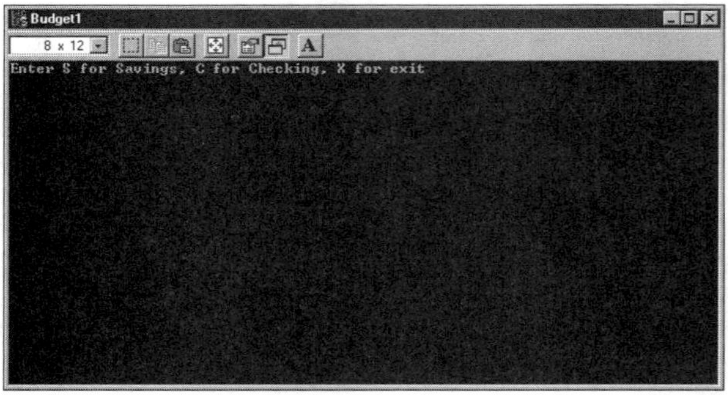

Figure 10: Executing a `printf()` statement under the Debugger updates the program display.

Continuing one more time, enter single-step, F10, to skip over the `scanf()` statement. Notice that the program appears to hang. What could be wrong? In fact, nothing is wrong at all — the program is simply waiting for you to enter something. Switch to the `Budget1` window again by clicking on the `Budget1` button on the task bar and enter an `S` for Savings account.

Enter F10 to single-step the `C/C++` switch statement. Notice that the program jumps to the `S` handler section. The Debugger is clever enough to follow the program through the logical twists and turns that it might take. Single-step one more time to pass through the `if()` statement to the call to `initSavings()`.

We have now run upon a problem. If we single-step now, should control pass over the call to `initSavings()` as if it were a single command, or should control pass into the function to begin single-stepping the code there? Depending on the condition either could be correct.

The Visual C++ Debugger offers two types of single-step. The F10 style single-step just demonstrated is called the Step Over single-step. It can step over the function. Another type of single-step is the Step Into single-step. This version, found under the F11 key, steps into the function and begins single-stepping the C++ code found there.

Since we don't know where the problem is, let's just stay at the `main()` level. Enter F10 to execute the `initSavings()` function. Budget1 is now waiting for you to enter an account number. It doesn't really matter what account number you choose — enter 1234 if you like.

As soon as you enter the account number, the program crashes and a message appears. (Aha! We're zeroing in.)

I'm not sure what that error message is, but it can't be good. Click OK to remove the window. At this point, the Debugger goes a little squirrelly. First, it asks you for the source code to some function that you've never heard of. Click Cancel and the Debugger opens an Assembly window with many four-letter words. The Debugger is trying to show you the point of failure. Since the crash (not the problem) lies somewhere in a library routine, this isn't much help.

We now know a lot more about where the problem rears its ugly head. Halt the Debugger by entering the Stop Debugging command, Shift-F5 (once again, there's a cute little button but it's hard to describe).

Let's start executing the program again only this time, let's single-step into the function rather than over it. Since we know that the crash lies within `initSavings()`, there's no need to single-step our way through the function.

Set a breakpoint by putting the cursor on `initSavings()` and then entering F9. Now clear out the breakpoints that you've already set by clicking the breakpoints and then clicking the Hand icon used to set them with (or press F9). Begin execution of the program by entering F5. Enter S for savings account. The program halts at the call to `initSavings()`. Enter F11 to enter the `initSavings()` function. Resume single-stepping F10-style through the `initSavings()` statements. Executing the call to `scanf()` causes the Debugger to pause until you enter an account number just as during the earlier pass.

As soon as you enter an account number, the program crashes again. The problem lies either in the call to `scanf()` or the arguments passed to the function.

Repeat the experiment (all this going around in circles is making me dizzy). Set a breakpoint on the `scanf()` call within `initSavings()` (the cursor is already there waiting for you) and restart the program. After halting at `initSavings()` (the old breakpoint we left behind), enter F5 again to proceed directly to our newer breakpoint.

If `scanf()` were a function that we had written, then I would enter F11 to step into the function and keep going. However, `scanf()` is a C++ Standard Library routine. You can't single-step into these functions since the Debugger doesn't have the source code to display.

In any case, let's look around to see if we can see the problem. There are two arguments to `scanf()`. The first argument, the `%d` can't possibly be the problem. What about `pSavings`? Let's check to see what it points to. Look back at the Variables window. Under the local tab, find the variable `pSavings`.

A small plus-sign next to the name implies that there's more to be seen. In fact, `pSavings` points to a structure. Click the plus sign (+) to reveal the members of the Savings structure. Notice that none of the members can be displayed. This includes the `accountNumber` member which was being passed to `scanf()`. This appears to be the problem. The `pSavings` pointer passed to `initSavings()` is invalid. Reset the breakpoint back at the beginning of this section, `/initSavings()`, so we can track our variables this time.

Let's return one more time to the scene of the crime. Restart the program by entering Shift-F5 to stop the Debugger and then entering F5 to start over. After entering the requisite `S`, the program halts at the breakpoint on the call to `initSavings()`. Use the Variables window to scan the local variables. Pay particular attention to `noSvgAccounts` since this variable is used in calculating the pointer passed to the `initSavings()` function. The Variables window is shown in Figure 11.

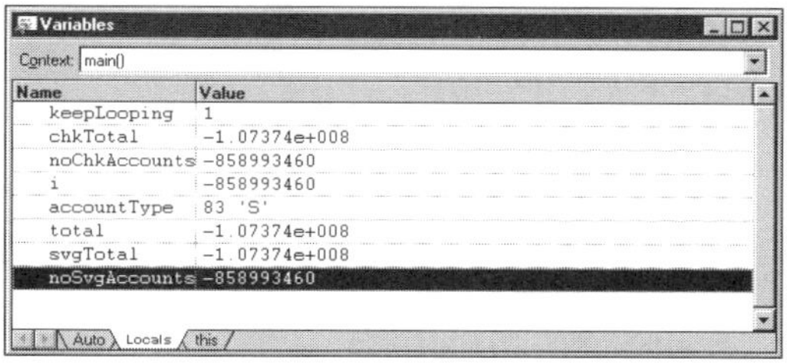

Figure 11: The Variables window showing the value of the local variables immediately before the call to `initSavings()`.

From this, you can see that the value of `noSvgAccounts` could not be correct. Because `noSvgAccounts` is an index, we would expect a non-negative number less than `MAXACCOUNTS`. Looking back, we notice that `noSvgAccounts` is never initialized (it isn't because we commented out the initialization steps). Restore the statements that initialize `noSvgAccounts` and `noChkAccounts`. Now rebuild the program and re-execute. The program now executes the same as it did before.

Remove all breakpoints by entering Ctrl + Shift + F9 before executing the program again.

Voila! The problem is solved.

Installation Instructions

To install the items from the CD to your hard drive, follow these steps.

1. **Insert the CD into your computer's CD-ROM drive.**

   Give your computer a moment to take a look at the CD.

2. **When the light on your CD-ROM drive goes out, double click the My Computer icon. (It's probably in the top-left corner of your desktop.)**

   This action opens the My Computer window, which shows you all the drives attached to your computer, the Control Panel, and a couple other handy things.

3. **Double click the icon for your CD-ROM drive.**

   Another window opens, showing you all the folders and files on the CD.

4. **Double click the file called License.txt.**

   This file contains the end-user license that you agree to by using the CD. When you are done reading the license, close the program, most likely Notepad, that displayed the file.

5. **Double click the file called Readme.txt.**

   This file contains the most up-to-date information about the code.

6. **You can copy individual folders from the CD to a appropriately named folder on your hard drive, or you can run the self-extractor, CODE.EXE.**

The self-extractor will place all the files on your hard drive and maintain the folder structure of the CD. The default location for the files to be installed is C:\C++ FD CODE, but you can change the name of this folder in the self-extractor dialog box.

IDG BOOKS WORLDWIDE BOOK REGISTRATION

Register This Book and Win!

We want to hear from you!

Visit **http://my2cents.dummies.com** to register this book and tell us how you liked it!

- Get entered in our monthly prize giveaway.
- Give us feedback about this book — tell us what you like best, what you like least, or maybe what you'd like to ask the author and us to change!
- Let us know any other *...For Dummies*® topics that interest you.

Your feedback helps us determine what books to publish, tells us what coverage to add as we revise our books, and lets us know whether we're meeting your needs as a *...For Dummies* reader. You're our most valuable resource, and what you have to say is important to us!

Not on the Web yet? It's easy to get started with *Dummies 101*®*: The Internet For Windows*® *98* or *The Internet For Dummies*®, 5th Edition, at local retailers everywhere.

Or let us know what you think by sending us a letter at the following address:

...For Dummies Book Registration
Dummies Press
7260 Shadeland Station, Suite 100
Indianapolis, IN 46256-3945
Fax 317-596-5498

...FOR DUMMIES™
BESTSELLING BOOK SERIES